WHO WILL CARE FOR GRANDMA?

WHO WILL CARE FOR GRANDMA?

Critiquing Ageism in Medicine

Brent Robert Kelly

WIPF & STOCK · Eugene, Oregon

WHO WILL CARE FOR GRANDMA?
Critiquing Ageism in Medicine

Copyright © 2009 Brent Robert Kelly. All rights reserved. Except for brief quotations in critical publications or reviews, no part of this book may be reproduced in any manner without prior written permission from the publisher. Write: Permissions, Wipf and Stock, 199 W. 8th Ave., Suite 3, Eugene, OR 97401.

ISBN 13: 978-1-55635-913-2

Manufactured in the U.S.A.

This work is dedicated to Christ Jesus to whom be all praise.
To my wife Rhonda, a woman of rare beauty and grace.
To Lori, Nick and Elissa, my treasures and fellow heirs of Christ
Thank You.

Contents

Preface ix
List of Abbreviations xiii

CHAPTER ONE
Introduction
Statement of the Problem 1
Thesis 3
Preliminary Orientation 4
Methodology 9
Other Avenues of Research 11
Chapter Content 12

CHAPTER TWO
Health Care Must Have Allocation
Allocation's Modern Development 17
Trends That Have Revealed a Need for Allocation 19
Attempts to Control Health Care's Problems 35
QALYs as a Basis for Allocation 48

CHAPTER THREE
QALYs Are Problematic as a Basis for Health Care Allocation
Using QALYs for Allocation Objectivity 52
Defining Denominators 61
QALY's Objectivity is Difficult to Obtain 71

Utilitarianism and QALY Calculations 79
QALYs and the Elderly 82
Conclusion 90

CHAPTER FOUR
The Biblical Basis for Elder Care
A Common Reading of Scripture 95
Identifying the Elderly 103
Biblical Guidelines for Elder Care 109
New Testament Living 130
Principles in Elder Care 153
Honor, Respect and Old Age 156
Responses to Community and Honor 159
Conclusion 161

CHAPTER FIVE
Comparing the Models
Foundations 165
Economic Strategies 173
Justice 183
Priorities in Health Care Distribution 190
Conclusion 201

CHAPTER SIX
Conclusion and Applications
Review of Conclusions 205
Application 217

Bibliography 227

Preface

IN THE early stages of this work, I realized that much of the Western medical community was in a love/hate relationship with Quality-Adjusted Life Years. QALYs are used in guiding many medical decision makers in the allocation of limited medical resources. It seems that deciding who will receive limited medical resources is a task filled with moral and ethical difficulties, even for those depending on the information obtained from QALY calculations. These moral and ethical difficulties are beyond the scope of sound-bites that tout the benefits of "universal health care," "affordable insurance," or the safety of the "free-market economy." The breadth of the difficulty is found in the wide-spread disagreement concerning how the health care system should be fixed, because most agree that there is a problem. It seemed obvious that some difficult decisions will need to be made which few are both willing and able to make. Nowhere is this more true than the issues surrounding health care allocation, and that is where QALYs have been found useful and problematic.

The Christian church in the West has not been oblivious to the health care crisis. Christianity has a long history of addressing social issues, unfortunately it has only been recently has the church made an effort to present a biblical position for addressing the complex issues in health care and health care allocation. One reason that the church has not addressed some of the issues involved in health care allocation is that there was not a problem. Limiting of medical care for the elderly, based upon their age, did not occur until the mid-twentieth century possibly because the elderly held a unique position of respect in the Western community. It is no longer the case that the elderly are given a unique position of respect and dignity. Rather, it seems that with the increased use of QALY calculations the elderly are in danger of receiving less medical care than they are warranted.

The problem of QALYs and the elderly have been addressed in the secular market, but it is a rare topic in Evangelical circles. Few Evangelical texts discuss the role of the elderly, caring for the elderly or attempt to formulate a Theology of Aging. Those who have so written are truly trailblazers. Unfortunately, in recent years, concerns in bioethics, such as human embryonic stem cell research and human cloning, have seemingly caused the discussion of resource allocation for the elderly to be set aside.

To defer the issue of resource allocation at this time seems unwise since the problem of limited medical resources will most likely become worse. Therefore, if Christians are going to be serious participants in the discussion concerning medical resource allocation, it seems imperative that they respond to the ethical implications of significant models of resource allocation that currently assist decision makers in the allocation process, such as QALYs. As a Christian I pray that this work adds a meaningful contribution to this important conversation.

This work could not have occurred without the patience of my wife Rhonda who has been an example of godliness and diligence. My bride of many years continues to be a source of friendship and counsel. This work also could not have been completed without the great patience of my children Lori, Nick and Elissa. Thank you for your patience, and belief that Dad would one day finish. A special note of gratitude needs to be expressed to Alice Rickman whose support through the years has helped Rhonda and me in the ministry and beyond.

This preface cannot be brought to a conclusion without a word of appreciation to my dissertation committee who guided this book in its original version. First, to Dr. E. David Cook, who suggested this topic and who has been an example of Christian scholarship. His tutorials will never be forgotten, and are now greatly appreciated. Next, Drs. Bruce Ware and Theodore Cabal, whose Christian lives have continually displayed grace and patience. I have treasured my dissertation committee's timely encouragement during my days of writing. To Lori Kelly whose literary scholarship completed the final editing. Finally, I want to express my appreciation to The Southern

Preface

Baptist Theological Seminary for providing a context where true biblical scholarship and comradery is able to flourish.

Brent Robert Kelly
Louisville, Kentucky
December 2004

Abbreviations

ADL	Activities of Daily Living
AKA	Above the Knee Amputation
BKA	Below the Knee Amputation
COPD	Chronic Obstructive Pulmonary Disorder
EQ-5D	A generic measure of health status used in five European countries to provide a single descriptive profile and index value that can be used in clinical and economic evaluation of health care.
EuroQol	European QALY
HALY	Health-Adjusted Life Years
HI	Hospital Insurance
HLYs	Healthy Life Years
HeaLYs	Healthy Life Years
HMOs	Health Maintenance Organizations
HRQofL	Health Related Quality of Life
SF6D	A generic measure of health status used in the United States for clinical and economic evaluation in health care.
OASDI	Old Age Survivor and Disability Insurance
QALYs	Quality-Adjusted Life Years
QofL	Quality of Life

Chapter One

Introduction

Statement of the Problem

A VARIETY of social developments in the last half of the Twentieth century, which will be discussed later in this chapter, have brought the American health care system to the point that it must explicitly allocate its services. In response to these developments a number of attempts have been made to limit the cost of health care and the services provided. Socialized medicine, Health Maintenance Organizations (HMOs), Medicare/Medicaid, and service-for-pay have been presented as options that could decrease the cost of health care. Although there are strengths to each of these plans, they experienced only limited success in their application because they were unable to stop the decrease of medical resources or limit the increase in medical consumption in America. Other methods of limiting cost for medical services were developed which try to assign resources based upon a variety of methods, such as allocations based upon healthy year equivalent (HYE), saved young life equivalent (SAVE), and person tradeoffs.[1] These ideas have had limited success in determining who should receive health care and treatment.

One contemporary and popular method of health care computation that assists in determining allocation is Quality-Adjusted Life

---

1. Donald P. Marazzo, "Quality of Life, "*Quality of Life Series—Summary Report* (1998), Dialogue Series 1997 [on-line]; accessed 1 August 2002; available from http://pitt.edu/~uclid? QOL.htm; Internet.

Years (QALYs). "QALY (Quality-adjusted life years) is a mathematical concept designed to measure the quality of life of defined illness states."[2] QALYs are utilitarian, allocating patient care and treatment based upon such calculating variables as healthy life years and quality of life. These denominators were developed by health care economists as a method of measuring the various possible outcomes of medical treatments, medication costs, physician's expenses and a variety of medical related expenses and, in so doing, allow for a common analysis of the cost effectiveness of a potential treatment.

QALYs take the two denominators, healthy life years and quality of life, and place them into a mathematical formula. That formula generates a sum which assists allocation decision makers in deciding where funding should be directed, or which treatment in what circumstance should be allowed. In one sense the mathematics of QALYs are straightforward. QALYs combine the quality and quantity of life in the following manner;

> It takes one year of perfect health-life expectancy to be worth 1, but regards one year of less than perfect life expectancy as less than 1. Thus an intervention which results in a patient living for an additional four years rather than dying within one year, but where quality of life fell from 1 to 0.6 on the continuum will generate: 4 years extra life at 0.6 quality of life values 2.4, less 1 year at reduced quality (1-0.6) equals 0.4. QALYs generated by the intervention 2.0. QALYs can therefore provide an indication of the benefits gained from a variety of medical procedures in terms of quality of life and survival for the patient.[3]

After quality of life and healthy life years scores have been determined, a number is assigned to the patient, or to the medical treatment project. If a health state is compromised, then the QALY

---

2. A. J. Wing, "QALY," in *New Dictionary of Christian Ethics & Pastoral Theology*, ed. David Atkinson and David Field (Downers Grove: InterVarsity, 1995), 714.

3. Ceri Phillips Newport, "So what is a QALY?" *Bandolier Library* [on-line]; accessed 1 August 2002; available from http://www.jr2ox.ac.uk/bandolier/band24/b24-7.html; Internet.

score will be lower than if the person was in full health. If a person is older, with fewer potential years of healthy life remaining that too will lower the person's QALY score.

The QALY method of deciding where allocation would best be directed, while cost beneficial, has its problems. In light of the denominators, especially that of healthy life years, it can place the elderly at a distinct disadvantage. Though QALYs are affected by patient preferences identified through multi-attributed utility instruments which ask people to identify health state preferences, it seems that the problem with the elderly is based upon their age more than any other factor. In one sense, discrimination is exactly what QALYs are designed to do: they are designed to assist in deciding where limited medical resources would best be used. However, the type of discrimination that is actually found in QALYs is not beneficial to all who are impacted by its calculations. The limited benefit of QALYs can be seen in how it uses age in its calculations. Age calculations are used as a primary measurement in QALYs and that use of age determines health care services for the elderly. Because chronology is considered a health state, the elderly are placed at a disadvantage and negative discrimination must inevitably result. The reason for this discrimination is that the elderly, primarily by nature of their age, would usually present a lower QALY score than those who are younger, although their quality of life may be the same. It is contended that this focus upon age as a method of measurement in health care allocation is inherently ageist.

Thesis

This work will claim that the biblical principles of community and honor can rightly and justifiably be used as a basis, or application, for impacting the ageism in QALYs. The purpose of this research is to demonstrate the deficiencies of quality-adjusted life years, and to demonstrate that the biblical model provides a better moral basis for medical allocation and the treatment of the elderly than the present utilitarian computations of QALYs. It adds to the field of scholarly work by contributing an evangelical perspective to the issue of health care allocation and the distribution of limited medical resources.[4]

4. Allen Verhey, *Reading the Bible in the Strange World of Medicine* (Grand

Preliminary Orientation

Since the 1960s the inability to control rising medical costs has caused a crisis.

> After failed efforts at price controls in the 1970s and only minimal success with managed care more recently, human resource managers and policy experts say individual workers will bear an increasing share of the financial burden. Nationwide, insurance premiums rose 11 percent in 2001 and are projected to climb 13 percent this year (2002), according to an analysis by the Center for Studying Health System Change. A survey by the Hewitt Associates consulting firm found that HMO rates increased an average of 15.3 percent this year (2002) and could increase 20 percent in 2003.[5]

A health care crisis looms before the American patient. This crisis may have been brought about by an increase in cost of medical care, frivolous lawsuits, greedy lawyers and patients, increased malpractice insurance, the decrease in available services and resources, a changing of demographics or a combination of all of these. The health care crisis has revealed the necessity of using wisdom in allocating limited medical resources. In light of the above circumstances, the problem that developed was in determining how the medical community could decide who should receive medical care and how that medical care would be distributed and financed.

QALYs were developed in the above context as it became clear, because of health care resource limitations, that a need for the development of cost effective measures to determine the value of health outcomes now existed. As these health care outcomes were analyzed, it was found that a method was needed by which the various and seemingly unrelated outcomes could be compared. QALYs were

---

Rapids: Eerdmans, 2003), 19. Verhey discusses at length the hesitancy of theologians to appeal to theological tradition or religious conviction. It seems that the works of Paul Ramsey and James Gustafson in the 1970's were among the first that attempted to break this unwillingness to include God in discussions of bioethics.

5. Ceci Connolly, "Health Care's Soaring Cost Takes a Toll Squeeze Hits Workers, Firms and Government," *Washington Post*, 9 July 2002, 10 (A).

designed to resolve the problem of comparing different outcomes, such as functional improvement and differing symptom relief, in a common value scale. By this method of valuation it became possible to compare the various outcomes.[6]

Over the years, QALYs have also been seen as a useful means of comparing cost effectiveness, cost benefit, and risk involved in medical procedures.[7] And, because the focus of QALYs is economic, in the sense that they seek to maximize limited resources, they have been considered by some to be fair and preferable. Those who hold to this position acknowledge the possible utilitarian basis for QALYs, and they see the utilitarian basis for QALYs as preferable to the struggle to define health care limitations by other methods.[8] As well documented as these benefits of QALYs are, the ability of QALYs to help determine health care preferences has not negated its many nagging problems.

Some of the problems of QALYs that have been identified are its lack of sensitivity within a given disease area, over-simplification of complex healthcare issues, an inability to show the variables in quality of life, a disregard for the poor, and the question of whose values are used in determining the QALY.[9] As early as 1992, these

---

6. Eric Nord, *Cost-Value Analysis in Health Care: Making Sense Out of QALYs* (Cambridge: Cambridge University Press, 1999), 18.

7. Joshua Cohen, "Preferences, Need and QALYs," *Journal of Medical Ethics* 22 (1996): 267–72.

8. Victor R. Fuchs, *Who Shall Live? Health, Economics, and Social Choice*, expanded ed. Economic Ideas Leading to the 21st Century, vol. 3, ed. Lawrence R. Klein and Vincent Su (Singapore: World Scientific, 1998). Fuchs' conclusion is marked by an understanding that economists have to take into account cultural peccadilloes when disseminating economic counsel. He does not hide his enthusiasm concerning the prospect of integrating economics with cultural values of, "the media, politicians, and health professionals" (ibid., 243).

9. Mo Malek, "Implementing QALYs," *Hayward Medical Communications* 2, no. 1 (March 2001) [on-line]; accessed 02 August 2002; available from http://www. evidence-based-medicine.co.uk; Internet. This is part of a series of articles which are sponsored by an educational grant from AVENTIS Pharma, a major pharmaceutical company. The advantages and disadvantages of QALYs are presented in this paper and in the AVENTIS Pharma paper by Ceri Philips and Guy Thompson, "What is a QALY," *Hayward Medical Communications* 1, no. 6 (May 2001) [on-line] accessed 02 August 2002; available from http:// www.evidence-based-medicine.co.uk; Internet. Much of the research done on

problems in QALYs were being discussed, and the problem of discrimination within QALYs was being acknowledged.[10] The type of discrimination under discussion was not that of deciding who would receive care based upon need, but that of unfair discrimination based on one's stage of life.

The discrimination in QALYs comes from the way in which a QALY is produced and applied. The computation of QALYs focuses upon healthy life years and quality of life. The weight given to age makes QALYs discriminatory toward the elderly in that the elderly will usually have a lower score than those who are younger simply by virtue of their age. Another discriminatory issue is found in how the idea of "quality of life" is defined. Depending upon how quality of life is assayed those whose health improves may not receive a beneficial QALY score because they are being compared to an unfair model of health which produces a lower score based upon the length of benefit from a given medical procedure. An older person, because of their age, will statistically not have as many healthy life years as a younger person. The utilitarianism that is the basis of QALYs is thus itself problematic. To attempt to counter this weakness in the QALY system, recent attempts have been made to modify the utilitarianism of QALYs with a deontological approach.[11] Thus; in seeking to infuse a moral basis into QALYs the idea of duty has been presented. However that concept of duty is defined, it would become the moral basis for QALYs. Others have tried to correct the problem of age

---

QALYs presume their usefulness and acknowledges, but fails to respond directly to their deficiencies. Both of these works have useful charts that demonstrate the simple mathematics involved in the generation of QALYs and tables stating the advantages and disadvantages of the QALY method of resource allocation.

10. Ann Michele Holmes, "Uses and Abuses of QALY Analysis" (Ph.D. diss., University of British Columbia, 1992). Holmes states that "QALY based measures probably discriminate against certain types of individuals, including those who are risk adverse with respect to health and in poor health (ibid., ii). Her final analysis is that this discrimination is no worse then any other model and so does not disqualify QALYs as a viable economic model to direct treatment in health care.

11. Gina Diane Safranyik, "Macro-allocation of Health Care Resources: A Computer Simulation Comparing a Utilitarian and a Deontological Approach" (Ph.D. diss., University of Victoria, 2000).

discrimination in QALYs by using societal values as a moral basis.[12] Thus if society agrees that ageism is economically acceptable then it is a morally worthy position.

Although some may see the age discrimination as problematic, others see it as the inevitable result of the health care crisis. In the current economic and medical climate a complete lack of consensus on the issue exists. Little agreement can be found regarding whose values, if any, can be used to correct the age discrimination that is found in QALYs.[13]

Economists have weighed in on the problem of cost allocation in health care through the introduction of QALYs, but they have not been alone. Some have attempted to use virtue ethics to correct the age discrimination in QALYs. Surprisingly, although economists and moralists have sought to deal with the problem of the distribution of limited health care resources, during much of this discussion the church has been amazingly quiet. This is not to say that the church has been silent about all health care issues. There have been some Christians who have written on cost allocation in health care.[14] But, few books have been written by Christians dealing specifically with QALYs.[15]

---

12. Paul Menzel, et al., "Toward a Broader View of Values in Cost-Effectiveness Analysis of Health," *Hastings Center Report* 29 (May–June 1999): 7–15.

13. John McKie, Peter Singer, and Helga Kuhse, *The Allocation of Health Care Resources: An Ethical Evaluation of the 'QALY' Approach* (Hampshire, UK: Dartmouth Publishing Company, 1998). This book written by economists and ethicists defends the core tenets of QALYs. They discuss the issue of whether all lives are of equal value, the basis of need, and adequate fairness and justice.

14. Gregory W. Rutecki, "Guidelines for Gatekeepers," *The Changing Face of Health Care*, ed. John F. Kilner, Robert D. Orr, and Judith Allen Shelly (Grand Rapids: Eerdmans, 1998), 141; John Kilner, *Who Lives? Who Dies? Ethical Criteria in Patient Selection* and *Life on the Line: Ethics, Aging, Ending Patients Lives, and Allocating Vital Resources* (New Haven: Yale University Press, 1990); John Wyatt, *Matters of Life and Death: Today's Healthcare Dilemmas in the Light of Christian Faith* (Leicester, UK: InterVarsity, 1998). These works present an analysis of health care from a Christian worldview.

15. The Christian Medical Fellowship has published a booklet on QALYs by A. J. Wing, *Quality-Adjusted Life Years* (London: Christian Medical Fellowship, n.d.). This book identified because of its Christian worldview, and as such it is in the minority when dealing with QALYs from a Christian perspective.

The changing demographics of the United States and the commands of Scripture ought to motivate Christians to respond to the age discrimination found in QALYs. Some works have been written on the need to care for the elderly, the theology of the elderly, and what the Bible says about the elderly, but the economics of health care and the ageism that occurs in QALYs have not been addressed from a biblical perspective.[16]

In the analysis of QALYs there is seemingly revealed a clear moral problem that directly relates to its use of utilitarianism as a basis for its ethic. This presents a situation where the elderly, among others, are discriminated against. The current medical market emphasizes cost benefit rather than patient care, and this too is problematic. The elderly are incrementally being marginalized because of their age rather than any other state or condition.[17] Numerous organizations have been formed to organize and support the elderly as they respond to medical limitations based upon age. The church has not addressed the issue of quality-adjusted life years and because of this lack of confrontation, "the care ethic given to us in the Christian tradition

---

16. Daniel I. Block, "Genesis: The Beginning of What?" (paper presented at The Southern Baptist Theological Seminary SME Seminar, 20 August 2001). William L. Hendricks, *A Theology of Aging* (Nashville: Broadman, 1986). Frank Stagg, *The Bible Speaks on Aging* (Nashville: Broadman Press, 1981). Paul Tournier, *Learn to Grow Old* (Louisville: Westminster/John Knox Press, 1972). John F. Kilner, *Life on the Line: Ethics, Aging, Ending Patient's Lives, and Allocating Vital Resources* (Bannockburn, IL: Center for Bioethics and Human Dignity, 1992). These works are representative of the efforts by the Christian community to assess issues that impact the elderly they do not provide an analysis of QALYs. A Christian analysis of health care allocation has been attempted, but that work focuses on the thoughts of Paul Ramsey and Daniel Callahan. It does not deal specifically with the issue of ageism in QALYs. Edward R. Carder, "A Christian Ethical Analysis of Health Care Allocation in the United States in the Thought of Daniel Callahan and Paul Ramsey" (Ph.D. diss., Southwestern Baptist Theological Seminary, 1995).

17. Stories abound concerning the neglect of the elderly. Elder protection laws have been passed in Missouri. The AARP actively oppose discrimination of the elderly. Nursing home abuse is widespread. Many elderly complain about being treated as non-persons when dealing with medical personnel. The issue of ageism seems to be an example of a common problem when dealing with the elderly, manifested by a lack of consistent care and commitment by caregivers.

has been marginalized in the current market model of health care systems."[18]

The church needs to present a better moral basis for health care allocation than the QALYs model. It needs to present a biblical model that provides, at least, a minimal basis for elder care. If the health care system continues to be in crisis, this ethic could become the basis for future health care decisions among the body of Christ. If QALYs in its present form, or some other type of utilitarian based economic indicator is used then there needs to be presented an alternative Christian moral basis for care that is able to impact the problem of ageism in QALYs, and which will provide hope for those who are elderly and in medical need.

The need for a biblical basis to counter the ageism in the QALY method directs this dissertation. The goal is to demonstrate the impact of the biblical principles of elder care as seen in inclusion into community and honor on the ageism problem in QALYs. This work is the result of fifteen years in the medical/nursing profession working in direct patient care.

Methodology

This book will focus on five areas: (1) the identification of the health care crisis and quality-adjusted life years; (2) the identification of QALYs and their problem of functioning as a basis for health care allocation; (3) a biblical model of elder care; (4) a comparison of QALY philosophical foundation and health care priorities; and (5) the impact of the biblical model on the ageism in QALYs, which provides a better foundation for health care allocation among the needy elderly and which will address QALYs' problem of ageism. The path of this work will follow the areas of focus with the goal of identifying the biblical model and demonstrating that model's applicability to the current problem in health care allocation as it relates to ageism in QALYs.

QALYs have been in use for many years, and there is much support for their utilitarian base. The fact that its use has not stopped

---

18. Patricia Benner, "When Health Care Becomes a Commodity," in *The Changing Face of Health Care*, ed. John F. Kilner, Robert D. Orr, and Judith Allen Shelly (Grand Rapids: Eerdmans, 1998), 125.

or slowed the problems of medical cost and health care allocation in some sense demonstrates its inadequacy. In order to substantiate that it is necessary to go beyond economics and seek a moral basis for health care allocation, one must review the plethora of plans for cost containment. Over the last forty years, Health Maintenance Organizations, socialized medicine advocates, Medicare, and groups such as the Veteran's Administration have tried to control the rising cost of medical care and treatment. In so doing the elderly seem to have been marginalized as can be identified in the ageism found in the QALY model.

If quality of care is to take precedence over market forces then a model will need to be presented which is derived from a higher moral plane. Thus the focus of this work is to find a biblical model of elder care and compare it to QALYs in order to see which one deals better with the problem of ageism.

This biblical model will focus on inclusion of community and honor as part of the basis for elder care. Because the elderly are in a position of dependence, it is necessary for other members of the Christian community to seek to meet their needs proactively. These needs are to be met though the inclusion of the elderly in the greater community. The biblical model presented will argue against the disconnectedness found in American culture.

The Fifth Commandment will be used as a basis for the idea of honoring parents. Additionally biblical principles found in the Old and New Testaments will be used to support the idea of honor for the elderly in general. This idea of honor will include the concepts of respect and care. The purpose of these principles will be to demonstrate the way people ought to treat the elderly.

This biblical model will be compared with QALYs, and areas of agreement and disagreement will be noted. Before the conclusion and application it will be seen that when the QALY model is calculated it has a problem of ageism that does not exist in the biblical model.

In order to accomplish the goals of this work research was necessary during its dissertation stage in order to obtain critical data concerning QALYs, its medical and economic applications, and the biblical basis for elder care. This information was obtained at the James P. Boyce Centennial Library, the E. M. White Library

Introduction

at Louisville Presbyterian Seminary, William Ekstrom Library and Kornhauser Health Sciences Library at the University of Louisville. Medical ethics organizations have also been consulted, such as the Center for Bioethics and Human Dignity and the Christian Medical Fellowship. As was needed on-line information, dissertations, serials, journals, and interviews with health care professionals have been sought and used.

Other Avenues of Research

Although this work will deal with the problem of ageism in QALYs; it will be limited in that it will not deal with other important issues concerning the elderly. Specifically, exceptions to the principles of elder care will not be addressed in this work. It is beyond the scope of this work to evaluate family dynamics that may impact the principles provided, or whether the American Christian church is actually applying the principles found in Scripture.

The dynamic of the elderly naturally includes issues surrounding a decrease in function, but this work will not specifically deal with the issues of chronic illness, the process of dying, or death. It will not directly address the need for long term health care for some patients or the problems of neglect, both familial and professional, that are pervasive in nursing homes.

This book is designed to evaluate and contrast two moral guides for health care allocation. Direct patient care, or the specific decisions that impact direct patient care, will not be addressed in this work. This piece will not solely focus on the problems of utilitarianism, but it will focus most of its energy on the ageist problem found in QALYs.

This book is limited in its scope to the impact, or application, of the biblical principles of community and honor on the problem of ageism in QALYs; however, other areas of research could be pursued. One of the areas of research that could be developed is the question of whether medicine ought to be for-profit. Many of the issues surrounding QALYs and health care limitations, in general, seem to spring from the desire for a greater financial return for stockholders' investments. Problematic on a number of fronts this could provide a fruitful area of research, such as an analysis of whether the medical community is too focused on profit in a consumer culture. This issue of for-profit medicine could also encompass research that could address the seeming inability of the market driven economic system to curtail the rising costs of medical care.

Another avenue of research that needs to be followed which will not be addressed in this work is the question of socialized medicine. Evangelicals must evaluate carefully, from a historical and biblical perspective, whether Christians should support socialized medicine. This research could dovetail into other areas of study such as whether socialized medicine would be capable of dealing with the commercially driven forces within healthcare. It might focus on whether it is right for the church to support non-benevolent medicine. Other areas of research might address the church's response to uninsured members.

While these ideas might have merit, they extend beyond the scope of this work. It is hoped that others will see the importance of the church addressing issues in medicine. In so doing, it would prevent the Christian tradition from being marginalized more than it already has been in medical policy determination.

Chapter Content

Chapter 1: Introduction

The context surrounding problems of ageism in Quality-Adjusted Life Years are set forth and the thesis statement will be set forth in this chapter. Some preliminary information concerning the development and current state of health care are presented as a means of orienting the reader to the subject. In the section on methodology, the five areas of development in this dissertation are noted, along with the two primary biblical principles of elder care that will be assessed in this work: the Fifth Commandment and inclusion in community. The limitations of this work are identified by what areas are beyond the scope of this work. Finally, a short development of the contents of this dissertation is given.

Introduction

Chapter 2: Health Care Must Have Allocation.

In this chapter the context of the problem of the necessity of some type of medical allocation is developed. It is noted that the American system of health has developed from a primarily altruistic vocation to one that is increasingly dependent upon economic incentives. When trends concerning the need for allocation are assessed it is readily discerned that American health care does not have the resources to provide comprehensive coverage for every person under its jurisdiction. Some of the trends that will be noted will reveal a shortage in health care staff, a limited amount of hospital beds as well as medical resources point to a need for purposeful allocation. The assessment of trends will show that health care costs continue to rise, and that rise in cost has impacted the availability of doctors, prescription drugs, and access to medical facilities.

After establishing this need for allocation, it will be noted that a number of solutions during the past forty years designed to deal with the challenge of resource limitations have been tried, all of which had very limited success. Some of the attempted solutions and current methods of dealing with limited resources will be noted such as HMOs, socialized medicine, Medicare, and the Veterans Administration. Quality-Adjusted Life years is then presented as a current and popular method of allocation that has become useful in attempting to control health care cost and guide allocation of medical resources.

Chapter 3: QALYs are Problematic as a Basis for Health Care Allocation

QALYs computational schematics are developed and the effort to provide an objective method of medical assessment for those making resource allocation decisions is provided. The denominators in QALYs, which are quality of life and healthy life years, are identified as discussed as is the difficulty in actually providing an objective resource for allocation decision makers through QALYs. It will be noted that QALYs then have only a limited benefit when it comes to being a basis for health care allocation because its selective criteria, quality of life and health life years, by their very nature focus on one's length of life. It is the criteria of age which ignores the issue of health improvement from a patient's starting point.

The reason for the difficulty in providing an objective criterion for health care allocation is that QALYs are based upon a utilitarian ethic. This idea of primarily focusing on the necessity to maximize resources through profit and productivity assessments has limited usefulness as a means of health care allocation. Because of QALY's commitment to a utilitarian basis, QALYs are unable to distribute fairly health care resources. This unfair distribution is a particular problem for the elderly. The potentially unjust distribution of health care resources which chooses, through computations, the elderly as the ones to carry the burden of correcting the health care resource problem is ageist, biased towards the young, and is therefore an unacceptable method of health care allocation.

Chapter 4: The Biblical Basis for Elder Care

This section begins with a discussion concerning how the Bible will be read and used as a resource in this dissertation. Because the issue of health care allocation is not simply a religious, or Christian, issue, hermeneutics, objectivity, and biblical ethics are reviewed. After identifying who the elderly are in Scripture, there is a basic outline of the Bible's view of elder care. References will be made to Genesis and to a variety of biblical personalities, but the primary Old Testament focus will be on two texts; Exodus 20:12, which is commonly called the Fifth Commandment, and Leviticus 19:32, which expands upon the principle of honor. Some Rabbinical sources will be evaluated in order to provide a broader perspective on this topic and to demonstrate that the present interpretation of honor is consistent with other scholarly analysis of this subject.

The New Testament will then be evaluated with particular emphasis given to Jesus and the Corban issue. After that analysis the broader New Testament will be assessed. It is from this point that two primary principles of elder care are presented, which are honor and the inclusion into community. The principles of honor will be shown to include the extent of what it means to respect and care for the elderly. Next, the importance of community as a place where there is interconnectedness and mutual responsibility is reviewed.

Introduction

After noting the foundation for the principles of community and honor which are found in the Image of God, the commands of God, and the principles of justice and love, objections to these minimum principles are noted, evaluated, answered.

Chapter 5: Comparing the Models

Since the QALY model and the biblical model have both been presented and evaluated, this section is designed to bring the two models together for comparison. Here the areas of agreement may be seen. The foundational principles and philosophies of the two models are compared. The issue of justice as used in QALYs and in the biblical model are presented showing the different emphasis of each model. There are important fundamental differences between the two models. Where the QALY model is concerned primarily with the maximization of economic interests, the biblical model will show that it is concerned with more than economics. The different priorities in each model show that there are distinct emphases in each model which make areas of agreement between the two models limited. The biblical model reveals that caring for the elderly is an ethic that rises above utilitarian maximization of resources. It is shown that the QALY model is unable to escape its problem of ageism, while the biblical model provides a framework for decision making that shows that ageism does not need to exist in health care allocation. By the very nature of how QALYs are calculated they produce a numerical product is ageist. This ageism also reveals that the QALY model has difficulty providing and identifying a holistic definition of quality of life.

Chapter 6: Conclusion and Applications

In this final section, two points will be made. The first will be the conclusions and the second the applications. In the section concerning conclusions, the differences in how funds are directed when relying on the two models is seen. It is also noted that the reason for the different economic direction is that there is a different focus. The economic implications of the two models and the need to choose a moral position that may not maximize resources but care is established. The need for medicine to be moral, even above economic incentives is discussed.

In the conclusion, it is the opinion of this author that the Bible provides a better foundation for health care allocation than QALYs in its present form by providing a corrective basis for the ageism in QALYs. It is concluded that the biblical model goes beyond what is the most economically efficient condition or treatment and focuses on the health state of the individual, which can be impacted through holistic methods of care. It is noted that the biblical model does not by necessity shift funds away from the elderly population. The biblical model is better able to deal with the variables involved in individual medical cases, than the QALY model. Finally, it is shown that the objections to the biblical model as simplistic and impractical do not negate its superiority over QALYs, since it provides a moral basis for honor inclusion which can be broadly applied.

The second point will be the application which will show that given that the Bible provides a better moral basis with which to allocate health care. Then a moral foundation is provided which is able to make sense of the conflicting ethical arguments for medical allocation. The biblical model is seen as providing a minimum standard which can be established for the treatment of the elderly. A moral choice needs to be made concerning health care allocation decisions between maximization of resources and caring for the elderly. The minimum standards of care for the elderly will be seen as a good and necessary basis for holistic health care. The shift in focus from maximization to the biblical model will allow the public to become aware of trends and policies which can be identified as ageist. Through the biblical model the elderly can receive respect in medical care as individuals of inherent worth and valued members of society. Finally, these applications will show the impact of the biblical model on the problem of ageism in QALY calculations.

Chapter Two

Health Care Must Have Allocation

SINCE THE purpose of this work is to see how the biblical principles of community and honor apply to the issue of ageism in Quality Adjusted Life Years, it seems reasonable to identify some of the factors that have brought about the need for health care allocation. In this section, some of the factors that led to health care allocations in America will be identified and then QALYs will be evaluated as a method of allocation.

Allocation's Modern Development

There is some debate as to when modern health care began in America, but it is generally agreed that it originated no later than the latter part of the Twentieth Century. Since the 1960's health care in America has struggled through a myriad of difficulties. The increase in demand for services coupled with the advances in medical technology, have presented at least one unique problem that applies most Americans: that of allocation of limited medical resources.[1] The result has been that everyone in America cannot have access to every health care procedure which they may want or, in some cases, need. One reason that this need for allocation has occurred is that economics are ever increasingly applied to medical care decisions. It is difficult to overstate the affect that the economic development of

---

1. John F. Kilner, *Who Lives? Who Dies?: Ethical Criteria in Patient Selection* (New Haven: Yale University Press, 1990), 3.

medicine has had on the American health care system. As Bradford Gray has aptly observed,

> A continuing transformation—some would say revolution—is taking place in the economics, organization, and control of health care in the United States. Although charitable institutions and selfless professionals have not disappeared, health care has become an increasingly commercialized and competitive set of activities that make up the fastest-growing element in the service sector of the nation's economy. The behavior of both providers of health care and third-party purchasers is driven more and more by the dollar.[2]

Because health care became "driven more and more by the dollar" the decisions concerning how medical care came to be distributed were affected. Medicine changed from being rooted in altruism as described in the Hippocratic Oath to a more pragmatic approach to medical care which included, in part, an understanding of medicine as a business.[3]

The increasing commercial focus of medicine was also seen in the emergence of investor owned hospital companies in the 1970's. Hospitals had become, "more oriented toward economic performance."[4] There was a concern that the consumer pay for the services rendered in some manner. A loss of profit became an inescapable and undesirable issue for the hospitals, physicians, and stockholders. While the physicians and the stockholders may have had different motivations for being involved in medicine, they both had a vested interest in the hospital's economic solvency. Although physicians might have been concerned with the needs of their patients and their own economic security, the privately owned hospital ultimately had to be obligated to its stockholders. Soon decisions were increasingly concerned with basic economic issues. Some may object to this statement, arguing that physicians and other medical personnel still follow "codes of ethics," such as the Hippocratic

2. Ibid., 5.

3. Bradford H. Gray, *The Profit Motive and Patient Care: The Changing Accountability of Doctors and Hospitals* (Cambridge: Harvard University Press, 1991), 3.

4. Gray, The Profit Motive of Patient Care, 6.

Oath, so that the argument that they were increasingly concerned with economic issues is unsubstantiated. Although many physicians did, and still do, follow their corporate, vocational, and personal "codes of ethics," this does not change the ultimate focus of a heath care company. Health care became more focused on economics, and that focus directly influenced medical personnel. However, the profit motive in health care did not make a problem, it only accentuated the new economic priorities.

In the development of modern health care in America, economic factors have increasingly taken priority, revealing a profit motive involved in medical care. This profit motive caused various aspects of health care to vie for the same health care dollars. Profit became an integral part of medicine, which meant that issues beyond medical care needed to be considered. It is not that these issues were ignored before this situation occurred. But now, with this increasing economic priority, the health care industry found it necessary to deal with stock holders, salaries, facilities, economic trends, medical development, research, and patient care more then it had in the past. A balance needed to be maintained between economics and medical care. Balancing economics and medical care is a complex process that also includes the issue of limited resources. How complex this is, is seen in the current factors that influence American heath care.

Trends That Have Revealed a Need for Allocation

Fiscal Responsibility

The emerging financial market surrounding current health care practices promoted business moves that made fiscal sense. "Fiscal sense" here means allocating funds in light of the economic incentives and the resource limitations in the health care industry. For this reason, when confronted with fluctuating patient loads, physicians contracted with health care organizations. HMO's offered the ideal of consistent accountability for patients and physicians alike. Consistent accountability meant that the patients experienced a medical community that, in theory, was accountable to them to meet as much of their medical needs as possible, and physicians experienced a medical community, in theory, that was accountable to provide manageable patient loads and adequate compensation packages. This medical community attempted to promote an organization that was able to make responsible economic decisions.

An accountable medical community could not occur in a vacuum. The increase in medical costs coupled with the organizational development of health care communities developed a need. That need was for administrators, such as healthcare managers, to play an increasing role in making healthcare decisions. The increasing role of administrators in health care decision making was seen in their surprising growth. "Since 1983, the number of practicing physicians has risen about 50 percent, while the number of healthcare managers has risen 683 percent. Medical priority has shifted from connecting with each person to holding down medical costs, to improve profitability."[5] The purpose of the rise of healthcare managers is seen in their task. They were tasked with the responsibility to hold down costs, which meant that they have to decide how to fund medicine in such a way as to provide the greatest financial benefit for their employers while providing for the patient's needs and avoiding harmful negative publicity. Another way of saying this is that healthcare managers were responsible to allocate resources in directions that they decided were appropriate for their company's mission statement. Their decisions to allocate resources were complex because these resources were limited. The breadth of the limitation of resources in the medical care and the need for fiscally responsible decisions reveal the need for some method of allocation.

Staff Shortages Limit Care

One of the ways that the limitations of medical care reveal the need for allocation is seen in the problems in health care staffing. Medical staff shortages continually plague most medical institutions, limiting the quality and quantity of care that patients receive. The medical community is not only dealing with staffing shortages, but also with low morale and a decrease in workplace loyalty. Along with these

---

5. Beth Witrongen McLeod, "Relationship—Centered Care," *Noetic Sciences Review* 48 (1999): 36.

problems is the plight of physicians. Like ancillary medical workers, physicians have to deal with unique pressures which limit their capacities to care for their patients while fulfilling their employer's economic wishes. Although ancillary medical workers and physicians function in the same medical community, their issues are unique, and each adds to the problems of staff shortages in health care.

At the patient care level, staff shortages are noticed by the consumer. This is one of the reasons why nurse shortages came to the attention of the medical community. The present problem concerning nurse staffing looks bleak.

> Today, there are more than 125,000 nursing vacancies. The American Hospital Association estimates that 11 percent of nursing positions are vacant. A chronic lack of staff is impairing the ability of U.S. hospitals to respond to rising demand for inpatient beds, and emergency and intensive care. Short-term recruiting strategies like bonuses and BMWs are quick fixes at best.[6]

This want of nursing staff influences the current ability of a hospital to care for its patients, but also presents a problem of meeting future consumer needs.

Some estimate that the shift away from acute care to an increase in administrative duties for registered nurses, which occurred in the Nineties, has also contributed to this shortage of nurses. This shift has contributed to fewer hospital admissions and shorter hospital stays for patients in order to reduce the total nursing workload.[7] Although this might be an admirable goal in itself it reveals the medical communities' attempt to deal with the shortage of nursing staff while maintaining fiscal viability. Nurses were placed in a situation

---

6. Russell C. Coile Jr., "Futurescan 2002: A Forecast of Healthcare Trends (2002–2006)" *Great Boards* May 2002: 3–4 [on-line]; accessed 05 April 2003; available from http://www.great.boards.org; Internet.

7. Barbara J. White, "A Nurse's Experience," in *The Changing Face of Health Care: A Christian Appraisal of Managed Care, Resource Allocation, and Patient-Caregiver Relationship*s, ed., John F. Kilner, Robert D. Orr and Judith Allen Shelly (Grand Rapids: Eerdmans, 1998), 21. In the early 1990's the vast majority of RNs were employed in hospitals. By 2000, the emphasis has shifted to an increased usage of outpatient settings, ambulatory care centers, and extended care facilities.

where their employers were attempting to maintain the same patient load while using personnel assigned to multiple tasks or with fewer personnel. The issue here is not necessarily the conservation of hospital stays by individual patients, but as with the issue of economics it reveals the reality of limited medical resources and nursing staff that exists in the American medical system. That the medical community should have a method of allocation which directs the existing staff to where they are most needed is vital.[8]

The staffing shortage includes not just registered nurses, but also radiologists, pharmacists, and related health support staff, the numbers of whom have decreased markedly in the last decade.[9] As a result the allocation of medical resources, in light of staff shortages, has become an important and timely issue in health care.[10] The specific issue at this point is not how human resources will be allocated, but that they need to be allocated.

Physicians are not immune to the pressures that point to the need for allocation. In the past there may have been enough physicians to cover basic medical care, but the trend is toward a precipitously deceasing doctor patient ratio. A recent study argues that the United States is going to face an increasing shortage of doctors over the next twenty years. Citing that most studies rely on evidence obtained from

---

8. "The Nursing Shortage and You," *USA Weekend*, 29–31 August 2003: 6–7. This article reveals the despair in the medical community concerning the nursing shortage. There is a 126,000 shortfall in nursing personnel. Some of the recommendations are importing foreign trained medical personnel. Nine suggestions to patients on how to navigate in the hospital in light of these staff shortages are also offered.

9. Karen Pallarito, "US Health Worker Shortage Endangers Public," *Yale New Haven Health*, Health News, Today's Health News, Reuters 05 Sept 2002 [on-line]; accessed 05 April 2003; available from http://yalenewhavenhealth.org/HealthNews/ Reuters/ NewsStory0905200240.html; Internet. Pallarito points out the there is a serious shortage of nurses, pharmacists and other health professionals across the United States and links patient death and injury to this nursing crisis. She also cites evidence that the US population is growing beyond the rate of graduating physicians, which presents a potential staffing crisis that is rare for the United States.

10. Coile, "Futurescan 2002," *Great Boards*. Labor shortages are not limited to nursing. Pharmacists, technicians and therapists are all in short supply. Labor force availability was the No. 2 priority in the AHA's annual Leadership Survey of key issues facing healthcare executives.

the 1990s Richard A. Cooper, Prakash Laud, and Heather J. McKie at the Health Policy Institute of the Medical College of Wisconsin and Thomas E. Getzen at Temple University state that, "medical services over the past 70 years has grown 50% faster than GDP."[11] At the current rate, there will be a fifty-thousand person shortfall of physicians by 2010, and by 2020 an overall shortfall of twenty percent. This explains a trend away from physicians to the use of a number of cheaper and more available substitutes such as midwives, nurse practitioners, and physicians' assistants.[12] The decrease in staff physicians means that their time, experience, and talents will need to be directed where they will be most effective.

The problem of physician shortage is not simply a numbers issue. In some areas of medicine there is a shortage of physicians because of collateral problems. Thus physicians are becoming discipline selective. Some doctors have steered away from specific specialty areas, such as emergency medicine, obstetrics, OB/GYN, orthopedic and orthopedic surgery. The reasons for these selective choices are varied. High malpractice rates have caused, among many things, a shortage of physicians in various fields of medicine, as mentioned above.[13] Others have chosen not to serve in specialties, such as psychiatry, geriatrics, and palliative care medicine, that are seen as depressing or which do not pay as well as other specialties. An important example of this need for allocating physicians based upon discipline selectivity is seen in the specialty of geriatrics. A Rand Corporation study shows the trend, "that the U.S. needs 20,000 physicians trained in geriatric care. There are just 7,000."[14] Others have noted that the elderly pose particular problems that some potential physicians find unattractive. "Young physicians see geriatrics as depressing and not as well-paying as other specialties. In a medical system that is acute-care-based, the

11. David Fairlamb, "No Doctor in the House: The Shortage Will Only Get Worse," *Business Week Online*, 4 February 2002 [one-line]; accessed 16 October 2002; available from http://www.businessweek.com:print/magazine/content/02_05/c3768044. htm?mainwindow; Internet.

12. Ibid.

13. Sandy Sims, "Medical associations say that exodus of California doctors is epidemic," part 2, *The Sun*, 07 Feb 2001.

14 Korky Vann, "Nation Faces Shortage of Doctors to Treat Geriatric Patients," *Hartford Courant*, 20 February 2001 [on-line]; accessed 11 October 2002; available from http://www.HartfordCourant.com; Internet.

emphasis is on diagnosis and cure. Geriatricians have to think beyond the treatment of disease to the issues of promoting function, preventing decline and preserving independence."[15] The shortage of geriatric physicians is a symptom of the need for responsible health care management.

An objection that may be raised is that these problems concerning physician shortages do not directly relate to the need for allocation. Certainly further research concerning how the various pressures apply to the career longevity of physicians is needed, but this does not make the point moot. A decrease in doctors as a whole, or in a specific field of practice, means that hospital administrators will have to direct those physicians that are available to those areas that are of priority. There is a clear trend pointing to a decrease in physicians which will present an even greater challenge in the coming years. The method by which decision makers choose which medical event is a priority is not the issue here as much as the point that is revealed by this need to make a choice. Worse staff shortages are just one example of the types of problems that are driving administrators increasingly to regulate medical personnel.

Those who have been observing the American heath care industry have not been oblivious to the realities of the system's problems. Dr. Floyd Bloom, the president of the *American Association for the Advancement of Science* declared in February, 2003 at the Association's annual meeting, that the American health care system is, "in imminent danger of collapse."[16] In light of the present clinical

15. Ibid. Vann goes on to show that the shortage goes beyond the physician to patient ratio. In the same article Dr. Robert Butler, former director of the National Institute on Aging and founder of the International Longevity Center, a New York City think tank on aging issues states, "There are not even enough geriatricians to teach medical students and residents who have chosen other specialties," As a result, elderly people often receive substandard care. In a new study conducted by the Longevity Center on the need for geriatrics training, Butler writes: "Care of older adults is disorganized and confusing; symptoms are often misunderstood or dismissed . . . diagnoses are often extraordinarily late, and doctors have limited understanding of the proper use of medications in older persons."

16. Jonathan Amos, "US Healthcare in Danger of Collapse," *BBC News World Edition*, 14 February 2003, In Depth: Denver 2003 [newspaper online]; accessed 15 February 2003; available from http://news.bbc.co.uk/2/hi/in_depth/sci_tech/2003/ denver_2003/2760101.stm; Internet.

shortage of medical personnel, at all levels, some type of resource allocation method is necessary to rescue the American health care system from this, "danger of collapse." A resource allocation method is needed which is able to address the various competing issues in the American health care system.

Staff shortages in medicine are not a peripheral issue. Additional numbers of skilled personnel will be needed in order to avoid substandard care. At this juncture, the issue of importance is that staff shortages in the medical community point towards the need for allocation of limited human medical resources.

Current Economic Issues That Display the Need for Allocation

Fiduciary responsibility and staff shortages are not the only areas that demonstrate a need for health care allocation. There are a number of other issues, specifically other economic issues that also point to the need for allocation. Some of these issues are related to the rising costs of health care, while others are related to supply and demand. Economics has developed into a driving force in health care. How patients and professionals deal with economic movements as they currently exist reveal why health care allocation is needed.

The current rise in medical costs points to a future in which some type of strict health care allocation will become essential. This need is seen in a number of areas. Regarding the rise in medical costs generally, the 2003 Hay Benefits Report surveyed over one thousand American companies, and found that medical costs are rising dramatically.[17] Increasing numbers of companies are moving to PPO's in order to save money. PPO's, as opposed to HMO's, do not use referral services which are more expensive.[18] As with most economic issues in medicine actions are taken to keep the profit margins unchanged while shifting the increased costs to other involved parties. This shift has come in the guise of reimbursement rates that have been limited to hospitals and physicians, which means that these

---

17. "Study Predicts Another year of Sharp Increases in Medical Premiums," *SmartPros* [on-line]; accessed 29 August 2003; available from http://www.smartpros.com/x40106.xml; Internet.

18. Ibid.

costs will be passed on to consumers. As a result, the average employee premium rose fifteen percent in 2003. As a percentage of total payroll expense, employer costs for health benefits have risen steadily from 7.3 percent in 2000 to 7.8 percent in 2002, and then jumped a full percent to 8.8 percent in 2003.[19] Health care costs are steadily rising. Dr. Floyd Bloom provides an answer for why this inflation is adversely affecting health care when he stated at the *American Association for the Advancement of Science's* annual meeting, "The costs of medications are exceeding the ability of employers to pay for them."[20] More will be said about the increased cost of medication later, but the common problem is that increased costs of health care are limiting medical care for many patients who simply cannot afford to pay for minimal care.

Patients are not the only ones who are concerned with the rising costs of health care. Tim Rhondes, president of the intelligence firm *Provizio* states, "We found that most employers in this study believe their health plan vendors are not doing enough to stabilize and decrease insurance costs."[21] Both employees and employers see the increase in health care costs generally, and health insurance costs particularly, heading in a disturbing direction, one which will edge out many people because of its high costs.

The economic power exercised by patients in American's free market medical system reveals a problem with health care costs. While discussing genetic medicine, Francis Collins reveals the inequality of the American health care system regarding those who cannot afford health care insurance.

> The United States has a dichotomous health care system. While many have excellent health care, over forty million Americans do not have any health care coverage. New technologies that come along tend to be both very expensive and available only in certain places. Genetic technologies could well drive an even larger wedge between those who have access to good health care and those who

19. Ibid.
20. Amos, "US Healthcare in Danger of Collapse," [newspaper on-line].
21. "Employers Leading the Charge to Control Health Care Costs," *SmartPros* [on-line]; accessed 29 August 2003; available from http://www.smartpros.com/x38246.xml; Internet.

do not. Genetics is not the cause of this problem, but it could augment the gross inequality in our health care system.[22]

The need for resource allocation is seen in Collins' comments concerning genetic medicine. But, the concern regarding medicine goes beyond genetic medicine, as has been noted. Medical costs are becoming increasingly difficult to control. The development of a method of allocation which ethically decides who will receive often expensive and difficult to obtain medical care has become essential.

When health care costs rise above the consumer's ability to pay, problems occur, compelling some important decisions concerning the direction of health care. The difficulty of consumer payment for medical care is underscored when one notes that this gap in financial resources must also deal with the problem of limited medical resources.

> Thousands of people die annually—even in a developed country like the United States—for lack of access to organ transplants. Vastly greater numbers die worldwide for lack of access to immunizations, or antibiotics, or prenatal care. The inescapable question echoes around the world: When there is not enough for everyone, who gets it and who doesn't? Who lives and who dies? Sometimes the problem is that health care becomes very expensive, or the resources allocated to it become limited by other priorities—perhaps misplaced ones. So it may be a question of tight money. But it also may be a question of absolutely scarce resources.[23]

The problem that occurs when medical costs escalate is that resources become unavailable to patients, often to those who need them the most. Priorities are also revealed in the process of determining who will receive the resources that are available. It is the prioritization of health care offered that is the concern here. The reason

---

22. Francis Collins, "Human Genetics," in *Cutting-Edge Bioethics: A Christian Exploration of Technologies and Trends*, ed. John F. Kilner, C. Christopher Hook and Diann B. Uustal (Grand Rapids: Eerdmans, 2002), 15.

23. John F. Kilner, "Age-Based Rationing of Health Care," *Dignity* (Fall 2001), 1.

is that, "medical services are seen to be somehow nonoptional, and therefore a rise in prices is seen to be particularly threatening, because we are powerless to respond by trimming consumption—and thereby taking the steam out of the inflationary pressures."[24] The problem of healthcare being nonoptional is that medical resources usually cannot be limited by most patients by simply choosing not to be involved in the process. Although some may argue that some types of medical care are arbitrary, some are clearly not so. An individual who has a heart condition may choose to die rather then go through open heart surgery, but most reasonable patients in that condition would desire the surgery. The implications of essential health care, like this proposed heart surgery, are complicated by the problem of a patient's inability to pay for the needed services.

An increase in cost of medical care coupled with scarce resources means that some people who need it may not receive medical care, and in one sense this is a type of allocation based on economic status. A decision to devote resources to one patient or treatment means that the service provided will not be available to someone else. The issue is an increased cost in medical care, and how that medical care will be distributed. Few would advocate that only those who can afford to pay fully for a medical service should receive such care. Even though medicine is a business, it still must deal with its customers. The task, then, is to provide guidelines so that all who have concerns regarding medicine and its costs are dealt with in a just and equitable manner. This just and equitable distribution system would prevent the free market medical system from disregarding those who may be unable to afford medical care. This allocation method should allow patient care, treatment, medication, and other vital processes to continue to the point that it can maximize the care that is available while maintaining viability for all concerned.

Increasing Prescription Costs

Certain trends in medicine are particularly problematic when it comes to the current economic conditions of health care, and,

---

24. Charles Fried, "Health Care, Cost Containment, Liberty," in *Ethical Issues in Modern Medicine*, 2nd ed., ed. John Arras and Robert Hunt (Palo Alto, CA: Mayfield Publishing Company, 1983), 527–28.

when revealed, also support the need for resources to be allocated. Medication costs are increasing at an exponential rate. An example of this is seen in Medicaid's struggle with rising prescription costs. "Medicaid spending on prescription drugs grew on average, by 18% between 1997 and 2000. The program spent $21 billion in 2000."[25] Each day, it seems as if another increase in health care costs is announced by the press or by some government agency. Increased medical costs have become a constant concern for patients. This worry is not without foundation. Its basis is seen, for instance, in the increase in prescription drug costs which have risen at a rate of twenty percent.[26] Technology now allows very sick patients to live longer, which means that they will have to bear a heavier burden of medical expenses. For those who are not very sick, co-pays for prescription medications have doubled.[27] The need for prescription medications to be available for those patients who need these resources the most means that distribution of medication will need to be directed, or allocated to the areas where their use can be maximized.

Another reason why the increase in prescription medication is seen as a concern for many people is that they simply cannot afford to pay for all of the co-pays and deductibles that they are required to pay in order to receive their medications. This is especially true in older life where many patients are on "fixed" incomes. American "consumers increased their spending on health care by a modest 4 percent, but it sure seemed like more. That's because out-of-pocket spending in the category experienced the steepest increases: 26 percent for health insurance and 23 percent for drugs."[28] Somehow balance must be found between the profit margins in health care and the ability of patients to afford needed medication. How decisions are made concerning who will receive the limited care and how the

---

25. "Prescription Drugs," Center on an Aging Society, Georgetown University, *Data Profile* 5, (Sept 2002) [on-line]; accessed 04 August 2003; available from http:// ihcrp.georgetown.du/agingsociety/pubhtml/rxdrugs/rxdrugs.html; Internet.

26. "Study Predicts Another Year of Sharp Increases," *SmartPros* [on-line].

27. Ibid.

28. Michael J. Weiss, "Inconspicuous Consumption: Health Care: The Growing Cost of Feeling Good," *American Demographics* 24 (Apr 2002): 34.

resources will be distributed is the concern of health care allocation, and why it is so desperately needed.

Increased Malpractice Costs

Another economic reality that has affected health care and indicates the need for allocation is the rising cost of malpractice insurance among physicians. This issue is different from that of physicians choosing to opt-out of a specialty because of low pay or lack of excitement. Increased malpractice insurance costs are forcing some physicians to be selective about who they accept, and in some cases, to leave the profession altogether, but these choices are often determined by others who decide the amount of money a physician is charged for his or her malpractice insurance. Donald Zuk, the CEO of SCPIE Holdings, California's second largest malpractice insurer, places malpractice insurance within its current context. He stated in an interview in June, 2003 that, "the loss ratios were going through the roof," and so his company raised malpractice rates forty percent in 2001 and thirty percent in 2002.[29] With tort reform unable to keep malpractice costs under control, physicians and patients are in a situation where costs will continue to rise in the near future. Although tort reform and caps on economic damage are beyond the confines of this work, they point to a growing need for cost control between the malpractice insurers, the physicians, the hospitals, the patients, and the juries that decide on the malpractice award. Some have said that investment losses are to blame as much as jury awards for the malpractice crisis.[30] In either case the problem remains and physicians are caught in the middle where they must pay large malpractice premiums as well as sustain an acceptable income adequate to sustain a practice and to repay medical school loans. A balance must be reached between the rights of physicians to make an acceptable income, the needs of patients, and the reality of increased malpractice awards. Though tort reforms are an important part of this equation, there is also the need for a method of allocation which is able to take these competing factors into account.

29. Daniel Eisenberg and Maggie Seiger, "The Doctor Won't See You Now," *Time* 161 (9 June 2003): 47.

30. Ibid, 51.

Health Care Must Have Allocation

The increase in malpractice costs has caused many physicians to choose areas of service that do not have traditionally high malpractice insurance costs. Some physicians have chosen to leave their state or leave field of medicine because insurance costs have made medicine unprofitable.[31] Increased costs in malpractice insurance have had a negative influence on the availability of physicians. This negative influence means that fewer resources will be available for medical care. With fewer dollars available, and fewer physicians, the need for resource allocation becomes an increasingly important issue. The tension between profit and the availability of resources is revealed in the physicians' choices. This problem needs to be addressed through resources allocation that takes physician needs into account.

Weight of Medical Costs for the Public

The weight of health care costs is another problem that reveals the need for allocation of resources. The weight of health care goes beyond the plethora of elective surgeries available to Americans, and includes the total cost of a given health system as it applies to the daily lives of the average American. An example of this is seen in The Oregon Health Plan legislation that called for total coverage of medical care at the expense of a state's given ability to pay for those services. This legislation would have provided unlimited medical care for its state's inhabitants. The method of payment would have been a new medical tax.[32] The issue here is not whether Oregonians wanted

---

31. Ibid. Forty-six states were described as either near or in medical-malpractice crisis. It is no longer uncommon to read stories of physicians moving to states that have lower insurance costs, or leaving the field altogether. This type of pressure increases the scarcity of resources available to patients. Examples of both of these issues can be read in the following: Elizabeth S. Burkett, "Malpractice Problems Shouldn't Hurt Patients," *Business First* (29 July 2002). Joy Davia, "Doctors Struggle with Different Malpractice Problems: Some See Leaving as Only Alternative," *Sunday Gazette-Mail* (7 April 2002).

32. The Oregon Measure 23, which provides the tax base for the Oregon Health Plan, was defeated when put up for a vote. The Oregon Health Plan was estimated to cost $1.7 billion and was to be supported by a new tax of nearly 9% on every working Oregonian. The bill was designed to cover "medical necessary procedures." The physician of choice would have been designated as the arbiter deciding what treatment or procedure was "medically necessary." According to Barney Speight, a former state health administrator, the *Oregon Health Plan* was

to pay the new tax. The issue is that the state could not afford to pay for the medical care that the *Oregon Health Plan* proposed. There were a number of reasons why Oregonians supported this concept of medical care, but the weight of the medical care proposed was too much for Oregon's population to sustain. Even so, it garnered nearly twenty percent of votes from the Oregon's residents.[33] The desire for medical care caused them, at least in part, to disregard the potential economic hazards of this specific health care plan for the benefits that it offered. The weight of costs of this medical system would have been disastrous to the state's economy, which would have meant that health care would have been necessarily curtailed. Comprehensive medical care which allows the medical system to be financially overwhelmed will be unable to distribute resources where they will be needed the most. Allocation is needed to ensure that the medical needs of as many patients as possible are met within the economic ability of a given health care system. This method of allocation must go beyond the demand for the services to guide the allocation of limited resources.

In America's market driven medical system, health care allocation decisions will have to be made if the maximization of health resources is to be realized.[34] The method of allocation may be an *ad hoc* or well developed method of allocating resources, but that scarce resources be allocated is imperative. The reality is that the American health care industry cannot provide every medical procedure necessary for every individual in need even if it wants to do so because there are not enough physicians, nurses, and other medical personnel to meet the growing demands for health care. Funding for medical care is also limited because of a number of sources vying for the same dollars. Together these factors make a compelling case for the necessity of a fair method of allocation for health care resources.

---

expected to plunge the state into a fiscal crisis. Brad Cain, "Oregon considers Universal Health Plan," *The Telegraph*, 08 Oct 2002 [on-line]; accessed 04 April 2003, available from http//www.macon.com/mld/macon/news/nation/4239062.html; Internet.

33. Associated Press, "Oregon Health Care Plan Rejected" *The Olympian*, Front Page, 06 November 2002 [on-line]; accessed 04 April 2003; available from http://www. theolympian.com/home/news/20021106/ frontpage/3437_Printer.shtml; Internet.

34 Ibid.

Disparity in Supply and Demand

Discussions concerning health care allocation in the United States often center on two opposing concerns: the tremendous and rising costs of care on the one hand, and the fear that attempts to reduce these costs will deny sick people the care they need on the other.[35] These concerns are revealed in the inflationary nature of health care in its modern expression. Initially, the difficulty manifests itself in the problem of consumer sovereignty in supply and demand. One of the ways that consumer sovereignty has exercised its economic power has been by demanding a continual option of care. A problem with this approach is that free market economics is hindered if enough resources to meet the demand are not available. Demand for services is immaterial if the system does not have the resources to cover, or supply, those services. Consumer sovereignty has come to show that many Americans exercise their power in the free market by seeking an unceasing choice of personal physicians, specialists, and hospital beds. The clarity with which the problem of unceasing choice can be seen was demonstrated in a recent study that confirms the trend to identify choice of care with quality of care. In that study, consumers often viewed choice itself as a proxy for good quality.[36] This type of consumer would object to health care allocation because it could potentially limit their choice of sources of care. Choice does not correct the problem that there is not enough medical care for everyone. Thus the issue of choice needs to take a secondary place to that of allocating limited resources.

Another reason why choice is of importance when dealing with supply and demand is that this view of medicine has caused medical

35. Lisa Yount, *Patients' Rights in the Age of Managed Health Care* (New York: Facts on File, Inc., 2001), 3.

36. AARP, *Beyond 50, A Report to the Nation on Trends in Health Security* (Washington DC: AARP, 2002), 91. In 2000, 79 percent of Americans age 18 or older reported that they were "very confident" or "somewhat confident" that they had enough information to make the right choice in choosing a doctor. In addition, most adults over age 50 reported satisfaction with their choice of primary care physician (over 90 percent) in 1998/1999, as they did with choice of specialist physician. Looking toward the next decade, about two-thirds of consumers in 2001 are very confident of being able to choose a quality doctor in the future, with people age 50–64 slightly less confident (64 percent) than people over age 65 (70 percent).

care to be seen as an entitlement instead of as a benefit among many sectors of American society. As an entitlement, medicine is seen as a type of social contract in which the hospital, government, or employer is obligated to provide sufficient resources for each person's need because it is expected in the American consumer culture. In the past, American medicine has not been viewed as an entitlement, but recently "the older models of voluntary assistance have gradually given way to a controversial model of an *enforceable right* to health care."[37] By *enforceable right,* it is meant that there has emerged a social consensus that access to health care should be available to all citizens.[38] The result of the Social Security debates of the 1950's, the construction of that program, with its implicit promises, provided the basis for the notion of medicine as an entitlement.[39]

Although there may be an increasing belief that medicine is a "right" this does not mean that the health care system was, or currently is able fully to care for every patient. One reason for this is demographics. The medical community cannot provide a *carte blanche* for all Americans regarding medical care. An increase in the elderly population coupled with the staff shortages point to the potential for a system overload in the medical community.

> As the "baby boom" generation turns 65, beginning in 2011, the size of the elderly population will grow substantially. By 2050 it is projected that one in five Americans will be elderly.
>
> The aging of the population has important consequences for the health care system. As the elderly fraction of the population increases, more services will be required for the treatment and management of chronic and acute health conditions. Providing health care services needed

---

37. Tom L. Beauchamp and James F. Childress, *Principles of Biomedical Ethics*, 5th ed. (Oxford: Oxford University Press: 2001), 241.

38. Ibid.

39. Paul M. Romer, "The Politics of Entitlement," in Individual and Social Responsibility: Child Care, Education, Medical Care, and Long-Term Care in America, ed. Victor R. Fuchs (Chicago: The University of Chicago Press, 1996), 198.

by Americana of all ages will be a major challenge in the twenty-first century.[40]

What this means for this discussion is that an inordinate demand for health care could cause the system to collapse. Though some view medical care as a right or an entitlement, that position does not negate the problem of limited resources in the medical community, rather, it reveals its need. Allocation is necessary to direct consumers to make decisions that are the best for themselves and for the medical community at large. This would prevent perceived entitlements from overwhelming the medical community with patient "wants" rather than patient "needs."

The need for some type of heath care allocation method has not escaped the medical community. The real question concerning health care allocation has been how could the medical community best meet those allocation needs. Over the years there have been a number of attempts to deal with some of the issues discussed which relate to the need for allocation. Reviewing some of these efforts to control resource limitations will show that these allocation attempts have not been entirely successful.

Attempts to Control Health Care's Problems

A short examination has been presented of some of the past trends and present dilemmas that confront the health care system in the United States, and which reveal the need for some method of health care allocation. As the current situation developed, there were several attempts to meet the need to limit medical costs and gain control of the developing health care crisis. Each of the following attempts have been held up as a "cure" for the problems in the American health care system. These attempts have spanned the spectrum from various methods of cost control from socialized medicine to imaginative payment plans for hospitals and doctors. An overview of four of these methods of allocating medical care will provide a context for look-

---

40. Department of Health and Human Services, Centers for Disease Control and Prevention, and National Center for Health Statistics, *Chartbook on Trends in the Health of Americans, Excerpted from Health, United States, 2002* (Hyattsville, MD: Department of Health and Human Services, 2002), 19.

ing at QALYs, which will be seen as a basis for meeting the needs expressed in resource allocation.

Health Maintenance Organizations (HMOs)

One attempt to control medical costs has been the familiar Health Maintenance Organizations. An HMO is an organized system of health care which attempts to provide a defined, comprehensive set of services to a defined population for a fixed, periodic per person fee. HMOs are one of the more structured forms of managed care.[41] Since HMOs emerged in the late 1960s with the rise of for-profit health care institutions and fee-for-services, there has been a constant trade off between care needed by patients and the cost allowed to be incurred by HMOs for those services. For many physicians the equation was simple. The HMOs had more patients, and more patients meant more potential income. But the trade off for more patients was, and still is, an increasing accountability to the organization and limited choice of physicians, and in some cases, limited choices of medical treatment.[42]

Unfortunately this connection has brought about some ethical problems that directly influenced allocations.

> One of the problems is found in how physicians are paid by HMOs. The pay of a physician is directly connected to their ability to restrict hospitalization and prescriptions. Fee-for-service, capitation, and salary can be modified through the use of "withholds" and bonuses. Withholds refer to the practice of MCOs (Managed Care Organizations) keeping a certain percentage of the fee or salary (typically 5–20 percent) until the end of the fiscal

---

41. Scott E. Daniels, "Managed Care's Financial Incentives," in *The Changing Face of Health Care*, ed. John F. Kilner, Robert D. Orr and Judith Allen Shelly (Grand Rapids: Eerdmans, 1998), 93.

42. Gray, *The Profit Motive and Patient Care*, 4–5. Victor R. Fuchs, *Who Shall Live?: Health, Economics, and Social Choice*, Expanded Ed. (River Edge, NJ: World Scientific Publishing Co. Pte. Ltd., 1998), 138. There are two types of payment plans for HMO. One is a prepaid group-practice plan and the other is a fee-for-service that is monitored by a foundation. In each case the goal is to provide comprehensive coverage, prepayment, and an covering organization that cares for the availability and quality of services.

year. Withholds are used to pay for any cost overruns that may be incurred. Residuals are then disbursed. The assumed benefit of having physicians take on additional risk is that the physicians will be motivated to control costs so that they will receive payments that are due to them. Alternatively, MCOs can use bonuses as a way of attempting to control costs. In MCO plans that use bonuses, physicians are rewarded for effectively controlling costs.[43]

That physicians are rewarded for effectively controlling costs through restricting hospitalizations and prescriptions may seem like a conflict of interest. A physician may be unduly influenced by financial incentives to make decisions that are not necessarily in the best interests of the patient. Not everyone considers controlling costs through financial incentives problematic, but others have indicated major ethical conflicts of interest with this kind of incentive. Those who object find that one of the causes for concern is that of control, arguing that the person who holds the purse strings is, ultimately, the one in charge of decisions. Researchers like Melvin Jacob have concluded that the pressures of HMOs are too much to be ethically acceptable. Jacob would desire HMOs to follow simple guidelines such as, do no harm, the Golden Rule and promote the common good in order to stave off the economic pressures.[44] Yet there are others, like Victor R. Fuchs, who find that the cost benefit are worth the problems of limited care. The incentives are simply a method of reducing hospitalization while providing comprehensive care.[45] This conflict demonstrates that there are economic pressures causing conflict within the HMO system of health care. With their respective proposals Jacob and Fuchs are attempting to draw ethical boundaries in health care. In that attempt they try to address the issue of resource allocation. While there is great disagreement as to how these resources should be distributed, all seem to agree that there needs

---

43. Daniels, "Managed Care's Financial Incentives," *The Changing Face of Health Care*, 96.

44. Melvin R. Jacob, "Ethical Boundaries and Health Maintenance Organization (HMO) Expectations: Who Draws the Line?" *The Journal of Pastoral Care* 55 (2001): 281.

45. Fuchs, *Who Shall Live?*, 138–42.

to be a "gatekeeper." There needs to be a method of allocation that is able to address these competing concerns in the HMO system of medical care.

Physicians have been suggested as being the ones who ought to have the authority to determine who gets care, since they are the ones who deal directly with the patients. Physicians would serve as, "gatekeepers of medical resources."[46] HMOs have attempted to place physicians in this position, but this has proved problematic. To expect doctors to confront the issue of allocation while in the midst of direct patient care would be a conflict of interests. Physicians would be required to "trade off" the care of a patient in front of him for that of an anonymous patient elsewhere.[47] Theoretically, having the physician decide how medical resources would be distributed may sound workable; however, the ensuing conflict of interests could potentially cause chaos, both morally and legally, between the physician, the medical facility, the patient and patient's family. It has been said that there is a "fiduciary trust that patients place in physicians to make decisions that maximize the well being of their patients, and to act as advocates for their patient in the health care system."[48] The HMO method of compensation places physicians in a position where the perception would be that medical care is primarily a business. An allocation method is necessary because there needs to be a method of distribution of medical care that can detach itself from the influences of issues such as bonuses and pay backs. The method of allocation must be one that, when it is applied, allows objective methods of decision making options for the physicians, the insurance company, the patients, and their families.

Veterans Administration

A longstanding system of health care in the United States has been the Veterans Administration, which traditionally has struggled with allocative and productive efficiency. The disparity between what veterans want or need and what the VA can provide has produced

---

46. Milton C. Weinstein, "Should Physicians be Gatekeepers of Medical Resources?" *Journal of Medical Ethics* 27 (2001): 268.

47. Ibid.

48. Ibid., 271.

a continual state of medical uncertainty, even though it has been restructured a number of times in order to deal with the issue of limited resources.

The VA began in 1798 when the Federal government inaugurated a law which was designed to care for disabled seamen. During the Civil War homes were established to care for disabled veterans when Congress authorized a National Home for Disabled Volunteer Soldiers. In 1921 the Bureau of War Risk Insurance and the U.S. Public Health Service was consolidated into the Veterans Bureau. By 1930 the Veterans Bureau had forty-nine hospitals under its direction. The Veterans Administration was established in 1930 by President Hoover, who consolidated all veterans benefit programs into one independent agency. World War II saw extensive expansion and construction of Veterans Administration hospitals with eighty-two hospitals added by 1960. In 1989 the position of director of the Veterans Administration became a cabinet level post.[49]

Throughout the history of the various forms of the VA the goal has been to provide adequate medical care for the veterans of the United States. Different organizational alignments have attempted to, "enhance the care and service provided to the Nation's veterans, consistent with the economical use of scarce dollars resources."[50] The ability of the Veterans Administration to use scarce resource dollars consistently reveals the difficulties surrounding the limitation of funds. The VA is required to provide high quality care to all United States veterans relatively free of charge. As is common for any government controlled system the budget for the VA is fixed. "It forces health care professionals, health care administrators, and even patients to decide how best to spend scarce health care dollars."[51]

As with other government programs there is a need to decide who will receive the "scarce health care dollars." The problem is

---

49. "History of Facilities Management," *Office of Facilities Management* [on-line]; accessed 02 July 2003; available from http://www.va.gov/facmgt/aboutfm/history.asp; Internet.

50. Peter A. Ubel, "Understanding and Improving Resource Allocation Decisions," *VA Center for Practice Management and Outcomes Research* [on-line]; accessed 2 July 2003; available from http://www.hsrd.ann-arbor.med.va.gov/ubel_cda.htm; Internet.

51. Ibid.

that there is an increase in the number of veterans, but a leveling or even decrease in funding for VA medical needs. The Department of Veterans Affairs projected that 3.7 million veterans used VA medical services in 2002 and that in 2003 the number would climb to 4.9 million, which is projected to be a 31.5 percent increase.[52] The problem is that VA funding for medical needs is fixed through Congressional discretionary decisions. Thus, the funding is not guaranteed, and it may be adversely affected by pork barrel projects.[53] The American Legion, a veterans advocate group, argues that the VA health care needs to be a mandatory budget item. The reason why they are arguing in this manner is because the VA is increasingly forced to do more with less. The VA administrators are often placed in the difficult position of arbitrarily deciding where scarce medical dollars will be spent.

> VA health-care administrators have more pressing needs than bricks and mortar. They must come up with innovative new ways to hit their operating budgets, which require more aggressive collections from third-party insurance carriers than ever before, despite decisions in Washington to deny access for veterans most likely to have insurance. Directors nationwide start their budget years deeper in the hole every time the target is raised. Some are forced to tap into building reserves to cover the cost of treating patients.[54]

One of the great issues for the VA is how the limited medical resources available are going to be directed. One may argue that this

---

52. Christopher Smith, "Veterans Deserve Guaranteed Access to Health Care," *The American Legion Magazine* 154 (May 2003) [on-line]; accessed 08 Aug 03; available from http://www.legion.org/publications/pubs_2003/pubs_may03_healthcare.htm; Internet.

53. Ronald Conley, "Veterans health care funding slaughtered in rush for pork," *The American Legion Magazine* 154 (May 2003) [on-line]; accessed 08 Aug 03; available from http://www.legion.org/ pub_relations/pr_releasecontent.php?id=a59; Internet. Conley, much to his chagrin, observes that $1.8 billion was removed from the VA medical appropriations bill in order to fund other causes.

54. Ronald Conley, "A System Worth Saving," *The American Legion Magazine* 154 (May 2003) [on-line]; accessed 08 August 03, available from http://www.legion.org/ publications/pubs_2003/pubs_may03_ system.htm; [Internet].

is really a funding issue for the United States Congress. The problem is that other forces are vying for the same budget dollars before Congress. The current system of funding for the VA will constantly place them in a position to have to choose where to spend limited funding, where to use limited resources and when to restrict care to an ever increasing veteran population. The VA has tried to use co-pay methods and charging the insurance companies of veterans in an effort to recoup some of its revenue. In spite of these efforts to alleviate the problem of limited resources, the VA still has problems. That problem means, for this work, that it requires a method of allocation that functions within the confines of a limited budget, while maximizing scarce medical resources.

The Clinton Plan

HMOs and the VA have not been the only attempts to deal with issues surrounding limited funding and resources in the medical system. Another method of cost containment has been seen in the idea of socialized medicine which has been expressed in a variety of ways. At one time the passage of Medicare legislation in 1965 was seen as, "a slide toward "socialized medicine.""[55] Yet some have seen socialized medicine as the best method by which medical allocation problems can be addressed since it would direct, in a predetermined manner, where resources ought to go.[56] Probably one of the best known attempts in recent years at developing a socialized medical plan for America which would direct resources was the *Clinton Plan*.

In the 1994 State of the Union address, President Clinton proposed a plan which would provide insurance coverage for every American. Quite simply the *Clinton Plan* called for universal medical coverage, which would be a kind of socialized medical plan. When the President presented the plan to Congress, he envisioned a plan that would provide all Americans with the opportunity to have their basic medical needs met. It would have done this through a directive

---

55. "Health Maintenance Organizations," *Minnesota Historical Society* [on-line]; accessed 21 April 2003; available from http://www.mnhs.org/library/tips/history_topics/ 87hmos.html; Internet.

56. Martin Green, *Economics of Health Care*, 3rd ed., Office of Health Economics, (London: Industry Supports Education, 2003), 10 [on-line]; accessed 06 September 2003; available from http://www.oheschools.org; Internet.

or command model of health care. In order to offset the increase in expenditures, the *Plan* called for a ten percent payroll tax increase. This idea of increasing taxation was to offset intended increased medical expenditures by augmenting available funding. Unfortunately the *Plan's* fiscal support base became the basis for, among other politically volatile issues, a political free-for-all. The issues concerning what to do with limited medical resources were pushed aside in the public discussion.

One of the main problems identified in the *Clinton Plan* was its decision making process whereby politicians would have been given the authority to decide where medical care is directed.[57] Because of the American political process this particular style of allocation would necessarily struggle to obtain objectivity. The *Plan* also called for Congress to define the benefits of the *Plan* thoroughly.[58] Since most politicians do not have a medical background, their decisions would be questionable when it came to the parameters that they would have to choose for this medical plan. These ideas would have put into place a method of control for medical costs and would direct or allocate the available medical resources. The *Plan* would have set up a new, huge government bureaucracy. Few people would agree that a new government bureaucracy would have been the best way to objectively and effectively deal with the problem of limited health care resources.

Some opponents of socialized medicine contend that the issue is not socialized medicine's perceived inability to provide adequate and objective care, but that the government has no business being in the health care business. This attitude concerning the limitations of socialized medicine was presented by David Mayer of the Ashbrook Center.

> Medical care may be an important human interest or need, but it is not a "right." Considering it as one will create a multitude of problems and injustices. No matter how wealthy a society is, its resources are never equal to the totality of the demands placed in them. The experience of other countries with national health insurance

57. Ibid.

58. Victor R. Fuchs, "The Clinton Plan: A Researcher Examines Reform," *Health Affairs* 13 (1994): 103–4.

shows that far from guaranteeing the "right," care is routinely denied to those who need it. Citizens not only do not have an enforceable right to any particular medical service; they don't even have a right to a place in line when health care is rationed. The 100th person waiting in line for heart surgery is not "entitled" to the 100th surgery, for example; and given the average wait in countries like Britain, New Zealand, and Canada, those at the bottom of the priority list are literally at the risk of their lives.[59]

Though some may see medical care as a "right" there is clearly a problem with that view in light of the supply of medical care meeting the demand. The fear that seems to be conveyed in Mayer's comments is that allocation of medical resources will be arbitrary. In light of some of the suggestions regarding the *Clinton Plan*, that may be a valid concern. Yet even if socialized medical plans do attempt to correct all of the problems of limited medical resources, it does not mean that this problem will no longer exist. There is still a need for an objective and fair method of resource allocation that can deal with the plethora of issues endemic to the American medical system.

Medicare

HMO's, the VA, and socialized medical plans have not been the only attempt to guide use of medical resources. A significant attempt has been the establishment of Medicare. Medicare is a government program that provides medical care for the elderly. In one respect Medicare is like socialized medicine in that it is influenced by the American government, but it is unique in its system of funding and payouts.

Some may argue that the elderly ought to have enough funds for medical care because they all have paid into Social Security which sets that money aside for the future needs of Medicare. Unfortunately, as has been previously noted, limitations in medical resources and funding prohibit every patient, even among the elderly, from receiving needed medical care.

---

59. David N. Mayer, "Clinton Health Plan: The Wrong Prescription," *On Principle* 2 (1994):1 [on-line]; accessed; 22 April 2003; available from http://www.ashbrook.org/publicat/onprin/v2n1/mayer.html; Internet.

When the issue of Medicare is addressed, the issue of limiting costs has never been far behind. Initially Medicare was enacted on July 30, 1965 by the United States President Lyndon Johnson. He was responding, in part, to a government survey which showed that nearly half of the elderly in America had no health insurance.[60] In this survey one needed to be sixty-five years old to be designated, "elderly."

Medicare, in its current form is split between Part A and Part B, representing the Medicare Hospital Insurance and the Medicare Supplemental Medical Insurance programs, respectively. These two plans cover different services. Part A is hospital Insurance which is the premium-free part of the program, available to all Social Security beneficiaries. Part B provides benefits for physician and outpatient services which receive pay from the federally-run Medicare program. Part B was originally made optional. "The beneficiary premium was intended to cover 50% of the plan's costs, with the remaining 50% coming from the general fund of the federal government. (Later legislation changed that ratio to 25% from premiums and 75% from the general fund.)"[61] The American economy and Medicare are interconnected. Because payroll deductions were designated to go into a Trust Fund for Medicare there was solvency as long as the number of people putting money into the Trust Fund remained significantly higher then those in need, as the Trust Fund was not used for other purposes, and as the American economy relatively stayed strong.

Since Medicare's enactment a number of events have occurred which have threatened Medicare's solvency. The most important of these is the demographic change in America's population. In the coming years the aging of the "baby boomers" will tax the Medicare system. "Sometime around 2010, costs are expected to outpace income in the Hospital Insurance Trust Fund, and the program will have to draw down trust fund assets to stay afloat."[62] The increase in the elderly population is already affecting Medicare. What this

60. "Medicare's 30th," *U.S. News & World Report* 119 (1995): 13.

61. "Medicare: Why Do We Have Medicare Part A and Part B?" *ElderWeb* [on-line]; last updated 22 September 2000; accessed 19 June 2003; available from http://www.elderweb.com; Internet.

62. Marilyn W. Serafini, "Medicare's Challenge," *National Journal* 32 (2000): 1602.

means for this study is that the gap between money flowing in and money going out is likely to continue to increase and this could bring Medicare close to bankruptcy. The ways that this problem could be corrected are by either increasing the amount of money going into the Trust Fund, by decreasing the amount of money spent on medical care, or both. These possible solutions are all easier spoken than accomplished. With the proportion of those over age 65 and eligible to participate in Medicare expected to increase, it is unlikely that there will be a decrease in the amount of money spent on Medicare. In light of the present economic realities in the United States, Medicare will have to struggle simply to maintain the amount of funding it currently has, let alone receive an increase in funding. While political winds may change, the situation, as it stands, reveals a need for allocating the resources that currently exist so that the value of resource dollars is maximized.

Economic slowdowns, along with decreased enrollment in Medicare HMOs have come to reveal that the managed care portion of Medicare, "intended to serve as the structural base for a modernized, market-oriented Medicare program, had major problems."[63] The cause of this major problem is that the method of allocating Medicare funds to hospitals and physicians is flawed. "While payments from the hospital fund are projected to increase from 1.39 percent of GDP in 2000 to 2.91 percent of GDP in 2074, payment from the physicians' fund are projected to increase from 0.94 percent of GDP to 2.36 percent of GDP over the same period."[64] The increase in payments is projected to be 1.42 percent and the increase in spending during that same period is projected to be 1.52 percent. Thus the physicians' fund will be depleted as baby boomers retire, and this could lead to significantly higher medical costs.

> While projected assets of the HI and OASDI Trust Funds are sufficient to pay projected Medicare and Social Security benefits under current law for another 23 and 39 years, respectively, such a perspective belies the enormous—and more immediate—fiscal challenge these programs pose. From a unified budget perspective, sub-

---

63. Ibid., 1603.
64. Ibid., 1604.

stantial fiscal pressure from Medicare and Social Security will appear in a decade and mount rapidly thereafter. At the time of OASDI Trust Fund estimated exhaustion in 2042, annual Social Security expenditures are projected to exceed annual tax income by 34 percent, with this excess growing to 49 percent by the end of the 75-year projection period. Similarly, at the time of HI Trust Fund exhaustion in 2026, annual expenditures are projected to exceed tax revenues by 37 percent, with this excess growing to over 200 percent by the end of the projection period. While SMI technically has no projected shortfall—because of the way in which it is financed—its costs nevertheless also will require a rapidly increasing draw on the Federal budget.[65]

Somehow funds are going to have to be allocated in such a way as both to provide equitable payments to hospitals and physicians, and to provide adequate care for those under Medicare.

Along with the problems surrounding the funding of Medicare are the use of the Trust Fund's perceived "surplus" for unrelated nonmedical causes and the fluctuating American economy. Policy makers debate as to whether the movement of surplus money in Medicare from Plan A to Plan B constitutes a decrease in actual Medicare dollars. In either case, it does reveal the vulnerability of the Trust Funds moneys. If these funds are allocated for other resources, then they will not be available for Medicare discretionary use.

The state of the American economy or the uses of "surplus" funds as such are not relevant. The issue is that, to remain solvent, Medicare needs to have a method of allocating the funds that are available, and a method that is flexible enough to respond to the shifting fortunes of the American economy. As with all other attempts to control the costs of medical care, Medicare has found it difficult to meet the increasing needs of those enrolled. How Medicare will decide to allocate the funds available to the elderly enrolled in Medicare is a question that still needs to be addressed.

65. John L. Palmer and Thomas R. Saving, A Summary of the 2003 ANNUAL REPORTS Social Security and Medicare Boards of Trustees," *Status of the Social Security and Medicare Programs* [on-line]; accessed 25 June 2003; available from http://www.ssa.gov/OACT /TRSUM/trsummary.html; Internet.

Limited Resources and Allocation

The inability of HMOs, socialized medical plans like the *Clinton Plan*, the VA and Medicare to control costs demonstrates, at least in part, that their attempts to deal with this problem have not been altogether successful. Few would argue against the need for the American health care system to control its spending in light of the limitations of resources, but this does not solve the problem. The problem centers on what method ought the American system of health care to use that will allocate resources in an ethically acceptable manner.

In one sense, a kind of allocation method is already occurring in United States. A market driven economy produces one type of allocation. Stuart Horner sees this economic rationing as a given in the American culture.

> How can a system, which excludes thirty-seven million Americans from any guaranteed health care provision, be described as anything else but a rationed system? Admittedly the rationing is by price, but rationing none the less. A free market which excludes individuals from participation within it is not only not genuinely free, but is rationing health care by excluding significant numbers of beneficiaries.[66]

In one sense, it is true that a lack of comprehensive health care partially due to financial inequities allows a select few to receive care. However, this method of allocation does not seem to be comprehensive enough to deal with the limitations of resources and the ever increasing cost of health care, because it only means that those who have limited income or access to medical care do not receive it. Thus, in the American system of health care economics matter, but economics is not the only issue that needs to be addressed.

> We first need to admit that the supply of resources available for health care is insufficient to meet the need because it is limited by other priorities. In the 1980s and early 1990s there was consensus that health care costs

---

66. Stuart Horner, "Conclusion: Change Health Care—A British Point of View," in *The Changing Face of Health Care: A Christian Appraisal of Managed Care*, 283.

were spiraling out of control, and that if they were not contained, they would constitute a disproportionate share of society's resources. This spiraling was due to a variety of factors, including overuse of expensive high-tech treatments, especially at the end of life, the legacy of aggressive treatment, and the phenomenon of third-party payer removing patients from payment decisions.[67]

A variety of factors point to the need for a method of allocation that can deal with the problems in the American health care system. Some of those problems such as limited funding and resources, are likely to remain. In light of this continuum, a basis for meeting the needs of the American medical community that is morally, ethically, economically, and medically appropriate needs to be developed.

Most hospitals and organizations have used a method of allocation as the basis for their health care decisions. In some respects, this method provides guidelines to alleviate many of the difficulties that the American health care system faces. The Quality-Adjusted Life Years model is a method of computing medical needs that assists the decision making process by presenting the two issues of need and resources in a single numerical sum. In light of the importance of QALYs, and their relationship to attempts to deal with limited medical resources, it seems appropriate to examine whether they accomplish their intended purpose of providing a numerical sum that assists in health care allocation decisions.

QALYs as a Basis for Allocation

One method of allocation that has come into consistent use as the basis for meeting allocation needs has been the utilization of calculated Quality-Adjusted Life Years. Some view it as having the potential to accomplish what other attempts to meet the allocation need have failed to accomplish. Specifically, the QALY model is said to have the potential to generate a numerical sum which, when calculated and applied, will assist in guiding decisions makers in the distribution of and the directing of limited resources.

67. Scott B. Rae, "Money Matters in Health Care," in *Cutting-Edge Bioethics: A Christian Exploration of Technologies and Trends*, ed. John Kilner, C. Christopher Hook and Diann B. Uustal (Grand Rapids: Eerdmans, 2002), 109–10.

Health Care Must Have Allocation

A number of definitions are available which clarify what QALYs are and how they function. For instance, Wing defines QALYs as, "a mathematical concept for measuring the quality of life of defined illness states."[68] QALYs are said to be, "a measure, developed by health economists, which incorporates an assessment of quality of life into life-expectancies. The aim is to facilitate resource allocation using cost-benefit analysis, by providing a single measure of the value of any medical intervention."[69] Finally, QALYs are seen as, "a quantitative measure, in terms of years of good-quality life, of the value of a medical procedure or service to a group of patients with similar medical conditions."[70]

By bringing together the economic, clinical, and patient needs and consideration the QALY model has become a commonly employed way of allocating medical resources. Alan Williams observes the following concerning the propriety of QALYs:

Collective priority setting requires us to be able to compare systematically the benefits of different kinds of health care, provided in different settings, by different clinicians, for patients with different characteristics, suffering from different conditions and different levels of severity. This requires a benefit measure which is extremely versatile and which has interval scale measurement properties (so we can compare the size of differences in levels of benefit between treatments). Any measure which fails to fulfill these rather stringent requirements will be inadequate in principle as an aid to the priority-setting.

---

68. A. J. Wing, "QALY," in *New Dictionary of Christian Ethics & Pastoral Theology*, ed. David Atkinson, and David Field (Downers Grove, IL: InterVarsity, 1995), 714.

69. "Quality Adjusted Life Years," *A Dictionary of Sociology*, ed. Gordon Marshall (Oxford: Oxford University Press, 1998). *Oxford Reference Online*, Oxford University Press [on-line]; accessed 08 August 2003; available from http://www. oxfordreference.com/views/ENTRY.html?subview=Main&entry=t 88.001836; Internet.

70. "Quality-adjusted life years," *A Dictionary of Nursing* (Oxford: Oxford University Press, 2003), *Oxford Reference Online*, Oxford University Press [on-line]; accessed 08 August 2003; available from http://www.oxfordreference.com/ views/ ENTRY.html? subview=Main&entry=t62.007626; Internet.

QALYs were designed to serve that purpose but they require one further prior commitment, namely that the benefits of health care relate to both a person's length of life and a person's quality of life.[71]

---

71. Alan Williams, *Being Reasonable about the Economics of Health*, ed. A. J. Culyer and Alan Maynard (Cheltenham, UK: Edward Elgar, 1997), 306.

CHAPTER THREE

QALYs Are Problematic as a Basis for Health Care Allocation

THE QALY model has been developed into a major factor in health care distribution because of its value in attempting to direct limited medical resources in an equitable manner. It has attempted to do this by using a computation that involves two important factors, quality of life (QofL) and healthy life years (HLY). Although QofL is important, the computations of QALYs attempt to include a calculation that can be applied in a comprehensive manner. The importance of QALY computation then is found in identifying QofL and also HLY factors. HLYs are identified in a computation which attempts potentially to identify how many, or the quantity of healthy life years that are likely to result from the performance of a given medical procedure.[1] When these denominators are graded and measured, they produce a QALY. The use of quality of life and healthy life years demonstrates the strengths and weaknesses of QALYs. One of the strength of the QALY model is that it provides a semblance of objectivity. However, these same denominators that are used in QALY calculations also reveal unsettling weaknesses. The premise of this work is that there are insurmountable problems as well as benefits to using QALYs as a method of health care allocation. If QALYs are to continue to be a useful tool for allocating America's

---

1. Years of healthy life and healthy life years will be used synonymously in this chapter. In the current literature on QALYs these two terms are used interchangeably.

limited resources then these issues need to be identified and, eventually, addressed.

Using QALYs for Allocation Objectivity

Those who use the QALY model have sought to provide an objective basis for health care allocation. Over the last fifty years America's health care requirements and demands have drastically outpaced its ability to supply health care. As the previous chapter has demonstrated there is now, more than ever, a need for impartiality in health care allocation. The scarcity of medical resources is why the QALY model in an attempt to provide an objective base for allocation, and that is an admirable undertaking. QALY calculations allow objective decisions to be made concerning the necessary distribution of limited medical resources. The distribution is necessary because demand has outpaced the supply of medical resources, therefore without some type of allocation, demand would quickly outstrip the resources available and some of those who need medical care the most would be unable to receive it. Some type of determination needs to be made concerning the distribution of those limited medical resources.

As discussed in the second chapter, the QALY model's initial development was seen in events that occurred in the 1960s. Health care planners sought to identify patients' preferences surrounding patient care, but the fluctuating opinions of patients along with those of other participants in the American medical system, made this method of directing health care needs unwieldy.[2]

During the 1970s, QALYs were proposed as a method of identifying patients' preferences in health states.[3] Those who developed QALYs presented it as a method of decision making which provided a computational model for incorporating medical and non-health

---

2. Martin Green, *The Economics of Health Care* (London: Office of Health Economics, 2000), 33 [on-line]; accessed 06 September 2003, available at http://www.oheschools.org; Internet. Not only were patients' opinions sought in the 60's which were subject to continual change, but doctors were said to have a monopoly over supply during that time. The result was a market that was unable to respond to the ensuing medical and economic changes. This version of *The Economics of Health Care* is available in its entirely via pdf.

3. Ann Michele Holmes, "Uses and Abuses of QALY Analysis" (Ph.D diss., University of British Columbia, 1992), 2.

related factors. This grading of "apples and oranges" assisted the health care industry in choosing where it was "best" to place limited resources.

QALYs' Background of Utility

QALY computations, which are developed by using the factors of years of healthy life and quality of life, are the result of the implementation of certain theories of game utility. "Utility requires that agents balance benefits and drawbacks to produce the best overall results."[4] A utility theory is "a theory of decision making according to which a decision maker chooses an alternative or strategy that maximizes the utility of the outcome."[5] The specific utility theory employed in the QALY model is an expected utility theory which can be defined as:

> A theory of decision making formalized in 1947 by the Hungarian-born US mathematician John von Neumann and the German-born US economist Oskar Morgenstern, according to which a decision maker chooses actions or strategies that maximize expected utility, and utilities are determined by revealed preferences. If the probabilities are subjective, then it is called subjective expected utility theory.[6]

Von Neumann and Morgenstern's utility theory was originally used in certain games, which is why it is called a "game theory," but health care economists found broader uses that were far less entertaining. Economists saw that this utility theory could be used in

---

4. Tom L. Beauchamp and James F. Childress, *Principles of Biomedical Ethics*, 5th ed. (Oxford: Oxford University Press, 2001), 165.

5. "Utility Theory," *A Dictionary of Psychology*, ed. Andrew M. Colman (Oxford: Oxford University Press, 2001), *Oxford Reference Online*, Oxford University Press [on-line]; accessed 08 August 03; available from; http://www.oxfordreference.com/views/ENTRY.html?subview=Main&entry=t87.008710; Internet.

6. "Expected Utility Theory," *A Dictionary of Psychology*, ed. Andrew M. Colman (Oxford: Oxford University Press, 2001), *Oxford Reference Online*, Oxford University Press [on-line]; accessed 08 Aug 03; available from http://www.oxfordreference.com/views/INTRY.html?subview=Main&entry=t87.002943; Internet.

QALYs to promote technical and allocative efficiency by addressing dissimilar factors simultaneously.[7] Thus patients, physicians and other health care concerns could be addressed concurrently with economic factors, and probable outcomes predicted through use of a developed computational model or sum. It is this sum that would give guidance to those making health care decisions by providing a scale by which the theoretical maximization of resources could be predicted.[8] Through the objective probabilities identified in the game theory, one can deduce certain outcome preferences. Thus the game theory is able to identify the point of maximization for preferred outcome. In the QALY model this point of maximization occurs through factors identified through preferences identified in QofL and the quantity measured in HLYs. The exact contents of QofL and HLYs will be assessed later in this chapter, but at this point, it is only necessary to understand that the sum obtained through these two denominators produce a QALY score which tends towards objectivity, and which is often used to assist in the decision process which seeks to maximize the allocation of limited medical resources.

The QALY model's utility formula attempts to provide a single measure of health care outcome, so that those who have responsibility for funding health care can compare various parameters of treatments and programs.[9] During the development of the QALY model, decisions concerning the allocation of medical resources were more "targeted," meaning that whatever price target or limit a medical community decided upon was in fact the target or limit.[10]

   7. Jack Dowie, "Analysing health outcomes," *Journal of medical Ethics 2001* 27: 248.

   8. *The von Neuman-Morgenstern Expected Utility Theory* [on-line]; accessed 10 December 2003; available from http://cepa.newschool.edu/het/essays/uncert/vnmaxioms. htm; Internet. In the game theory people's preferences are formed over lotteries and from these preferences over lotteries, combined with objective probabilities, one can deduce what the underlying preferences on outcomes might be. This means that in the von Neumann-Morganstern analyzing preferences over lotteries logically *preceded* preferences over outcomes.

   9. John McKie and others, *The Allocation of Health Care Resources: An Ethical Evaluation of the "QALY" Approach* (Dartmouth: Ashgate Publishing Limited, 1998), 64.

   10. John Rapoport and others, *Understanding Health Economics* (Rockville, MD: Aspen Publication, 1982), 171.

While the medical community attempted to decide upon a target, a competing idea for the directing of health care decisions developed through what has been identified as the *Arrow Impossibility Theorem*. The *Arrow Impossibility Theorem* stated, "a certain set of quite acceptable axioms on social choice orderings necessarily implied that there would be a "dictator" (i.e., that a single agent's own preferences over outcomes would dominate everybody else's)."[11] This theorem presented a single agent as the one who would direct resource allocation. Interestingly, in Arrow's later work he saw the government as the institution which should take the "risk-bearing role," a natural extension of his theorem.[12] Two sets of problems that exist with the idea of an agency existing which could take up the "risk-bearing role." First, the measurement of health outcomes is incomplete. Even when agencies use clinical trials, these trials are primarily a guide to likely benefits under certain controlled conditions so that their results can be unrealistic, subjective or subject to limited time constraints when applied. Second, there widely agreed upon method or metric for comparing the multitude of different outcomes currently exists.[13] Therefore the agency would be subject to the overwhelming pressure of interest groups vying for control of limited resources. The system of identifying "value" in QALYs is unique and different from the *Arrow Impossibility Theorem* in that QALYs attempt to provide a more objective method of identifying a measurement of health care outcome than that of an overseeing agency, like the government, as proposed in the *Arrow Impossibility Theorem*.

QALYs developed into a positive measurement tool through mathematical computations based upon preferences based research concerning QofL and the perceived quantity of life obtained through HLY computation. "QALYs are computed in a positive orientation, that is, "more is better." The computations are meant to describe the health-adjusted longevity of a population based on cross-sectional or

---

11. *Kenneth J. Arrow, 1921-* [on-line]; accessed 10 December 2003; available from http://cepa.newschool.edu/het/profiles/arrow.htm; Internet.

12. Ibid.

13. Jeff Richardson, "Linking Health Outcomes to Funding" (working paper presented to the Australian Outcomes Conference in July 1999, Centre for Health Program Evaluation, West Heidelberg, Australia), 1.

brief longitudinal observations of quality of life and longevity."[14] The positive orientation of QALYs is identified as the portrayal of health-adjusted longevity. Although the positive orientation is significant, it is not the only issue that must be addressed. Other important issues are the computations involved in QALYs which are identified as, "quality of life and longevity." The reason for their importance is seen in the fact that these two factors are critical in the computations by which QALYs are developed. Some view these two factors as the result of "recognition that years of life are more or less valued according to the quality of life."[15] Whether length of life equals a QofL may be debatable, but the issue of what these denominators mean will be dealt with later. Separately, these two denominators have become connected not only because they 'fit' the utility theory, but also because of their inherent interrelationship within the QALY model's utilitarian computational model. Their interconnectedness, along with QALY's natural relationship with utilitarianism, is one of the reasons these specific computations came to be placed on a scale so as to provide a basis for objective allocation decisions.[16]

QALYs' Mathematics

Having evolved throughout the 1960s and 1970s, the QALY model sought to combine quantity and quality of life in a single measure of health care outcome. Economists attempted to use the quality and quantity of unrelated elements of health care, such as treatments and programs, to formulate outcomes in a single measurement. When compared on a QALY scale, these various elements could be assigned

14. Dennis G. Fryback, "Methodological Issues in Measuring Health Status and Health-related Quality of Life for Population Health Measures: A Brief Overview of the "HALY" Family of Measures," Appendix C, in *Summarizing Population Health—Directions for the Development and Application of Population Metrics*, ed. M. J. Field and M. R. Gold (Washington DC: National Academy Press, 1998), 14.

15. McKie and others, *The Allocation of Health Care Resources: An Ethical Evaluation of the 'QALY' Approach*, 22.

16. Ibid., 61. While some may argue that there can be a place for other foundational models, such as those based upon Deontology, McKie objects to rival foundations stating that "the QALY method is more naturally conjoined with utilitarianism than with Kantian ethics or any other normative theory" (61).

a numerical value which could then be computed and given a priority or place on an allocation scale. Each QALY score would then be compared to a chosen cost per QALY. When the comparison occurred, the "value" of a procedure, treatment, or program would then be identified for those responsible for funding or distributing health care resources. Procedures that might *seem* unrelated could then be compared with one another on a cost analysis basis.[17] The cost of a treatment is then presented in terms of its expenditure per QALY. Cost effectiveness in a QALY computation does not necessarily mean cost savings, but it does attempt to identify the maximization of medical resources. Therefore, what the use of QALYs has attempted to do is enable the health care system, as well as those who are involved in the distribution of health care funds, to compare possible outcomes. Seemingly unrelated elements of health care can be compared through the use of QALY calculations.

The basic denominators and calculations of QALYs are commonly acknowledged:

> Each life year is rated (by patients or citizens in the community) on a scale from 0 to 1, where 1 represents perfect health and 0 represents the worst possible health state, (often death). If a year in poor health (e.g., severe chest pain) is rated 0.6, it means that the respondent believes that living 10 years with severe chest pain is of equal value to him or her as living 6 years in perfect health.[18]

It is important to note the interconnectedness of the two denominators. Years of life are compared with perceptions of QofL. If looked at with foresight, then the assumption is that a person would prefer to live a shorter period with less pain experientially than experientially suffering greater pain and living longer. Most Westerners strive for a life devoid of pain and suffering.[19] QofL could, in one sense, include a type of compassion that would attempt always to al-

17. Green, Economics of Health Care [on-line].

18. John D. Graham, "An Investor's Look at Life-Saving Opportunities," Risk in Perspective, *Harvard Center for Risk Analysis* 7 (Feb 1999) [on-line]; accessed 23 September 2003; available from http://www.hcra.harvard.edu/pdf/February1999.pdf; Internet.

19. Allen Verhey, *Reading the Bible in the Strange World of Medicine* (Grand Rapids: William B. Eerdmans Publishing Company, 2003), 102–3.

leviate pain. While the complete relief of pain in life is an unrealistic goal and reflects an inadequate definition of QofL, it demonstrates that popular expectations can be found in perceptions that equate less pain with a "better" life. This "compassionate" foresight that less pain is better is a speculation preference that allows the QALY measurement to provide data concerning quality of life and the quantity of life involved in healthy life years in a single computation. The addition of QofL and HLYs can then be compared with and prioritized against other medical expenditures for the maximization of resource utilization. In one sense, the use of QALYs endeavors to level the field between competing medical expenditures which may or may not be related in theory or application.

It has been noted that QALY computations are adduced by estimating how many years of life will be added or saved by a treatment or the administration of some medical resource. The QofL expected to result from the given medical expenditure translates into a factor that reflects the belief that the increased length of life should be a preferred life.[20] Because of the "positive" nature of QALYs, each additional year during which the patient experiences a higher QofL is identified through the calculations. When these quality and quantity adjustment coefficients for all the years gained are added up, the ensuing calculation becomes the number of QALYs gained.[21] Since QALYs are graded zero to 1, the greater the score the greater the calculated benefit or believed maximization of the medical treatment. It can be readily observed that use of QALYs brings together varying elements of health care under a single measurement of health care

---

20. Peter Singer, "What's Wrong with Killing," in *Writings on an Ethical Life* (New York: HarperCollins, 2000), 134. Singer discusses preference utilitarianism where one's preferences define what is "good" and therefore one's preferences also define what is ethical. He supports the notion that a healthy life is always preferable to a life in which there are significant physical or mental disabilities when he states that, "beings who cannot see themselves as entities with a future cannot have any preferences about their own future existence." The issue thus becomes not simply the maximization of pleasure and the minimization of pleasure. Singer's position demonstrates the determination of what constitutes an adequate QofL and it demonstrates that QofL is an issue in which egoist preferences become most important.

21. Alan Schwartz, *MHPE 494: Medical Decision Making*, Lecture notes (Spring 1999) [on-line]; accessed 23 September 2003; available from http://www.araw.mede.uic.edu/~alansz/ courses/mhpe494/week10.html; Internet.

outcome. The QALY score that is finally obtained reveals a statistical objectivity, which is in part the result of using principles derived from *The von Neuman-Morgenstern Expected Utility Theory*.

Monetary Thresholds of QALYs

The monetary threshold of QALYs is another factor that needs to be addressed if the QALY model is to claim legitimately to be an objective allocation method. The computation of QofL and HLYs produces a sum which is assigned a given fiscal value. What is idiosyncratic about the QALY model is that fiscal values may vary depending upon the need of the medical community. This means that the threshold, the limits of a QALY cost, may not be exact. How an economist decides what will be the value of a year of healthy life is the issue. Determining the value of a QALY is not easy. Some values may be as much as $100,000, while others may be as little as $20,000, depending upon the medical need.[22] What this fluctuation in QALYs means is that, based upon provisional economic evidence or hypothetical models, a given country decides what is an acceptable payout for a medical expenditure.[23] In a practical sense the value of a QALY then depends upon the country, the procedure, the potential results, the technology, and the willingness of taxpayers to pay for improvements of health.[24] Despite the existence of these variables, some proposals of what an individual QALY may be worth have been offered. In England the cost-effective ratio for the average QALY has generally been identified as L 30,000.[25] In

---

22. Elizabeth Davies, "How are thresholds used elsewhere?" in *Cost-Effectiveness Thresholds: Economic and Ethical Issues*, ed. Adrian Towse, Clive Pritchard and Nancy Devlin (London: King's Fund, 2003), 69.

23. Clive Pritchard, "Overseas approaches to decision making," in *Cost-Effectiveness Thresholds: Economic and Ethical Issues*, ed. Adrian Towse, Clive Pritchard and Nancy Devlin (London: King's Fund, 2003) 57.

24. Nancy Devlin, "An introduction to the use of cost-effectiveness thresholds in decision making: what are the issues?" in *Cost-Effectiveness Thresholds: Economic and Ethical Issues*, ed. Adrian Towse, Clive Pritchard and Nancy Devlin (London: King's Fund, 2003), 18–19.

25. Peter Littlejohns, "Does NICE have a threshold? A response," in *Cost-Effectiveness Thresholds: Economic and Ethical Issues*, ed. Adrian Towse, Clive Pritchard and Nancy Devlin (London: King's Fund, 2003), 31.

the United states this QALY cost is equivalent to that in England and equals approximately $45,000, depending upon the American dollar rate verses the English pound.[26] It seems that depending upon the economic value and influences placed upon medicine in various countries, the value of a QALY necessarily fluctuates. Economists and health care professionals constantly struggle to remain informed concerning the cost and complexities of given medical expenditures. In one sense, the decision making concerning the cost of QALYs is like triage, the choosing of which treatments or programs are most urgently needed and therefore should receive correspondingly more funding. The important thing about a QALY calculation is that it does present some type of grading whereby the cost of various medical regimens can be assessed.

Some may desire that the cost threshold of a QALY be more precisely obtained if it is to claim objectivity. However, while precision may be desirable, exactitude is not a necessity, and can be set aside for consistency, without compromising objectivity. QALY scores are estimates based upon perceived patient preferences regarding medical care. Others may object to the imprecision of QALYs because it suggests an arbitrariness that makes QALY calculations vacuous. The response to these objections may be deduced from the process by which QALYs are obtained. The QALY model is like comparing apples and oranges or like comparing diet therapy and heart transplants. Both calculations would employ the same computational model. The result may not be exact, but it is not unexpected. "An element of arbitrariness is inevitable. Any judgment about the appropriate cost-effectiveness threshold is in some ways an arbitrary one, made in the absence of knowledge about the cost-effectiveness of technologies that have not been evaluated and, more broadly about the value of investments elsewhere in the economy."[27] Thus an expected, though not exact, valuation of a QALY is possible by looking to economic models or hypothetical cases. The objection that QALYs are arbitrary can be addressed, in part, when it is realized that QALYs do have an expected and therefore a consistent threshold, which results from the variables involved in QALY calculations.

26. Schwartz, MHPE 494: Medical Decision Making [on-line].

27. Clive Pritchard, "Oversees approaches to decision making," in *Cost-Effectiveness Thresholds: Economic and Ethical Issues*, 67.

Since QALY thresholds are discretionary, some would state that it is not possible "to talk about the value of a QALY."[28] Though this objection acknowledges the variables in QALY thresholds, it does not take into account how QALYs are derived. When the computations of QofL and HLYs are compared with other QALYs, then the "monetary values" of QALYs are comparative. Consistency, then, is found in QALY valuation. Although the "monetary value" of a given QALY may be in flux, the QALY score allows for consistency while seeking a maximization of the utilization of limited resources or the optimal ordering of preferences. It allows for consistency because a single QALY cost threshold can be identified. When the threshold is identified, monetary expenditures can be compared and a decision concerning allocation preferences can be made. The maximization of resource utilization is possible because QALYs are the result of a mathematical computation, and as such an answer presented as a sum is available. Clues to how the QALY model uses quality of life and healthy life years in order to generate a given sum are found in assessing the actual denominators themselves.

Defining Denominators

In order to understand the use of QALYs as an allocation method, it is important to define what its denominators mean. Quality of life (QofL) and healthy life years (HLYs) are the denominators of the QALY calculation, and both of these terms have broad definitions. This works to the advantage of QALYs in that it allows the computations to have a broad based application. The focus of quality of life for QALYs is found in, "describing objectively measurable personal and relational skills, individual dignity, and the ability to interact in a meaningful way."[29] A healthy life year is a life year weighted

28. National Institute for Clinical Excellence and National Co-ordinating Centre for Research Methodology, *What is the Value to Society of a QALY? Issues Raised and Recommendations for How to Address Them* (Norwich: University of East Anglia, 2003), 2 [on-line]; accessed 23 September 2003, available from http://www.publichealth.bham.ac.uk/nccm/PDFs%20and%20documents/ GL_AQLY_report_Feb03.pdf; Internet.

29. E. David Cook, "Quality of Life," in *New Dictionary of Christian Ethics & Pastoral Theology*, ed. David J. Atkinson and David H. Field (Downers Grove: InterVarsity, 1995), 715.

by an index of quality of life or utility, which estimates how long a person will benefit from a given medical treatment.[30] HLYs is meant to identify the maximization of the health care outcome chronologically. Looked at from these perspectives a QALY can be simply defined as, "an exchange rate between the quality and quantity of life."[31] It may be that the term, "exchange rate" causes difficulty. In order to clarify any confusion concerning the identity and relationship of QofL and HLYs, it is now appropriate to look at these denominators individually.

Quality of Life

When taking a closer look at the idea of quality of life (QofL) one finds that attempting to describe what it means is complex. In the QALY model, quality of life factors are determined by comparing preference-based measurements which are obtained through questionnaires given to a patient, potential patients, or a community. While not easily defined QofL may be said to be, "a value judgment: the experience of living, as a whole or in some aspect, is judged to be "good" or "bad," better" or "worse."[32] As one of the denominators in the QALY calculation, QofL are value judgments which are obtained, through multi-attributed utility instruments.

Preference-based measurements obtain QofL data for QALYs. QofL data are obtained from patients through a questionnaire that functions as a multi-attributed utility instrument.[33] Examples of these instruments are the SF-6D used for QALYs or the EQ5D used for the EuroQol. All multi-attributed utility instruments ask people to identify health state preferences.

The goal of preference-based measurements is to provide a health related quality of life outcome measure that can be used in resource allocation calculations.

---

30. McKie, *The Allocation of Health Care Resources*, 22.

31 Ibid., 23.

32. Wesley Smith, *Culture of Death: The Assault on Medical Ethics in America* (San Francisco: Encounter Books, 2000), 27.

33. Eric Nord, *Cost-Value Analysis in Health Care* (Cambridge: Cambridge University Press, 1999), 19.

The SF-36 is one of the most widely used HRQoL outcome measures in the world today. It contains 36 questions measuring health across eight dimensions—physical functioning, role limitations because of physical health, social functioning, vitality, pain, mental health, role limitation because of emotional problems and general health. Responses to each question within a dimension are combined to generate a score from 0 to 100, where 100 indicates "good health."[34]

The SF-36 was revised and summarized in the SF-6D. The six health state classifications of the SF-6D are, "physical functioning, role limitations, social functioning, pain, mental health and vitality."[35] When used in conjunction with patient preferences there is a possibility of defining 18,000 health states. The EQ5D is the UK version of the SF6D. It focuses on five areas, mobility, pain/discomfort, self-care, anxiety/depression and usual activities (or ADLs). "Each of the five dimensions used has three levels—no problem, some problems and major problems—making a total of 243 possible health states, to which "unconscious" and "dead" are added to make 245 in total."[36] What both of these measurements are attempting to do via their questions is to identify preferences or values with which to define "good health" or what an acceptable quality of life would be for a given medical community in a specific context. This means that in the QALY model the SF6D measures the quality of life within the healthy years saved. The measurement is then used in economic evaluations or medical decision making models, demonstrating that interconnectedness of quality of life and chronological life. It has already been noted that, because of the way that QALYs are crafted, it is difficult to have one without the other. For this reason, when

34. Stephen J. Walters and John E. Brazier, "What is the relationship between the minimally important difference and the health state utility values? The case of the SF-6D," *Health Qual Life Outcomes* 2003; 1 (1): 4 [on-line]; accessed 25 September 2003; available from http://www.pubmedcentral.gov/articlerender.fcgi?tool=pmcentrez& artid=155547; Internet.

35. Nord, *Cost-Value Analysis in Health Care*, 5.

36. Ceri Phillips Newport and Guy Thompson, "What is a QALY?" *Aventis House* 1 (6) www.evidence-based-medicine.co.uk [on-line]; accessed 25 September 2003; available from http://www. jr2.ox.ac.uk/ bandolier/painres/ download/whatis/QALY.pdf; Internet.

quality of life issues are discussed, the length of life experienced through the medical treatment is also mentioned. Preference-based measurements provide a useful calculation because they not only define quality of life, but they also take into account the various chronological implications of potential medical treatments.

Some may object that this method of obtaining health preferences is untrustworthy because of its subjective nature, and, as such, would undermine QALY's efforts at objectivity.[37] Preference scoring is indeed subjective, in the sense that personal health preferences may be different for each person, this does not necessarily imply that this method of obtaining preferences is automatically unacceptable. While SF6D does not provide an absolute standard for quality of life, it does provide consistent, general guidelines of patient preferences to assist those responsible for making health care funding decisions. Since the QALY model seeks to be an objective basis for health care allocation decisions, it is essential that the QALY model, and those who employ the computations produced by the QALY model, take into account the preferences of the parties involved in the medical treatment or program.

Other methods for establishing quality of life scores than multi-attributed utility instruments are available. Among these are the standard gamble, the time trade-off (TTO), and the rating scale techniques. In the standard gamble, the patient is given two alternatives with two possible alternatives, such as optimum health and death. In other words if a person has a choice between death and a below the knee amputation (BKA) there is a high probability that the patient will take accept the amputation. However, if there is a possibility of the patient retaining the limb with limited mobility than that option might be selected instead of amputation even if death remains a possibility. The gamble is that there is the possibility that the limb may not be of use or that an infection may necessitate a more radical above the knee amputation (AKA) procedure, or that the less aggressively treated disease process may kill the patient. Thus the possible outcomes continued to be modified in their intensity until the patient is dispassionate about the two alternatives, the point at which the patient would be ambivalent concerning the

---

37. Walters, *Health Qual Life Outcomes* 2003; 1 (1): 4 [on-line].

partial amputations of the limb.[38] In time trade-off, the same general method is applied, but time is now the variable while of health outcomes are held constant. The rating scale technique simply asks a patient to point out on a rating scale what their values for various health states would be.[39] The public would be offered what they themselves desire as determined by their responses to direct questions related to "interpersonal trade-offs in health care."[40]

These three methods of obtaining health state preferences are not as objective as using the SF6D in that their respective methods of identifying quality of life and chronological maximization may include trade-offs that set priorities that are not held by their patients. TTO and standard gamble lack objectivity because they are not based on patient preferences or the objectivity that is based on consensus. Objectivity in scoring may be compromised by the desire for a particular outcome by those attempting to obtain outcome scores through TTO or standard gamble. Single variable methods which attempt to establish quality of life scores may not provide preferences that are as specific as multi-attributed utility instruments given the various medical situations experienced in the current system of medicine. That is the technology and promises of possible treatments make the scores obtained by the alternative outcomes of TTO and standard gamble difficult to sustain. Multi-attributed utility instruments, such as SF6D, seem to be a more reliable method of obtaining perceived quality of life scores than the standard gamble, the time trade-off, and the rating scale methods of establishing quality of life scores. The multi-attributed utility instruments are preferable because they are more reliable in determining optimum point regarding QofL in patient preferences. This ability to find consensus, based upon utility principles which are applied through the von Neumann and Morgenstern axioms make the QALY model with its

---

38. Brian Harris, *Quantifying Health Outcomes*, University of California, Berkeley (2004) [on-line]; accessed17 March 2003; available from http://psg-mac43ucsf.edu/ticr/syllabus/courses/10/2004/01/13/Lecture/notes/Utilities%20and%20QALYS.ppt; Internet.

39. Nord, *Cost-Value Analysis in Health Care*, 19.

40. Beauchamp and Childress. *Principles of Biomedical Ethics*, 258.

use of multi-attributed utility instruments the preferred method of identifying QofL.[41]

It may be argued that using multi-attributed utility instruments construction of a QofL score does not really address the problem of limited resources.[42] These preferences only provide a general basis for patient opinions. The issue of patient preferences will be addressed later in this chapter, but here it is important to understand the role of patient preferences in the area of health care allocation. Measurement of preferences offer an indicator of societal norms for health services, which allows for a greater level of objectivity in medical decision making in that society itself defines what is medically beneficial. Since one of the tasks of a QALY is to provide an objective basis for health care allocation, then the method of scoring that seeks multi-attributes seems to provide a more complete assessment of societal preferences. This is in contrast to other questionnaires, such as those that examine a single attribute or questionnaires that are disease or dimension specific.[43]

QofL scores are obtained in QALY calculations through multi-attributed utility instruments which are able to identify the median patient preferences. These scores are objective in that they accurately reflect a general consensus of the tested population at the time of testing. QofL scores identify the general values concerning acceptable or unacceptable states of health through testing and grading of possible health states.

---

41. Michael W. Kattan, and others, *Time trade-off utility modified to accommodate degenerative and life-threatening conditions*, Harvard University [on-line]; accessed 14 March 2004; available from http://www.mgh.harvard.edu/PDF_Repository/ D010001204.pdf; Internet.

42. Victor R. Fuchs, *Who Shall Live? Health, Economics, and Social Choice*, expanded ed. (Singapore: World Scientific Publishing Company, 1998), 164.

43. Andrew Garratt and others, "Quality of life measurement: Bibliographic study of patient assessed health outcome measures," *BMJ.COM 2002* 324: 1417 [journal on-line]; accessed 26 September 2003; available from http://bmj.bmjjournals.com/cgi/reprint/ 324/7351/1417; Internet. Examples of single attribute questionnaires are those that focus on an a single capability such as mental competency or activities of daily living (ADLs), scales may not be as objective in providing a method of obtaining quality of life preferences.

Healthy Life Years

QofL scores are not the only denominator of interest in QALY calculation. As previously noted, QofL scores affect and are affected by HLY calculations. Healthy life year scores may be defined as:

> A composite measure that combines the amount of healthy life lost due to morbidity with that attributable to premature mortality. It can be applied to individuals or to population groups to determine the impact of a particular disease, to work out the effects of an intervention, or to compare areas, populations, or socioeconomic groups.[44]

Those who employ QALY measurements use HLY scores by taking the chronological implications found in multi-attributed utility instruments, and unite that information with morbidity and mortality values to obtain a numerical sum, which is then used for QALY calculations.

When QALY calculations are implemented, the sum identifies a year of healthy life by the numerical designation of one. A year of unhealthy living would be calculated as proportionately less than one.[45] Thus, healthy life years are those years where healthy living occurs, as opposed to unhealthy or less than optimum health years. Any score that is less than one reflects the implications of morbidity and disability per year as perceived by the respondents. In regards to healthy life the potential morbidity and disability preferences of the individual apply directly to the calculations of their QALY scores.

In evaluating how healthy life years are calculated, one readily discovers how disability and morbidity are defined.

> In the HeaLY formulation, healthy life lost is based on all diseases with onset in a given year and on the stream of life lost due to disability and death thereafter in accordance with the natural history of disease. In the DALY

---

44. Adnan A. Hyder, Guida Rotlant, and Richard Morrow, "Measuring the burden of disease: Healthy life-years," *American Journal of Public Health* (1998) 88: 196.

45. Justine Jenkins, "The Ethical QALY," *Quality of Life News Letter* 7–8 (Jun 93–Jan 94):1 [on-line]; accessed 02 October 02; available from http://www.mapi-research-inst.com/pdf/art/qol7_1.pdf; Internet.

formulation, disability is calculated in an equivalent fashion but termed "life lived with disability," whereas mortality is considered for all deaths in the current year regardless of when onset occurs. In practice, this makes little difference in a steady state, since expectation of life is calculated on the basis of current estimates of age-specific mortality. HeaLY uses expectation of life from disease onset rather than the expectation of life at death, again in keeping with the natural history of disease; this results in slightly less loss attributed to the HeaLY proportional to the duration between onset and death, but even with a long interval the effect is minor.[46]

HLY scores are then seen as a combination of numerators which, when added, produce a denominator which forms part of the objective calculation of QALYs.

The HLY method of looking at health states through survey-based classification provides a measure of objectivity as well as validity to the QALY calculation sum.[47] The Center for Disease Control (CDC) provides the specific guidelines for the use of QALY sums in the calculations of HLYs. The CDC's particular method of arriving at the years of healthy life is helpful in that it provides a broad understanding of the dynamics involved in QALY computation generally and in determining healthy life years scores specifically, which is seen in their discussion concerning Health Related Quality of Life (HRQL).[48]

---

46. Adnan Hyder, "Measuring the Burden of Disease," *American Journal of Public Health* 88 (1998): 200–01. A steady state of health is identified as the "current estimates of age-specific mortality." (201) The objective of this approach to HLYs is the maximization of the total healthy life of a given population.

47. "Years of Healthy Life," *Bureau of Business & Economic Research, University of Madison* [on-line]; accessed 02 October 2003; available at http://www.bber.umt.edu/healthcare/healthyyears.htm; [Internet]. This site discusses how the Center for Disease Control combines the effects of mortality with the information about morbidity and disability through random, state-based telephone surveys of American non-institutionalized adults in order to assess health risks and behaviors, which then allows the CDC to have an age and state based healthy life year calculation.

48. Ibid.

The HRQL index was combined with lifetable functions to compute age-group specific lifetable number of total person-years lived by the average HRQL (range: 0.1–1.0) within each age group. The number of healthy person-years lived was summed for each age group and divided by the number of persons at each age. These data were adjusted using data from previous national estimates of the relative size and HRQL of institutionalized persons. Age-specific estimates of YHL represent the average number of YHL remaining to a person at a given age[49]

The estimates of the expectation of healthy life are continually being reevaluated and revised in order to keep up with current expectations of healthy life as determined from actuarial data. The calculations for QALYs which combine both numbers are able to provide sums that accurately reflect contemporary American culture. "YHL were calculated by first computing the index of HRQL for each respondent (HRQL ranged from 1.0 {for those in excellent health and with no limitations} to 0.1 {for those who were limited in self-care activities of daily living and who were in poor health})."[50] Years of healthy life and health related quality of life are necessarily related in the QALY computation, for good or for ill.

At this juncture how "health" is defined becomes important. For the World Health Organization "health" is said to be, "the state of complete physical, mental and social well-being; not merely the absence of disease and infirmity."[51] While it is true that health as a holistic concept is a desired state of existence that encompasses all aspects of one's being, including non-physical experiences, when it comes to QALY calculations, health may have more to do with an individual's perceived or acceptable state of physical well-being. While this emphasis on physical attributes is important when viewing health dimensions one's overall perceptions of health may not be

---

49. "Years of Healthy life—Selected States, United States, 1993–1995," *MMWR Weekly* 47: 5 [on-line]; accessed 02 October 2003, available from http://www.cdc.gov/ mmwr/preview/ mmwrhtml/00050833; Internet.

50. Ibid.

51. E. David Cook, "Health and Health Care," *New Dictionary of Christian Ethics & Pastoral Theology*, ed. David J. Atkinson and David H. Field (Downers Grove: InterVarsity, 1995), 435.

completely discounted, as has been previously noted in the discussion of the meaning of QofL. The perception of health allows for multi-attributed utility instruments to measure a perceived state of health that would be acceptable to the patient. What the perception of health as measured by mult-attributed utility instruments have to do with QALYs and healthy life years is that these measurements provide the health economist with calculations that seek to provide a general maximization of years of acceptable disabled life or acceptable healthy life that will potentially be experienced. Generally acceptable healthy life is then used to compare treatments and programs in different areas so that allocation decisions can be made concerning the limited medical resources available.

In QALY calculations, an attempt is made to show sensitivity and concern for both the quantity and quality of life. Some would "seek to reduce differences in quality of life to differences in quantity" and, in so doing, the breadth of life becomes the defining factor in the quantity of change packed into a given time.[52] The greatest totality of life chronologically is what becomes important in advancing a quality or a pleasurable life. Difficulties in the use of quality of life calculations seem to be comprised of more than simply the quantity of years that one lives. Still, there does also seem to be a connection between the length of one's life and the social definition of an advantageous life. This connection is important in demonstrating that for QALYs to be objective they need both of these calculations. Length of life and quality of life are, in part, interconnected. So when the calculation of a QALY is produced, the length of life that patients are likely to experience because of the expected treatment is assumed to be as important as their perceived quality of life.

The benefits of an objective resource allocation calculation may be seen in how QALYs are generated. Through the use of multi-attributed utility instruments, such as SF6D, quality of life preferences and perceived healthy life years are changed into numerical computations that provide an index which becomes the basis for decisions regarding maximization of health care resources. These calculations are not always hard and fast, but they do provide a measure of objec-

---

52. Owsie Temkin and others, *Respect for Life in Medicine, Philosophy, and the Law* (Baltimore: The Johns Hopkins University Press, 1976), 27–28.

tivity. Unfortunately within the denominators of QALY calculations lay some difficult factors which undermine that very objectivity.

QALY's Objectivity is Difficult to Obtain

Although QALYs are computed through the combination of healthy life years and quality of life, there are limitations to the benefits obtained by the use of these calculations. Some of these difficulties exist because of the denominators themselves and some because of the utilitarian philosophy that underlies the QALY model. Interestingly, the benefit found in QALYs' attempt at objectivity paradoxically generates much of the basis for its difficulties.

The Limits of Quality of Life Computation

When assessing the QofL computation a number of common difficulties arise. In QofL computation, the preferences fluctuate depending upon patient preferences. Though this issue has been addressed, there is another aspect of this fluctuating preference that needs to be approached. One reason why preferences are problematic is that the method by which the information is obtained is questionnaires. Individual preference questionnaires can inadvertently produce partiality or even disingenuous results, because when patients are filling out the EQ-5D, or SF6D, the patients' pre-treatment preferences are weighed as their selection. Needless to say, when a person has not experienced a certain disability, he or she has limited information upon which to base responses. Some patients will find the disability, compared to years gained, to be a benefit while others will find that post-allocation has produced a situation that they find unacceptable. No matter what the preference scale, there will always be a subjective element. This subjectivity, while allowing for a general quality of life denominator, can produce a false confidence in QALY computations.

The implications of this variable quality of life number are that QALYs struggle to compare similar disabilities in different contexts.

> Chronic diseases, where quality of life is a major issue and survival less of an issue, are difficult to accommodate in the QALY context and there is a tendency to resort

to the use of disease-specific measures of quality of life. Similarly, preventive measures where the impact on health outcomes may occur for many years, may be difficult to quantify using QALYs because the importance attached to each of the health dimensions is highly dependent on age, life context and life responsibilities.[53]

Preference scales ask pre-event values which represent only a current impression of a person's quality of life. Quality of life calculations must struggle to establish a calculation that incorporates the experience of time during which one has decreased health or is disabled versus chronological time. "There are still no quality-of-life rating scales that express the quality of life in the depths of the individual. So the QALY value only represents a superficial impression of a person's quality of life."[54] Although QALYs have attempted to present an objective basis for health care allocation through the use of QofL calculations, the comparisons of various unrelated diseases seem to be problematic.

Values assigned to the QofL component of the QALY may or may not reflect the preferences or values of the patients involved. If a large number of patients are surveyed to obtain a consistent QALY score for a given intervention, then it is likely that the majority of those who communicated their preferences will find that their positions have been, at least in part, not incorporated. The attempt to identify a median value undermines the objectivity of QALYs because as it identifies the maximization point it inherently distances itself from those preferences that do not fall into that median value. The result then is that those who participate in these questionnaires

---

53. Ceri Phillips Newport and Guy Thompson, "What is a QALY?" *Aventis House* 1 (5) [on-line]; http://www.jr2.ox.ac.uk/ bandolier/painres/download/whatis/QALY.pdf; Internet The example in this article is that of the health care status of a potential Olympic champion who suffers a hamstring twinge compared with that of an elderly person who has been restored to some measure of mobility as the result of a given intervention. This example demonstrates the difficulty of comparing, "diverse disease-specific measures of quality of life."

54. Soren Ventegodt, "Measuring the Quality of Life From Theory to Practice," *Quality-of-Life Research Center*, Denmark, (1995) [on-line]; accessed 10 October 2003; available from http://home2inet.tele.dk/fclk/mql_eng.htm; Internet.

may be put in a position where they unfortunately must follow the quality preferences of someone other than the patient.[55]

Another issue that causes difficulty with the quality of life denominator is the identity of "value," i.e., whose values will have precedence in allocation decisions? Allocation decisions are comprised of more than patient preferences for an estimated trade-off between various health states. Economists, health care professionals, administrators and other groups with a vested interest in the monetary outcome of medicine are concerned with implementation of the information gleaned from the quality of life calculations. The involvement of these various groups that have conflicts of interest can cause qualitative surveys to be viewed with suspicion. Researchers may inadvertently bias data that they have received based upon preconceived beliefs, prejudices or theories. Also, the researchers themselves may deliberately bias the surveys by imposing their own values, or succumbing to financial pressure.[56]

Another objection to the use of quality of life in QALYs is that the QALY value does not express what it means for a person to live life at a reduced quality. The question of identifying what quality of life means can be expressed in the disparity between institutional or societal perspective and the patient's perspective of what it means to have an acceptable quality of life.[57] One patient may be able to contribute more productively to society than another. However, the ability to contribute to society does not necessarily indicate that the first patient's life is of greater value. A society's perspective of quality

---

55. Mo Malek, "Implementing QALYs," *Aventis Pharma* 2 (1) [on-line]; accessed 8 October 2003; available from http://www.allgemeinmendizin.med.uni-goettingen. de/literatur/EBM/ImplementQALYsBandolier.pdf; Internet.

56. Soren Ventegodt, *Measuring the Quality of life from Theory to Practice* [on-line]; accessed 10 October 03, available from http://home2.inet.tele.dk/fclk/mql_eng.htm; Internet. An example of this would be a researcher who is an opponent of alcohol consumption surveying the quality of life of drinkers. That researcher's deep rooted notion that alcohol consumption would have the potential to influence negatively the quality of life in the long run may influence their research.

57. Alan Schwartz, "Cost-Effectiveness Analysis," *MHPE 494:Medical Decision Making*, week 10, University of Chicago [on-line]; accessed 24 September 2003, available from http://araw.mede.uic.edu/~alansz/courses/mhpe494/week10.html; Internet.

of life and that of a person who is experiencing a compromised quality of life can, and often do, conflict. Thus quality of life is unable to capture all that it means for a person to live in a state that is other than what he or she would choose.

An important philosophical question can be raised concerning the quality of life computation at this point: "Who has the better life?" Clearly from a utilitarian perspective, one is compelled to say that the individual who is able to function at a higher level of activity is generally the one who has the life that is more valuable to society. But, as has been seen with the rather broad definition of health presented by the World Health Organization physical properties are not the only criteria to be evaluated in this matter. The breadth by which health may be defined raises the question as to whether one may have confidence that QALYs are able to produce an accurate numerical value for quality of life for all people.[58] The quality of life computation, then, is problematic since it places quality of life calculations in a position of continual fluctuation resulting from QofL's varying definitions.

Other issues involved in the quality of life computation that need to be addressed further are the issues of quality versus possibility and futility. An explanation of how quality of life will measure and address such diverse issues as palliative care or the potential benefits versus liabilities of experimental treatment must be developed. The influence of political pressure to modify numbers to achieve sectarian ends needs to be addressed, as must the potential influence of unscrupulous scientists. It is important to address how much weight economics have in the computational process and the eventual allocation of scarce resources in light of the quality of life numbers.[59] These issues will need to be addressed more fully in another work, but they do demonstrate that the QALY model's quality of life computation can make attempts at objectivity problematic. The QALY

---

58. James G. Heller, "Will public health survive QALYs," *Clinical Pharmacology 2002* (Spring 2003) 9, 1 [on-line]; accessed 4 June 2003, available from http://www. pulsus.com./clin-pha/01_01/hell_ed.htm; Internet.

59. "Health Care Rationing: Needs and Options," *709 Health Law Syllabus* (19 Sept 2002), Boston University School of Public Health [on-line]; accessed 21 April 2003, available from http://www.bumc.bu.edu/Departments/PageMain.asp?DepartmentID=95 &Page=6616; Internet.

model is problematic in that QofL denominators lack the sophistication to include additional factors that may or may not be gradable as a maximization of value, but which are important because they influence a more comprehensive view of QofL.

The Limits of Healthy Life Computations

A QALY score computes the QofL and the extent, value, or utility of a given health care expenditure. QALY scores try to demonstrate how much benefit, both to the patient and to the medical system involved in the event, will be experienced because of the given intervention. The connection between the benefits of QofL scores and HLY scores indicate that 'value' is a difficult concept to define, and that chronological benefits of a health related event probably entail more than simply how many years more or less a patient may live.

Those who calculate chronological benefits struggle to prioritize all that is involved in experiencing time, while those who generate QofL calculations wrestle with fluctuating patient preferences. While preference based utility measurements are not the only method of self-perception, other measurements have the same failure to reflect the "quality" of years of healthy life. Some of the scales and studies that assist in this measuring self-perceived QofL are presented here:

> The Years of Healthy Life (YHL) measure from the US National Center for Health Statistics and the Medical Outcomes Study Short Form (known as the "SF-36") both explicitly include self-perceived health. The Quality of Well-being Scale (QWB), the Health Utilities Index (HUI), and the scale of disability used in the Disability-adjusted Life Years (DALY) measure, and the EQ-5D (the instrument being used by a multi-national collaboration on measuring health-related quality of life in Europe) do not use this dimension as part of the classification scheme.[60]

60. Dennis G. Fryback, "Methodological Issues in Measuring Health Status and Health-related Quality of Life for Population Health Measures: A Brief Overview of the "HALY" Family of Measures," Appendix C in *Summarizing Population Health—Directions for Development and Application of Population Metrics*, ed. M. J. Field and M. R. Gold (Washington, DC: National Academy Press, 1998), 7.

All of the multi-attributed utility instruments discussed are subject to the problem of the patient's subjectively identifying their preferences before entering into a compromised health state. Although their efforts at accuracy and general objectivity are commendable, they do not address the problem of subjectively choosing what the outcomes of future measures will be based upon past experiences. The "one size fits all" defining of healthy life years through preference based measurements that calculate every subsequent year as of less value than the present one is problematic.

The common use of multi-attributed utility instruments in calculating QofL and HLY scores places an undue burden on those who are either healthier than the projected HLYs measurement because they are using more resources than expected, and on those who are in the general category of living an expected amount of life years. Those in the general category, for instance, may feel a responsibility to waive treatment because they have used up their "time." Indeed, it has been suggested that there should be a distribution rule based upon a "personal identity approach" which would address the issue of a "prudential life span." A personal identity approach is an approach that views human beings at different "stages" of life. A prudential life span is an amount of life years that is expected for the average population. This approach promotes the idea that discriminatory distribution of limited resources should not be against different groups, but simply against the same group at different stages of life[61] It side steps the claims of discrimination against specific groups, such as people groups identified by their race, gender or class. Yet the prudential life span and the personal identity methods of distribution reveal at least one of the limits of HLYs. Because of its commitment to utility if a group is identified as using too much, as the distributors of resources count "too much," patients are potentially denied resources to benefit another group. The difficulty is twofold. First, as each "stage" is chosen for limitation of resources, the providers as well as

---

61. McKie, *The Allocation of Health Care Resources: An Ethical Evaluation of the 'QALY' Approach*, 70. In footnote 11 the authors compare personal identity and the prudential lifespan approach. In the text it is noted that utility maximization is the overriding principle in QALYs and as such it takes precedence over the accusation of ageism because it promotes social welfare through the maximizing of expected utility (59).

the consumer base dwindles. Some might suggest that a smaller base of consumers could correct the problem of resource limitation, but it would also cause a problem by limiting resource producers. Second, the method of choosing which "stage" should be refused the limited medical resources would be based upon societal preferences. In light of the utilitarian nature of these calculations, which find the "good" in utility through societal preferences, the choices as well as the identity of the "stage(s)" themselves would be relative and unstable.

Care for those who are living significantly longer than predicted may also become problematic. If members of a given population are not adhering to healthy life year guidelines, but are outliving the projected "prudential life span," then they could likely be viewed as an unexpected burden on the health care system. They may be viewed as a burden because, "The underlying idea of the approach is that medical technologies with low costs per QALY gained should be given priority over those with high costs per QALY gained."[62] With an increase in patient lifespan, the disability scale becomes skewed and the utility scores become less reliable. The scores become unreliable because HLY calculations are based upon current projected life spans. When life span exceeds expectations then the perception and projected figures are no longer trustworthy. In one sense, HLY calculations are an educated guess into the life spans of those who have taken or will take the multi-attributed utility instruments.

The Problem of Age

Healthy life years scores also struggle with the issue of age when it comes to calculating the value of treatments. Efforts have been made to lengthen the projected years of healthy life for those over sixty-five, but extended projections of life expectancy do not completely deal with the problem, which arises from the method by which healthy life years are calculated. What is sought is the number of years of healthy living that will occur after the treatment or procedure is applied to a given patient. The difficulty is that the estimated healthy life years for a twenty-five year old will be longer than that of a sixty-

---

62. "Health Related Quality of Life—Questions & Answers," *The Quality of Life Instruments Database*, accessed 4 June 2003 [on-line]; available from http://www.qolid.org/public/http://www.qolid.org/public/questions.html; Internet.

five year old.[63] The difference in the potential healthy years will not occur because the medical event is or is not effective, but simply because a person at age sixty-five most likely will not on average live another forty to fifty years. Consequently, healthy life year numbers are progressively stacked against the elderly, and would result in QALY scores being used to discriminate against the elderly. All things being equal, the older patient will consistently have a lower QALY score than the younger patient, not because of medical status but because of chronology. In light of the demographic shifts that were noted in chapter Two of this work,[64] this particular problem is not one that can be easily dismissed.[65]

The reason for this computation of healthy life years that discriminates against older Americans ties in QALYs' design for cost-effectiveness.

> In a resource-constrained publicly-funded health care system this cost, while conventionally phrased and measured in terms of money (financial cost) is more appropriately conceptualized as the benefits forgone by the patient (or those patients) who would have benefited most from having the resources devoted to them instead. Only if this opportunity cost is less than the benefit received by those who do receive the resources are we in an optimal—and it can be argued, ethical—situation as far as outcomes are concerned. So the economist's conclusion, through rarely stated this bluntly, is that the only comprehensive form of evaluation in this context is a cost-effectiveness

63. "Years of Healthy Life—Selected States," *MMWR Weekly* 47 [on-line]; http://wwww.cdc.gov/mmwr/preview/mmwrhtml/00050833; Internet.

64. See chapter 2, p. 41of this book. Data is presented concerning the expected increase of the elderly population as consumers of medical resources and the decrease in the projected tax paying population available to finance their resource requirements.

65. McKie, *The Allocation of Health Care Resources: An Ethical Evaluation of the 'QALY' Approach*, 59–64. In these pages McKie argues against four common accusations leveled at QALYs as ageist. The arguments defending ageism in QALYs are titled: A Slippery Slope, Utility and Fairness, Rival Foundations, and Social Hijacking. It will be noted later whether any of these arguments are valid in refuting the charge of ageism against the QALY model. For now, the point is merely being made is that the accusation of ageism cannot be easily dismissed as an unimportant issue.

one. Any other form (for example clinical evaluation) can only be regarded as a limited and partial evaluation.[66]

The basis for this cost-effectiveness lies in an underlying philosophy rooted in utility or the utilitarian maximization of value. In one respect, what is meant is that the philosophical basis for healthy life years is a utilitarianism that seeks to identify the consequence of a given medical event and apply that perspective to the healthy life year calculation that seeks to maximize the benefits of limited resources. The results of the utilitarianism in the QALY model are either that the elderly may feel pressure not to receive resources that could be used for the younger patients who, by implication, deserve it more, or that the very old should feel guilty for living past their projected "expiration date."

Utilitarianism and QALY Calculations

The philosophical basis of QALYs presents a number of difficulties for those who advocate the use of QofL and HLY scores as a basis for decisions regarding limited medical resource allocations. Looking at the relationship between utilitarianism and QALYs can provide an understanding of how the variable numerical qualities used in QALY calculations respond to changes in patient demographics. Consequential utilitarianism is commonly regarded as the philosophical basis for QALY determination which, in turn, directs QALYs' computational model of QofL and HLY factors and serves as a basis for those who make decisions regarding the allocation of limited medical resources.

QALYs and Utilitarianism

That QALYs have a utilitarian basis is not seriously disputed. Eric Nord has stated, "The QALY approach assumes that the societal value of an intervention is proportional to the size of the health improvement. We may call this a utilitarian view."[67] Whether one is discussing the length of healthy life years, or how society should apply

---

66. Jack Dowie, "Analyzing health outcomes," *Journal of Medial Ethics* 27 (2001): 246–47.

67. Nord, *Cost-Value Analysis in Health Care*, 38.

QALY scores, it is important to realize that consequential utilitarianism is the guide, or directing influence within the calculations. In one sense, the utilitarianism in QALYs is not a negative thing in that QALYs are doing exactly what they are designed to do: to provide the American medical system and those concerned with the distribution of limited medical resources an impersonal measurement that will enable caregivers and their associated financing groups to compare diverse treatments and programs.

The cost to benefit ratio that is sought after through the computations of QALYs is a utilitarian computation. In consequential utilitarianism "the relevant consequences are identified in terms of amounts of happiness."[68] The relevant consequences or 'happiness' sought in QALYs is the maximization of medical resources and of patient satisfaction.[69] The idea is that the greater the maximization of medical resources the greater the "happiness" or "benefit" achieved "by society." The QALY approach makes the benefit of an intervention directly proportioned to the potential maximization of limited resources. This process of medical allocation is, "firmly based on utilitarian considerations."[70] The problem is the tension that exists. If perceived happiness is the basis for maximization then a means to identify whose happiness takes precedence must be established. One may argue that QofL calculations are able to identify what the typical measurement of happiness is, but that measurement excludes the specific wishes of many and may actually work against the general happiness of members of the larger population who have not been asked their preference concerning QofL. The difficulty for the advocates of the QALY model, as well as for the adherents of any utilitarian allocation scheme, is how the needs and desires of the few can be balanced with the needs and desires of the many. It seems too altruistic to assume that those whose desires are not acknowledged and acted upon will graciously accept their diminished role in society. The allocation method selected must be one that is not subject to

---

68. "Utilitarianism," in *The Oxford Dictionary of Philosophy* (Oxford: Oxford University Press, 1994), 388.

69. Nord, *Cost-Value Analysis in Health Care*, 38.

70. John Arras and Robert Hunt, *Ethical Issues in Modern Medicine*, 2nd ed. (Palo Alto, CA: Mayfield Publishing Company, 1983), 446.

QALYs Are Problematic as a Basis for Health Care Allocation

the tension of the happiness of a few, that is patient satisfaction, and the happiness of the general population.

Not everyone agrees with utilitarianism as being the natural basis of the QALY model in the sense that it serves as the philosophical guide for QALY calculations. Some have argued that patient preferences are more likely the basis for the QALY model than is utilitarianism.[71] This argument fails to convince because the QALY's maximizations are "defined in terms of life extension and/or improvements in the quality of life."[72] This defined measurement is utilitarian, whether patient preferences are or not. Another reason utility rather than preferences is the basis for the QALY model is that Von Neuman and Morganstern's game theory is based upon a utilitarian maximization of probabilities. Though more will be discussed concerning Von Neuman and Morganstern's game theory in chapter Five the inescapable fact here is that the choice to rely on a Mixed Strategy of maximization within Von Neuman and Morganstern's game theory demonstrates a commitment to utilitarianism. Consequently, a commitment to the decisions resulting from calculations based upon their game theory is unavoidably utilitarian.

The Implications of Utilitarian Allocation

That there will be those who do not receive adequate medical care because of limited resources is an important point that needs to be fleshed out. The focus of this work is different so discussion of allocating limited medical resources will address not the general problem of who should receive limited medical resources, but the issue whether the QALY model, in limiting care, does so in an inequitable manner. When allocation is based upon the utilitarian ethic, those who have a decreased potential for maximum health can experience discrimination.[73] What then is presented as a method of allocation can become a method of discrimination against those whose conditions,

---

71. McKie, *The Allocation of Health Care Resources: An ethical Evaluation of the 'QALY' Approach*, 36–37. Another example can be found in "Preference or Utilities," Quality of Life Resources, *American Thoracic Society*, (2003) [online]; accessed 10 October 2003; available from http://www.atsqol.org/utility.asp; Internet.

72. Ibid., 36.

73. Nord, *Cost-Value Analysis in Health Care*, 39.

whether by nature or by accident, penalize them by giving them a lower priority in medical care. The lower priority assigned can generate great controversy over which individuals are the most productive, and what it means to be less productive and therefore of less value. In part, this issue will be addressed in the next section. Yet an even more disturbing problem exists that cannot be ignored. The utilitarian values that are inherent in the QALY model discriminate against a particular group not because of ability, race or gender, but because of a natural state or stage of life. The elderly would be discriminated against because they have the greatest potential for generating lower dividends in response to medical interventions. If the QALY model, as a utilitarian computation, does discriminate against the elderly because of their age, this seriously undermines the claim that the QALY model functions as a just and objective resource allocation modality, because it has been shown to discriminate not on the basis of perception, preferences or acuity, but on predicted potentiality.[74]

QALYs and the Elderly

When one looks at the computational development of the QALY model, it is easy to predict the potential problems that could occur related to care for the elderly. In many respects, the problem with the allocation of resources to the elderly resides in both the assessment of quality of life and in the computations that define healthy life years. These computations set the elderly apart, because their quality of life is never as high as that of their younger counterparts. The QALY model is unable to protect the elderly from unfair distinction as "burdens" to the medical system. The QALY model must provide an affirmative response to the question "when the care of the elderly imposes emotional and financial burdens on others—family, society, the middle-aged population—should the elderly be treated with less vigor for similar medical problems than, say, the middle-aged and

---

74. Peter Singer, *Rethinking Life and Death* (New York; St. Martin's Press, 1994), 131. While repudiating Ronald Reagan's sanctity of life ethic Singer suggests that the worth of a life can be defined by a quality of life ethic. In his work Singer, like other utilitarian ethicists, choose to define what quality of life means and where the line ought to be drawn which identifies a life as no longer worth living.

the young?"[75] Though adherents of the QALY model would affirm the position that a decrease in quality of life should mean a lower score and a lower probability of resource use, the final choice remains in the hands of those who decide how to use QALY scores. In light of the data providing general information concerning preferences and probable years of benefit a cost conscious resource distributor would tend not to choose those with lower QALY scores. The elderly will be consistently placed into that category of having a lower QALY score. That situation does not correct the problem of ageism in QALYs nor does it protect the elderly from undue discrimination.

It seems that the elderly cherish many of the same things that every other age group values such as choice, independence, dignity, privacy, personal rights and fulfillment.[76] They may perceive life in a slightly different manner than those who are younger because of their greater experience, and they may be willing to be more self-sufficient. The elderly are, for the most part, well aware of their decrease physical function and ability; they are not unaware of the implications of their aging. The difficulty in the QALY model arises when the computation of healthy life years makes age difference the variable that determines the difference in QALY scores. While some might argue that discrimination against the elderly is not like sexism or racism because the elderly are simply at a different "stage" of life that does not mean that such discrimination is acceptable.[77] If anything, the fact that the elderly are at a different stage of life ought to place them in a position to receive necessary resources to complete ADLs as they are capable. Like gender and race, age is a feature that is shared by all. Stating that the elderly are in a different "stage" does not negate the issue that they are still human beings involved in the medical system and subject to judgments of allocation that apply to all subsequent "stages" of life.

75. Mark Siegler, "Should Age Be a Criterion in Health Care?" *The Hastings Center Report* 14 (1984), 25.

76. M. J. Moss, "Ageing," in *New Dictionary of Christian Ethics & Pastoral Theology*, ed. David J. Atkinson and David H. Field (Downers Grove: InterVarsity, 1995), 148.

77. McKie, *The Allocation of Health Care Resources*, 70. The discussion is found in Footnote 11.

When QALYs are computed, it is believed that, through obtaining quality of life preferences, it can be understood that,

> If an extra year of health (i.e., good quality) life-expectancy is worth one, then an extra year of unhealthy (i.e., poor quality) life-expectancy must be worth less than one. On this scale, if the value of a healthy year of life is one, the value of the condition of death is zero. Various states of illness or disability better than death but short of full health receive a value between zero and one. The value of particular health outcomes depends on the increase in the utility of the health state and the number of years it lasts.[78]

The focus at this point is the words "the number of years it lasts," which are what health life years describes in its mortality score. The problem at this juncture is that based upon the utilitarianism of QALYs this state of years will always favor the young, because of an inherent assumption that they will live longer. Therefore, all things being equal, if a thirty-eight year old man and a sixty-eight year old woman enter a hospital for a kidney transplant the younger patient would receive a higher priority for treatment because his QALY score would be greater. It would be greater not because the possibility of his contributing to society would be greater, although some may argue this point, but only because the woman was sixty-eight. Herein is not discrimination based upon acuity, but this discrimination is based solely upon chronology. Age then presents neither a necessary benefit nor a liability, other then the natural development that occurs in a given life span. What age does do is it presents a probability that a person may not experience the perceived benefits of a medical event as long as another. This probability is also suspect because HLYs are based upon pre-determined calculations concerning "today's" age demographics.

---

78. Beauchamp and Childress, *Principles of Biomedical Ethics*, 209. Here Beauchamp is using analysis presented by Alan Williams and Eric Nord. Alan Williams, "The Importance of Quality of Life in Policy Decisions, in *"Quality of life: Assessment and Application*, ed. Stuart R. Walker and Rachel M. Rosser (Boston: MTP Press Limited, 1988), 285, and Erik Nord, *Cost-Value Analysis in Health Care*, 20.

One purpose of QALYs is to discriminate medically. The QALY calculations are designed to discriminate in the sense that they provide numerical guidelines for the maximization of limited resources; however, it is not in this regard that discrimination is being criticized in this work. Rather, here it "is not discrimination in the original sense of the term but a newer use of discrimination, which means an unfair or injurious distinction, as, for example, a difference in treatment made between persons or classes with respect to the same services."[79] Using the chronology as a ground for allocation selection seems to be a type of discrimination that is unfair and problematic. In light of the problems with the QALY model's discrimination against the elderly those problems will now be reviewed and critiqued.

The Problem of Age Discrimination

In discussing the problem of ageism as a criterion for making medical allocation decisions, Mark Siegler states that there are three particular problems. The discussion of these three problems is not intended to be an exhaustive critique of ageism, but it does lay the groundwork for a case against the age discrimination in QALYs.

Siegler first states that ageism in health care is wrong because it has a "Dump the Poor" perspective.[80] Unless the elderly have enough money to pay for their own services, insurance providers will eventually raise rates so high as to render the elderly uninsurable. The drastically increased rates demanded of those who need more medical care is cruel and unfair. It is cruel because it targets the population who, as a whole, most needs medical insurance, and it is unfair because it penalizes a whole class of people, the elderly, for a perceived lack of health more than it does any other age category.

Ageism is a wrong method of controlling costs because it will "Blame the Victim."[81] Here Siegler notes that age is not like some avoidable "voluntary health risks" such as smoking, alcoholism or drug abuse. When people get older they should not be set aside as burdens because they are . . . older.

---

79. Mark Siegler, "Should Age Be a Criterion in Health Care?" *The Hastings Center Report* 14 (1984): 25.

80. Ibid., 26.

81. Ibid.

Finally, Siegler states that this type of discrimination fosters a "Kill the Dying" philosophy. The "high cost of dying" comes to be regarded as too much of an economic burden to others so the seriously ill elderly may feel pressured to step aside for those who are younger and possess a higher "quality-of-life."[82]

Summarizing Rick Moody, Seigler presents his argument for an ethical obligation *for* the elderly. He states that universal human rights, compassion for the weak, prior contributions of the elderly, compensatory justice, the elderly as victims and the universality of aging all present an ethical obligation for the elderly. Finally, he states that providing for the elderly is "consistent with medical tradition."[83]

Seigler argues for a nobler obligation than that of the utilitarian ageism in the QALY model. The strength of his position seems to be that it is based upon virtue rather than utility. It considers the broader contributions of the elderly rather than their potential future economic or present demands on limited medical resources. The slippery slope of utilitarian QALYs promotes ageism as conducive to "more good generally." Yet in promoting a social welfare that discriminates against the elderly, one might question what benefit would be aroused in a society that promotes the general welfare by discrimination against those whose welfare it is responsible to uphold.[84]

Age discrimination also works against QALYs' attempts at objectivity in two ways: First, it discriminates based upon a presumed benefit of youth and an assumed liability of old age. That is, that the utility of the elderly is seen as less than that of the younger. While it is agreed that the elderly do experience a degree of natural deterioration of function because of their age, age in itself may not constitute a medical liability that affects expected QofL. Second, it is problematic because it seems that in QALYs there is inequality based upon a productivity argument. Adherents of this view reject a holistic view of what it means to be elderly.[85] It seems to ignore the possibility that

    82. Ibid.
    83. Ibid., 26–27.
    84. McKie, *The Allocation of Health Care Resources*, 59.
    85. John F. Kilner, "Ethical Legitimacy of Excluding the Elderly When Medical Resources Are Limited," in *On Moral Medicine: Theological Perspectives*

the greatest contribution to society in a person's life may come in the later years. To state that the elderly may continue to contribute to and receive from society as long as they do not consume a particular amount of medical resources in excess of a certain threshold dollar amount assumes that youthful people have higher productivity and are entitled to more medical resources.

In one sense, the issue of discrimination in the QALY model is one of fairness. QALY calculations have demonstrated a decrease in justice and a reduction of equity for the elderly. However, this is not to say that some type of allocation model is unnecessary. When charges of injustice or unfairness are leveled against the QALY model it means that a perception exists that basic social relationships involving trust and fidelity have been violated. Some may protest that QALYs are, in fact, fair and just. "Allocation on the basis of QALYs is fair in the sense that programs are prioritized on the basis of their potential to produce improvements in the quality and quantity of life (within budgetary constraints), without regard to the way these benefits are distributed among particular individuals and groups."[86] The problems with this defense are that it ignores the function of QALYs as a single measurement of health care outcomes that is employed in cost-benefit analysis by those who have to make health care allocation decisions. In one way this argument seems to negligent. If a person left a loaded pistol out in the open in an area where there were known to be criminals present that person would be held liable because he or she should have known what a criminal would do with an available weapon. Likewise, to state that QALYs are fair because they come up with a particular calculation but that it does not actually use the computation demonstrates the same logical fallacy. It seems to lack consistency for the QALY model to define "fairness" in the above manner. When accusations of being unfair are leveled the implication is that the accusers, assuming honesty, perceives that they have note been given what is, "due to them."[87] Fairness means

---

in *Medical Ethics*, 2nd ed., ed. Stephen E. Lammers and Allen Verhey (Grand Rapids: Eerdmans, 1998), 980.

86. McKie, *The Allocation of Health Care Resources*, 60–61.

87. Nicholas P. Wolterstorff, "Justice and Peace," in *New Dictionary of Christian Ethics & Pastoral Theology*, ed. David J. Atkinson and David H. Field (Downers Grove: InterVarsity, 1995), 16.

that there is an obligation to give to the elderly that which is given to every other member of society.[88]

Some have argued against the idea that QALYs are unfair on grounds different than potential health improvements. They argue that quality of life deteriorates with age and that makes the use of chronology as an allocation parameter acceptable.[89] The problem with this perspective is that it assumes that all individuals over a certain age have the same rate of deterioration in their ability to carry out activities of daily living (ADLs). This runs together quality and chronology. Of course it is true, that "with increased longevity, more people are developing chronic diseases that require extensive medical services."[90] Nevertheless, while increased longevity may bring chronic illness this does not necessarily mean that the majority of individuals' perceived QofL deteriorates to such a level that they consider life no longer worth living.[91] The issue here is whether those who are living longer, with or without chronic disease, ought to have medical services as needed, or should a limit to their medical consumption be established? It seems that if QALY calculations are going to look at QofL from a utilitarian perspective, then it is difficult to conclude how the elderly will not feel as if they are "burdens" to society. The elderly are know to consume a large amount of resources in the last few years of life. If their lives could be limited then there would be more for others. As former Colorado governor, Richard Lamm,

---

88. Clarke E. Cockran, "Health Policy and the Poverty Trap," in *Toward A Just and Caring Society: Christian Responses to Poverty in America*, ed. David P. Gushee (Grand Rapids: Baker, 1999), 237. Health care should be primarily distributed according to need for health care rather than distributive principles.

89. Des O'Dea, "Putting a value on 'a life saved': Should the value vary with age?" Paper given at the *New Zealand Association of Economists' Conference*, Wellington, NZ, 26–28 June 2002 [on-line]; accessed 12 October 03; available from http://nzae.org.nz/ files/no.43(PAPER)-odea.pdf; Internet.

90. Lisa Yount, *Patient's Rights in the Age of Managed Health Care* (New York: Facts on File, Inc., 2001), 20.

91. Ibid., 57. Yount quotes a December 2000 study which claims that fifty percent of Americans have one chronic disease, and twenty percent of Americans have two or more such diseases. Seventy percent of Americans are in this category of having a chronic disease. According to this study it seems that having a chronic disease cannot in itself define whether the elderly have a high or low QofL.

insisted that some denial of treatment to some people is necessary to make society's limited medical resources available to the greatest amount of people.[92] If the "greatest good" for society is to deny treatment to those who probably need it the most, especially because of the perceptions associated with age, then that policy comes dangerously close to an ethic that is not just encouraging wisdom in the utilization of limited resources, but also a duty of the elderly to die. Although many reasons for the opposition to the notion of a duty to die have been offered, it is interesting that one author sees Christian ethics as the primary religious block to such an ethic.

> An example of the first line of argument [that there is a higher duty that always takes precedence over a duty to die] would be the claim that a duty to God, the giver of life, forbids that anyone take her own life. It could be argued that this duty always supersedes whatever obligation we might have to our families. But what convinces us that we always have such a religious duty in the first place? And what guarantees that it always supersedes our obligations to try to protect our loved ones?[93]

Hardwig does not think that religious considerations are weighty enough to set aside the duty to die when one has become a burden to family, society or self. Neither chronic illness nor the prospect of being a potential burden is unique enough problems to warrant only age as being used for calculating HLYs. What Hardwig's argument proves is that there are at least two potentially opposing worldviews in this discussion. The first is utilitarianism which supports the view that the elderly place an unacceptable burden on available medical resources, and that age should thus be an integral part of QofL because age includes the possibility of debilitation and of an increased consumption of medical resources. Adhering to the utilitarian view argues that the burden of the elderly occurs when there is a potential for illness, but does not necessarily conclude that the elderly identified will be dying any time soon.

---

92. Ibid., 30.

93. John Hardwig, "Is There a Duty to Die?" *Hastings Center Report* 27 (1997): 35.

Fortunately, a very different ethic exists which takes the burden of caring for the aged and considers it in the context of family and community in a more positive light. The next chapter will look at how the Bible addresses the issue of allocation and the treatment of the elderly. At this point, one can conclude that the elderly are potentially in a position where their care is considered by some a greater burden then that of someone younger based on age, and it probable implications. It can also be concluded that the choice not to care for the elderly is not a morally neutral position. When QALY calculations are used to place elderly patients in a position that they are discriminated against because of their age there is a presumption that this quality makes them a burden, or that older age is a "problem" to society in general and to those allocating limited medical resources, in particular. That the elderly are forced into this position reveals a discord that makes the QALY model problematic as a basis for health care allocation.

Conclusion

In the quest for the QALY model to have an objective basis for assisting in medical allocation decisions, distribution of limited medical resources those who have developed QALYs have come to rely on two denominators, quality of life scores and healthy life years. Although these denominators do provide a workable basis for health care allocation they both have inherent problems. The quality of life score is currently inadequately standardized and insufficiently inclusive to be used as a method of assessment. Little standardization in the use of QofL measurements is employed within clinical trials, and reports concerning QofL vary considerably according to the health problem.[94] Its method of assessing preferences cannot incorporate all of the data necessary to make a conclusive calculation.

In the consideration of healthy life year scores it was noted that the connection between the quality of life and quantity of life is an intrinsic part of the QALY calculation. Though the length of life

---

94. Andrew Garratt and others, "Quality of life measurement: Bibliographic study of patient assessed health outcome measures," *British Medical Journal* 324 (2002) [on-line]; accessed 11 February 2004; available from http://bmj.bmjjournals.com/cgi/reprint/ 324/7351/1417; Internet.

provided by a medical event is important in assessing the benefits of that event it seems to also present some difficulty.

If the QALY model is to provide an objective basis for health care allocation, then the denominators used will need to be redesigned to be more inclusive. As was noted in the discussion of QALYs and fairness, equality entails more than looking at a common "potential to produce improvements."[95] That potential is based upon pretreatment assumptions as well as a utilitarian basis which often finds the elderly to have less potential than younger people regardless of the health status of either.

This evaluation of QALYs does not suggest that its calculations are entirely without merit, only that the use of QALY calculations needs to be tempered to offset their ageist components. Those who use the QALY numbers in their allocation process may need to develop a method of correcting this problem. Andrew Garratt and his colleagues offer a suggestion for the proper use of QofL measurements in QALYs.

> The huge growth in the numbers of patient assessed measured of health outcomes has obvious benefits in terms of the availability of measures for specific populations. However, potential users require guidance particularly when faced with multiple measures. Structured reviews together with recommendations based on patient and professional consensus are required for effective application of measures. Concurrent evaluation can also help to determine the most suitable measure for a particular application.[96]

Thus, users of QofL measurements and the QALY calculations that use them, must be careful to recognize the limitations of the QofL measurements in comparing various populations. Without such caution, it is all too easy to dismiss as a computational anomaly the ageism that results from its calculations.

---

95. McKie, *The Allocation of Health Care Resources*, 60.

96. Andrew Garratt and others, "Quality of life measurement: Bibliographic study of patient assessed health outcome measures," *British Medical Journal* 324 (2002) [on-line].

HLYs also contribute to the problem of ageism in QALYs by weighing healthy years gained against the probability of mortality. Given the tendency to look at the elderly as a drain on the medical resources available those who live beyond the proposed life span may feel a burden either to limit their medical care or to commit suicide at a certain point to avoid using "more than their share" of medical resources. It is unfair to penalize elderly people for illness they do not yet have. Moreover, even if a large subpopulation of the elderly does have chronic illnesses this does not mean that it is morally acceptable to limit their access to needed medical care. It seems that QALYs subject the elderly to a utilitarian ethic where they are allowed only limited medical resources so that those who are younger, who are perceived to have a better chance of obtaining a positive outcome because of their age, may benefit. Perhaps this is the optimal economic choice. As with the *Mixed Strategy* of von Neuman and Morgenstern's game theory there is a point of maximization when one is committed to a utilitarian philosophy. While that choice finds the maximization point, it also excludes other choices. Many of those choices may not stretch the limited medical resources the farthest but, on the other hand, some of the other choices would allow the medical community to serve a broader population in a better manner.

Finally, it may be argued that the ageism in the QALY model will be corrected through the give and take of the free-market economy. There are two problems with trusting the market to correct the ageism in QALYs. One is the profit motive that now dominates healthcare. The Hippocratic Oath has been replaced by cost-benefit analysis in many medical venues, and there is increasing pressure for medical revenues to increase. This brings up the second problem, which is conflict of interest. It would be unrealistic to expect the American system of free-market enterprise to become altruistic. "Numerous observers have stated that at some level, obligations to the bottom line will directly conflict with duties to serve the needs of patients."[97] It is the inability to adequately deal with this conflict

---

97. Scott B. Rae, "Money Matters in Health Care," in *Cutting-Edge Bioethics: A Christian Exploration of Technologies and Trends*, ed. John F. Kilner, C. Christopher Hook and Diann Uustal (Grand Rapids: Eerdmans, 2002), 105. In developing this issue in his footnote Rae quotes Arnold Relman who states, "Medical care is in many ways uniquely unsuited to private enterprise. It cannot

of interest, as it involves the elderly in QALY calculations, which has come to be an ever worsening allocation problem.

---

meet its responsibilities to society if it is dominated by business interests." (Footnote 2). It seems that this statement sums up the conflict in health care allocation.

Chapter Four

The Biblical Basis for Elder Care

Those who use QALY calculations in the decision making process for determining allocation of limited medical resources are confronted with the challenge of distributing those resources in a fair and just manner. On one side, the moral principles and calculations that need to be used in directing the decisions to allocate funding for treatments and programs should be able to withstand the majority of economic forces, but conversely they need to be simultaneously inclusive and discriminatory. That they should be able to deal with many of the economic forces that influence health care has been discussed in the Conclusion of chapter Three. The allocation of limited medical resources must be discriminatory in that principles and calculations should be fair guides for those making health care allocation decisions. They should be inclusive in that they include those who have a legitimate need for health care. The problem, as was noted in the last chapter, is that not everyone agrees with what can be considered a legitimate need for health care. In certain QALY calculations, age alone makes certain medical treatment options illegitimate.

The discrimination against the elderly in the QALY model stands out as a unique and serious problem that warrants consideration. The ageism in the QALY model calls for a competing ethic that will act as an alternative moral basis for the allocation of health care. The Judeo-Christian ethics found in the Bible provide a basis for conceiving of a philosophy of care that can challenge the ageism found in the QALY model. For this to occur, the Bible will need to be considered and used as a noteworthy collection of documents which offers principles that can provide an alternative philosophy of care for the elderly, and one which can provide a basis for holistic resource allocation. This competing biblical philosophy of elder care found in the Bible will now be addressed.

A Common Reading of Scripture

It is important to understand where one starts because, as has been demonstrated in the case of the utilitarian underpinnings of the von Neumann and Morgenstern game theory as it relates to the QALY model, it will directly influence one's conclusion. For this reason, it is important to discuss how the contents of the Bible will be interpreted, since the Bible will be the basis for identifying a competing ethic for elder care.[1] In this work the Bible will be looked at as a document which provides not only a historical, contextual and textual ethic for guiding the decision making process in health care, but also provides a basis for dialogue as well as analysis of the propriety of utilitarian based allocation, such as the QALY model.

There are some good reasons to use the Bible. The first is that it has been the basis for moral discourse within the Christian church throughout its existence.[2] "The Christian believes that Scripture has

---

1. Christians historically have had a high regard for Scripture. Since this work is being written from a Southern Baptist perspective there is a specific, presumed respect for the contents of the Bible which should be acknowledged before the evaluation of the representative texts is undertaken and is summed up in many documents, and one which many Southern Baptists agree upon is the *Baptist Faith and Message 2000* which states concerning Scripture, "The Holy Bible was written by men divinely inspired and is God's revelation of Himself to man. It is a perfect treasure of divine instruction. It has God for its author, salvation for its end, and truth, without any mixture of error, for its matter. Therefore, all Scripture is totally true and trustworthy. It reveals the principles by which God judges us, and therefore is, and will remain to the end of the world, the true center of Christian union, and the supreme standard by which all human conduct, creeds, and religious opinions should be tried. All Scripture is a testimony to Christ, who is Himself the focus of divine revelation." "The Scripture," *Baptist Faith and Message 2000* [on-line] accessed 22 March 2004; available from http://www.sbc.net/bfm/bfm2000.asp, Internet.

2. Allen Verhey, *Reading the Bible in the Strange World of Medicine* (Grand Rapids: Eerdmans, 2003), 63.

something to say to the world and to mankind and that something carries authority."³ The contemporary Christian church follows this tradition of using the words, principles and ideas of the Bible in private and public moral discourse.

A second reason for using of the Bible in moral discourse is that the Bible has been viewed in Western culture as a divinely inspired text that is seen by Christians as a document that contains divine wisdom which is generally believed among Christians to be able to guide humanity in making prudent decisions concerning relationships among people. The Christian community has traditionally used the Bible as a moral guide for itself as well as a basis for societal critique, which one can readily identify in Old Testament prophetic literature.

The inspiration of Scripture means that the Bible should be taken seriously. The implication of the inspiration of Scripture for this chapter is found in the implications of Scripture as a document that is "without any mixture of error" and "totally true and trustworthy."[4] It is believed that the Bible is a document that has a divine origin and can be trusted and used for practical wisdom. The steps to obtain this "practical wisdom" occur when the representative texts are analyzed in light of their social context. Then the overriding principles are identified and applications are gleaned from the principles found in the text. Thus practical applications will be available from texts which may not directly deal with health care allocation, but which do provide principles of care for the elderly, or social justice for those in need. What such a statement implies is that the Bible itself contains principles which may apply directly or indirectly to the care of those who are sick, in general and the care of the elderly, in particular. Biblical principles are useful not only for the medical care and compassionate treatment of the sick, but also as a moral basis for decisions concerning health care allocation.

The church does not exist in isolation. The community of Christianity exists within the greater social community, and as such it is called to be "Salt and Light" (Matt 5:14–6). The church is called

3. David Cook, *The Moral Maze: A Way of Exploring Christian Ethics* (London: Spck, 1983), 45.

4. "The Scripture," *Baptist Faith and Message 2000* [on-line] accessed 22 March 2004; available from http://www.sbc.net/bfm/bfm2000.asp, Internet.

to engage in dialogue with those outside the church and to discuss what courses of action are the best for all of the citizens, Christian and non-Christian, within that society. An example of this is seen in the church's critique of child labor in the 1800's.[5] The West has had a tradition of staying in conversation with the Christian church regarding morality and ethics. This work fits into that tradition in that there are some new and extremely difficult decisions that loom on the horizon regarding the allocation of health care resources. For Christians, as well as secular authorities, to abandon the longstanding tradition of amicable dialogue regarding important social issues would be disastrous.

There is general agreement that the Bible is good for the Christian community and that Christians should be in dialogue with secular authorities concerning morality and ethics, but some may argue that it is difficult to come to a consensus on biblical ethics in light of the problems of variant readings, hermeneutic difficulties and how contemporary Western Christians selectively interpret and apply biblical teachings. It is certainly true that each generation or culture looks at the Bible with a unique perspective, but that does not imply that a sufficient level of objective knowledge of the content of the text is impossible to obtain.[6] This present work views the text as clearly presenting the intent of the Divine author through the eyes of his human servants. This is not to say that the issue of epistemology can easily be dismissed, but that a thorough discussion of the objectivity or subjectivity of knowable truth is beyond the scope of this work. It will be postulated that there is a level at which truth can be known, and so there is also a level at which Scripture can be understood and used as a basis for formulating Christian principles of ethics and morality. An example of the complexity of this issue is seen in the following discussion concerning the possibility of knowing historical truth. The discussion concerning historical truth directly applies to this present work as is seen in the comments of

---

5. See, Charles Howard Hopkins, *The Rise of the Social Gospel in American Protestantism, 1865–1915* (New Haven: Yale University Press, 1940; reprint, Brooklyn, NY: AMS Press, 1967).

6. Kevin J. Vanhoozer, *Is there a Meaning in this Text?: the Bible, the Reader, and the Morality of Literary Knowledge* (Grand Rapids: Zondervan, 1998), 26.

Michael J. Wilkins and J. P. Moreland regarding the gulf that exists between interpreting history subjectively or objectively.

> The idiosyncrasies of modern scholarship promote what Oxford New Testament scholar N. T. Wright dubs the "cultural imperialism of the Enlightenment," an attitude that assumes it is only in the last two hundred years that we have discovered what "history" is, "while writers in the ancient world were ignorant about these matters, freely making things up, weaving fantasy and legend together and calling it history. When it comes to the Gospel records, critics like those in the Jesus Seminar contend that the evangelists were so influenced by the early church's portrait of Christ that the records of Jesus' life must be treated with skepticism. Such skepticism is undue with regard to history in general and to the records of Jesus' life in particular. Standard historiography is applied to other ancient religious documents with profit and the same rules of validation of historical data should be applied to the biblical record.[7]

A type of objective historical truth is possible so that with the evidence presented one can reasonably know truth. In the same way, it is also possible to know what Scripture says about the subject at hand, elder care as it applies to resource allocation.

What the Christian should do in the midst of all of the potential confusion of subjective or conflicting biblical interpretations is to look for the "evidence" of the principles found in the text and verified by historical/traditional interpretations. There are some things that are up for question, but there are numerous events, statements, artifacts, documents, people, activities, ethical statements that are verifiable. These facts make it difficult to reject obvious conclusions unless one desires to descend into the realm of the deconstruction or postmodern reader response. None of these options provide a basis for common reading or constructive dialogue concerning the moral contents found in the Bible.

---

7. Michael J. Wilkins and J. P. Moreland, "Introduction: The Furor Surrounding Jesus," in *Jesus Under Fire: Modern Scholarship Reinvents the Historical Jesus*, gen. ed. Michael J. Wilkins and J. P. Moreland (Grand Rapids: Zondervan, 1995), 3.

The Biblical Basis for Elder Care

It is assumed, for the purpose of this discussion, that it is possible to know what is communicated in the Bible. There is sufficient documentation to provide a reliable basis for knowing biblical content sufficiently to agree on what was said and in what context. For those who object to the present view of biblical truth regarding the elderly, they should present their evidence and then allow others to render a verdict. Without this open interchange of ideas which seeks out evidence, biblical truth is relegated to propaganda, a result that neither side desires. As Nicholas Wolterstorff has advised, "The Christian scholar ought to allow the belief-content of his authentic Christian commitment to function as control within his devising and weighing of theories."[8] It behooves the Christian scholar to see how her or his faith is verified textually, contextually, historically and culturally. Then can Christians, and only then, challenge other views legitimately. If Christians have done their homework well, they have nothing to worry about when it comes to an open examination of the evidence by unbelievers or other Christians. Thus an exchange of ideas between proponents of a biblical basis for elder care and the problem of QALY's is desirable.

The Christian influence on American culture has been, and continues to be, noted in the applications of the representative texts found in this work. Pluralists may object, saying that the Bible is a nice book that could be used as a discussion point in moral discourse among church people, but it is only one voice among many and deserves no greater esteem than the Koran or any other religious text.[9] In response to this objection, it should be noted that the applications of the biblical texts are comprehensive enough to remain a basis for discussion in the current American culture.[10] The Bible has had an unequaled effect upon Western culture and it has long been viewed as a symbol of honesty, truth, and Western culture's most cherished

---

8. Nicholas Wolterstorff, *Reason within the Bounds of Religion*, 2nd ed. (Grand Rapids: Eerdmans, 1984), 76.

9. Verhey, *Reading the Bible in the Strange World of Medicine*, 33. Also, in footnote 2, Verhey states that using the Bible in community discourse is appropriate, but it is not unique because there are other competing voices involved in social discourse.

10. Ibid., 40.

values.[11] Also, "It is at the heart of the biblical vision of the human situation that the believer is a witness who gives his testimony in a trial where it is contested."[12] In light of its moral and ethical influence on American culture, the influence of the broader Christian church on society and the appropriateness of the biblical vision to be contested it ought not to be a voice that is quickly dismissed.

In this work, the initial step to a common understanding of Scripture will be to examine some texts which have principles which clearly pertain to the problem of ageism. An impartial reading of Scripture will be attempted through an analysis of the texts from varying perspectives. This work is not an exegetical commentary on any of these texts, but an effort will be made to minimize biased perspectives in an effort to find a common understanding of the texts. After a common reading of the text is obtained, an effort to identify and then apply the principles found in that reading will follow. Thus an attempt will be made to employ a hermeneutic that not only supports the authors' original intent, but one which takes their intent and extracts some of the moral principles found in the relevant texts.[13] Finally, the text will be applied humbly, with the understanding that the texts were written for a particular reason and that it would be disingenuous to deduce from them what thing they were never intended to say.[14] Every effort will be made to verify the textual contents through comparison with other texts, commentaries on those texts and historical application of the representative texts under scrutiny.

---

11. Kenneth Schenck, *Jesus is Lord: An Introduction to the New Testament* (Marion, IN: Trinity Publishing, 2002), 1.

12. Leslie Newbigin, *Foolishness to the Greeks: The Gospel and Western Culture* (Grand Rapids: Eerdmanns, 1986), 63–64.

13. See, D. A. Carson and John Woodbridge, ed., *Scripture and Truth* (Grand Rapids: Baker,1992); Moises Silva, *Biblical Words and their Meaning: An Introduction to Lexical Semantics*, Revised and Expanded edition (Grand Rapids: Zondervan, 1994).

14. "Modern Hermeneutics: Lesson 1: Legitimate Contrasted with Illegitimate," *Bible Studies at The Moorings* [on-line]; accessed 30 March 2004; available from http://www.themoorings.org/doctrine/issues/hermeneutics/intent.html; Internet. Cf. James Callahan, *The Clarity of Scripture* (Grand Rapids: InterVarsity Press, 2001).

The Biblical Basis for Elder Care

It is respectfully understood then that the Bible is not universally accepted as an authoritative document, and that some people find that the principles of the Bible impede their desire to actuate medicine as they consider best, especially regarding certain ethics which have direct application to the elderly.[15] It is true that in modern America, all people have a right to express opinions concerning various aspects of medical practice. The desire to follow a competing ethic which may deal with the elderly in an innovative manner is not forbidden any more than following a biblical ethic is prohibited. Rather, what this objection does is to challenge those who are struggling with the issue of allocation to look beyond a single ethic, such as cost-value analysis, and consider competing ethics which may otherwise influence the issue of health care allocation. It challenges those who regard allocation decisions as being based solely on utilitarian values, such as those expressed in the QALY model, to advance a more holistic method of evaluating health care.

There may be a concern at this juncture that the following discussion of the application of biblical principles on ageism as applied to QALYs will be a polemic which commands obedience. The texts of Scripture might be commands, but in a pluralistic society each person has the right to the beliefs of their own choosing. Therefore the Christian community has the same rights as any other group discussing moral issues, and is free to draw upon Scripture in the process. The point here is that discussions of morality need not be uncomfortable simply because there is a religious dimension. If anything using the Bible in moral discourse allows for a common reading and a common place of discussion concerning issues, such as ageism in the QALY model.

The Bible will be used as the primary source for identifying a biblical ethic of elder care. The ethic that will be developed will not be isolated to how individuals should act, but it is intended for a broader audience.

> The behavior with which biblical ethics is concerned is not simply the behavior of individuals; the principles

---

15. John Hardwig, "Is there a duty to die?" *Hastings Center Report* 27 (1997): 35. Harwig notes that the Christian principles regarding a duty to God impede his challenge for people to die at such a time as to not "burden" their families, societies, or selves.

of society bear intimately upon all ethical studies and it bears also upon biblical ethics. Hence the biblical ethic takes account, not only of individuals as individuals and of their behavior as such, but of individuals in their corporate relationships. There is corporate responsibility and there is corporate action.[16]

Thus, biblical ethics should not only influence the religious community, but its application should be presented to secular audiences who may or may not be supportive of its propositions, even on "nontheological" matters, such as health care allocation. In light of the dilemmas resulting from the rapid advances in medicine without commensurate financial resources to offer these to everyone, it would seem prudent for secularists to consider alternative models, included those presented in the Bible. If a broad-based critique of the ageism in the QALY model is to occur then the biblical model deserves a place in the discussion.

Examination of the Christian Scriptures will reveal that there are many biblical texts that deal with the treatment of the elderly in both the Old and New Testaments. Also, "in biblical perspective and in observable evidence, there is no necessary correlation between quality of life and length of life. The direction of a life and not its duration is decisive for its quality. It is not how long but how one lives that matters most."[17] The biblical record does not say that there is no connection, but that the connection is such that it pales in comparison to the issue concerning how one lives life, and that temporal existence, however long, comprises a negligible fraction of one's eternal existence. The separation of QofL and chronology seems to present at least two opposing ethics. The Utilitarian-based QALY model computes with the presupposition that there are always direct correlations between QofL and length of life, in contrast, the biblical model sees that QofL is not directly connected with chronology.

It is neither the aim of this work to evaluate every text in the Bible that relates to the elderly, nor to develop a full blown theology

---

16. John Murray, *Principles of Conduct: Aspects of Biblical Ethics* (Grand Rapids: Eerdmans, 1957; reprint Grand Rapids: Eerdmans, 1999), 13.

17. Frank Stagg, *The Bible Speaks on Aging* (Nashville: Broadman, 1981), 182.

of what the Bible says about the elderly.[18] This chapter will examine the biblical ethics of elder care in an attempt to postulate a moral basis for health care allocation through an analysis of some important texts of Scripture. In light of the importance of the Torah, and in particular the Ten Commandments, to biblical ethics, the Fifth Commandment and a Levitical clarification of how the elderly are to be honored will serve as a basis for analyzing the principle of elder care in the Old Testament. It will also serve as a reference point for the rest of Scripture. The texts themselves will be evaluated and then other supporting texts within the Law will be examined when clarification is necessary. Various theological viewpoints will be presented to identify the boundaries of the principles and applications available in the representative texts. In the New Testament, some of the comments that Jesus makes concerning elder care will be discussed, along with the general perspectives on treatment of the elderly described in the New Testament. A common theme will be sought which honestly and accurately represents the intent of Scripture regarding the treatment of the elderly. After identification and evaluation of the biblical principles, the church's responsibility towards God and its neighbors will be evaluated and some responses to the primary principles uncovered will be considered. In the process, this work will seek to clarify what the Bible presents as the basic principles of elder care.[19]

Identifying the Elderly

Since the chapter seeks to identify a biblical ethic of elder care it seems expedient to define what is meant by the term, "elderly." *The Merriam Webster New Collegiate Dictionary* defines "elderly" as "rather old." This definition is simplistic, and that is true to some extent. But there is a reason for caution when defining "elderly";

> Old age is often defined as beginning at 65, but people grow old at such different rates that chronological age

---

18. See, William L. Hendricks, *A Theology of Aging* (Nashville: Broadman, 1986).

19. Unless otherwise noted all Scripture texts will be taken from *The Holy Bible*, New International Version, (c) 1973, 1978, 1984, International Bible Society.

does not accurately reflect a person's capacity for work and play. There are two distinct groups of older people. The "young-old," aged 55–75, include many people who may be regarded as middle-aged. They are generally comparatively healthy, active, and economically comfortable. However, for those in the "old-old" group-over 75 years of age-health, mental abilities, and general life-style may deteriorate.[20]

Most elderly stereotypes focus on the old-old which have been called, "sexless, demented, incontinent, toothless, and childish."[21] These derogatory remarks reveal the inherent phobia and prejudice that the West has with the elderly in general and particularly those elderly who are in need of continual care. Therefore, to be elderly has broad implications, but these implications do not make the term itself unwieldy. It can be affirmed that most of the time when the term "elderly" is used it carries along with it the idea of old age. Sometimes old age is seen in the use of euphemistic terms such as "white hair," or "elder." Although "white hair" seems obvious enough when used as a metaphor for old age, white hair itself is not unique to the elderly. In ancient times, "elder" may have referred to any male who was past puberty and about to grow a beard, but it more commonly applied to an older person holding some type of leadership position.[22] Though it is true that an 'elder' might not always be elderly the biblical context often reveals whether the elder is a 'young' elder or an 'elderly' elder.[23] In Scripture the word for elder has a broad application and can indicate, "a clan leader, a local official, and an older person, its feminine form also describes older women. The word normally in-

---

20. Robert N. Butler, "Old Age," in *Encyclopedia Americana International Edition*, vol. 20, Navajo to Opium (Danbury, CT: Grolier Incorporated, 1993), 701.

21. Betty Friedan, *Fountain of Age* (New York: Touchstone, 1993), 36.

22. J. Gordon Harris, *Biblical Perspectives on Aging: God and the Elderly* (Philadelphia: Fortress, 1987), 11–12.

23. Mary Pipher, Another *Country: Navigating the Emotional Terrain of our Elders* (New York: Riverhead Books, 1999), 28. Piper makes a distinction between young-old and old-old. The young old are in their sixties and seventies. She defines the old-old as those whose health has deteriorated, usually in the mid-seventies.

The Biblical Basis for Elder Care

dicates older persons, heads of family."[24] How the term is used is usually easily determined from the individual context. Sometimes, the context in which the words of the text are used reveal the subject to be the elderly even when age is not explicitly mentioned. Though context often reveals the meaning of "an elder," it should be noted that the word normally indicates an older person.

The idea of the elderly is associated with chronology is seen throughout Scripture. In Genesis 18:11 Abraham is considered, "Old and well advanced in years," at the age of ninety-nine. In Psalm 90:10, the psalmist states that humanity's life span is to be seventy years, but that if a person is particularly vigorous, then his or her life expectancy could reach eighty years of age or more. In 1 Tim 5:9 the Apostle Paul established age qualifications of sixty years old for widows in need of church financial support. In 2 Chronicles 27:1–7 the Old Testament makes a distinction between people of various ages when the issues of vows and the equivalent value for people of varying ages are discussed. The sum to be paid for the ages of twenty to sixty is set at fifty shekels of silver. If a person is over sixty years of age then the amount for a man is cut to fifteen shekels of silver and for a woman it is cut to one third of that of her working years. Thus it is noted that the possibility of living beyond sixty was a realistic possibility in both cultural contexts. Significantly, it is also noted that the responsibilities of those that become chronologically old were diminished. However, this in no way implied that their worth was diminished, instead, the elderly were to be honored, and this important command will be discussed later in this chapter.

The biblical data suggests the number of sixty years of age for a person being considered to be old, but the actual number of years that constitute being old is often based upon the common life span of the prevailing culture. For instance, one finds that in France in the 1600's the average life span of a person was twenty to twenty-five.[25] This median life expectancy can change from culture to culture.[26] This trend can be seen in America where a person living past one-hundred years of age is still considered special, but no longer unique.

24. J. Gordon Harris, *Biblical Perspectives on Aging: God and the Elderly*, 12.

25. Pipher, *Another County*, 41.

26. Ibid. In light of the high rate of infant mortality life expectancy was pulled down, but a given culture may still have significantly different life expectancy.

To be considered elderly not only involves age, but often incorporates commonly associated changes in capacity. In 2 Sam 21:15, King David is said to have become, "exhausted." He was in danger of attack and he needed help against his enemies during combat. This was the last time that King David went out to battle, and it placed him in the category of being old (2 Sam 21:17). It was not only his decrease in strength but also his age affecting his strength that identified him as what he was; elderly. David's decrease in fighting ability is indicative of the change in physical capacity that occurs as a person ages. Today, someone like David might be considered semi-retired. He was still able to carry out administrative functions, but it was clear that he was heading towards the fall and winter years of his life when he was no longer able to go out into battle and defend himself adequately in battle.

It rightly has been said that, "ageing is a physiological process, which occurs at different chronological ages."[27] Some people experience decreased physical ability much earlier than others. Eventually, a variety of changes occurs in the elderly, such as a decrease in mental/intellectual capacity, a change in emotional responses, and a possible increase in wisdom, or at the very least, a greater understanding of the consequences of life's experiences.[28] In other words, the elderly experience transition, but this transition does not necessarily denote a decrease in quality of life. As has been noted, QofL is a holistic concept involving multiple dimensions of one's being. Transition is a common human experience but, for the elderly, it carries unique anticipation and apprehension.[29] Apprehension may come when they realize that they are weaker, slower, and at times, marginalized by those younger. The old are then those who have reached such an age and capacity that a given society readily identifies them as old.

A biblical understanding of elder care not only needs to know who the elderly are in a given society, but it also needs to clarify what the Bible means by the term, 'elder' or "elderly." In the present

27. Ian S. Knox, *Older People and the Church* (London: T & T Clark Ltd., 2002), 17.

28. "Aging," *American Medical Association Complete Medical Encyclopedia* (New York: Random House Reference, 2003), 126.

29. Charles G. Oakes, *Working the Gray Zone: A Call for Proactive Ministry by and with Older Adults* (Franklin, TN: Providence House Publishers, 2000), 80.

context the term "elder" or "elderly" will not necessarily fall into an ecclesiastical context. This does not suggest that there are no connections between the idea of the elderly and the biblical elder. The initial elders of Israel probably had the recognition of being old, and were probably the heads of their tribes, and they may have been a valuable source of wisdom. The idea of an elder, "was first applied to senior adults whose age apparently was considered a likely advantage in counseling."[30] It is not assumed that age always brings wisdom, but that the original Old Testament elders were wise and their age contributed to this state of spiritual maturity. These characteristic, became part of the Hebrew understanding of the idea of being "elderly."[31]

In the New Testament, in 1 Peter 5:1, Peter calls himself a fellow elder, again combining an office with age. In 2 John 2:1, the opening words, "the elder," denotes, as this word was originally used, seniority in age. This perspective is recaptured in Luke 15:25, where the older brother, in the story of the Prodigal Son, is referred to using the same term. Later, "elder" came to refer to rank, as seen in 1 Peter 5:1. "Elder" is used when referring to members of the Sanhedrin in Matthew 1:21 and Acts 6:12. The term is also applied to those who preside over churches and Christian assemblies, as well as to the twenty-four members of the heavenly court in John's vision are called "elders," (Acts 11:30; 1 Timothy 5:17, 19 and Revelation 4:4, 10; 5:5, 6, 8, 11, and 14).[32] This quick overview reveals that there is a connection, in part, between the term "elder" and age, but also a connection between the word, "elder," and leadership roles in church government. However, the focus of this work is not on church government, but on those who are chronologically old and their need for medical care. The idea of one who is elderly does not in and of itself refer to a person of wisdom or godliness, nor does it always refer to an office in the church. Originally, it referred only to seniority, and seniority is the context that will be sought when discussing the biblical basis for elder care.'[33]

30. Frank Stagg, *The Bible Speaks on Aging* (Nashville: Broadman, 1981), 25.

31. Charles G. Oakes, *Working the Gray Zone*, 55.

32. Marvin R. Vincent, "2 John 2:1, The Elder," in *Word Studies in the New Testament*, vol. II; The Writings of John (McLean: MacDonald, 2003), 392.

33. Harris, *Biblical Perspectives on Aging: God and the Elderly*, 16. Harris

The Bible acknowledges that old age is a time of diminished physical and mental ability. According to the Bible this was not part of humanity's original state. In Genesis 3, before the Fall, when Adam and Eve were in the Garden of Eden, the portents of old age were positive. An increase in years only pointed to an increase in their pleasure of God and of their labors. Reviewing how age is viewed in Genesis, one author states that, "Longevity is clearly viewed as positive, if not actually normal. It is short life and not long life which is abnormal."[34] Understanding the view that a short life was considered atypical, it is easier to understand the implications of the punishment meted against of Adam and Eve when they sinned in the Garden of Eden. After the Fall and God's judgment of these seminal parents, life in general, and old age particularly, became a potential burden.[35]

Other Scripture texts discuss the limitations of old age. In Genesis 27:1 poor eye sight is associated with old age, and in Genesis 42:38 and 44:29 gray hair is mentioned. In 2 Samuel 19:31–40 the story of the eighty year old Barzillai, who helped King David, reveals a man who had become content with his age and limitations. The opposite of this was King Saul whose old age seemed "empty and miserable" because he was jealous of losing his royal position to David, when David was young.[36] Old age is also seen as a blessing from God, or the lack of it is seen as a potential curse. In 1 Samuel

---

makes the comment that in ancient Israel an elder/leader may have been as young as thirty or forty. It is not the age that is as significant as the issue of transition. Elders are in a situation where they have passed from youthful energy and interests to that of encroaching weakness with a lowering of production and, eventually, of status. Their perceived quality of life may be affected by their age and physical status, but this does not mean that they are to be discounted or marginalized. In light of their positions of leadership and their potential for decreased productivity, the Bible places the elderly in an elevated and protected status.

34. Frank Stagg, *The Bible Speaks on Aging*, 9.

35. The potential of enjoying a continual and unbroken relationship with God would have placed Adam and Eve in the enviable situation where their potential old age mean more time 'walking with God in the cool of the day.' The trespass of Adam and Eve in Genesis 3 not only interrupted that fellowship with God, but it also placed a physical burden upon all of humanity that it was not originally meant to experience. That is the afflictions experienced in old age.

36. Frank Stagg, *The Bible Speaks on Aging*, 56.

2:31–32 the elderly Hebrew high priest Eli was cursed by God, who condemned Eli's family by stating that "there will not be an old man in your family line." While in this case, a curse is given, this is not meant to suggest that in every situation the length of one's life is based upon a whether or not one has incurred God's wrath. Rather, the diminished physical states of the elderly place them in a context where their enjoyment of the "golden years" is based upon their outlook on life.

> In biblical perspective and in observable evidence, there is no necessary correlation between quality of life and length of life. The direction of a life and not its duration is decisive for its quality. It is not how long but how one lives that matters most. If the direction of a life is wrong, it does not help to speed up or just keep going. The quality of life improves with aging or deteriorates with aging, depending upon what qualities are built into it.[37]

In light of the above texts, where it states that from a biblical perspective there is not a direct observable correlation between quality of life and length of life it seems that the Bible does present old age as a stage of life that has the potential for both positive and negative experiences. Quality of life may change focus, but it may not necessarily diminish when one grows old. Indeed, as the inevitability of infirmity and death for the elderly draw near, what is needed is increased assistance. How the elderly should be treated in light of their increased need for assistance is an important issue to be addressed when seeking to understand the biblical basis for elder care.

Biblical Guidelines for Elder Care

When the Bible presents admonitions concerning elder care, they are almost always connected to familial or communal relationships. Within these admonitions one finds that the major principle revolves around the word "honor," which is derived from the Decalogue, as will be noted later in this chapter, and can be broken down into two closely related concepts, care and respect. In poetic imagery, Ecclesiastes 12:1–7 describes both the process of growing old and

---

37. Ibid., 182.

the responsibility of the young to care for the aged. "The ancient Hebrews, in obedience to a natural feeling, and because of their superior moral discipline, entertained the highest regard for the aged; and this sentiment still prevails throughout the East, as it did among all ancient nations."[38] Caring for the elderly, in the ancient world was a priority, and in Scripture it was a command. The care of the elderly has a unique requisite in Scripture. "The young were accustomed to rise and give place modestly, whenever an old person approached. Want of reverence for the aged was severely rebuked."[39] The responsibility of the young to care for the elderly in the ancient world was pretty much universal.[40] Two important Old Testament texts may be considered exemplars of the Jewish perspective of elder care, Exodus 20:12, which is the Fifth Commandment of the Decalogue, this is also repeated in Deuteronomy 5:16, and Leviticus 19:32, which provides a more general command to show respect to the elderly. Later in this chapter, a number of New Testament texts, beginning with Jesus' reiteration of the Fifth Commandment, will demonstrate the consistency of the New Testament in reaffirming the Old Testament perspective on elder care. These New Testament texts were chosen because they uniquely reaffirm the principle of honor and the concepts surrounding community found in the Old Testament.

Old Testament Care and Respect

Honor and respect are often used synonymously in the Old Testament. ""Honor," would seem to demand behavioral concretization, while "respect" might primarily describe an inner feeling."[41] Thus to honor

38. "Old," in *Cyclopedia of Biblical Theological, and Ecclesiastical Literature*, vol. III, New-Pes, ed. John McClintock and James Strong (Grand Rapids: Baker, 1981), 330. Job 12:12 and 15:10 are examples of a high regard for the aged.

39. Ibid., 331. Deut 28:50 speaks in condemning tones regarding an invading country that does not respect the elderly. This lack of respect seems to be a characteristic of wickedness.

40. David Padfield, *The Care of the Elderly*, (2001) [on-line]; accessed 24 March 2004; available from http://www.padfield.com/tracts/elderly.pdf; Internet. Philo and Aristotle saw a moral and legal duty to support parents in their later years.

41. Gerald J. Bildstein, *Honor Thy Father and Mother: Filial Responsibility in Jewish Law and Ethics* (New York: KTAV Publishing House, Inc., 1976), 37–38.

the elderly is to show outwards signs of deference, while to respect, or revere the elderly would mean to have an authentic inner emotion of deference towards them. They are in effect two aspects of the same attitude, one relating to outward behavior and the other to internal motivation. The principles to honor and respect the elderly are illustrated in a number of biblical texts, but the clearest examples of this deference are observed in the stories found in Genesis. These stories illustrate the connection between honor and respect, and provide a context for the analysis of the Exodus 20 and Leviticus 19 texts. As these texts are evaluated filial responsibilities to parents will first be evaluated, and it can then be shown that the principles involved in honoring the parents can be extrapolated to encompass all elderly people to the elderly in the community.

Genesis

It is difficult to discuss honor and respect of the elderly without understanding that the Bible presents these principles within the context of the family. In the Old Testament, the family is always seen as an extended unit. This is particularly true in the book of Genesis where one finds that families were described as including multiple generations. This perspective runs throughout the Scriptures whether the context is an urban or an agrarian society. The common family unit was usually a monogamous relationship that included the extended family.[42] The extended family commonly included family members and servants as well.

That the extended family included a variety of relatives is seen in a number of texts in Genesis. It is seen when Terah left Ur and took his son Abraham in Genesis 11:31, and when Abraham took his nephew Lot with him when they went to Canaan in Genesis 12:5. Isaac and Rebekah lived with their sons until Jacob stole his brother Esau's birthright and had to flee for his life (Gen 27). Laban cared for his grown family, including Isaac and Laban's daughters, Leah

42. Brent R. Kelly and E. Ray Clendenen, "Family," in *Holman Illustrated Bible Dictionary* (Nashville: Holman Bible Publishers, 2003), 557. Occasionally Scripture discusses polygamous marriages, but this was an uncommon occurrence. Polygamous marriages in the Bible are often identified as those having relational difficulties, such as treachery, as well as problems of infertility and going after other gods, e.g., King Saul and Solomon.

and Rachel, whom Jacob married (Gen 29). Laban's extended family included Laban's grown sons, and daughters as well as their spouses and children. The extended family is also seen in Jacob's family life. After Jacob's son Joseph was made second in command to Pharaoh in Egypt, Jacob is said to have brought all of his extended family to live in Egypt (Gen 46:26). The existence of the extended family in ancient Israel does not in itself demonstrate the necessity for the care and respect of the elderly, but it does provide a context for the commands of the Law that give specific guidelines regarding the care of the elderly. By the time of the Exodus, Israel had developed into a community which was held together by close knit tribal and familial allegiances. "There is evidence that apart from the periods of rampant paganism and moral decadence (such as the reign of Manasseh) average Israelites shared a common ethos which was substantially informed by the major distinctiveness of the Mosaic law."[43] That Law permeated the commonly accepted values of the society, and Israelite society was a community that was familial to the core, the role of filial respect for parents mirroring that of Yahweh's chosen people for Him.

The Fifth Commandment

Among the families of Israel and in the Law of the Old Testament care and respect were important issues. The first text, which is the fifth injunction given in the Ten Commandments, will be examined as presented in Exodus 20:12. This command is repeated by Moses when the Ten Commandments, and the fifth commandment in particular, are repeated in Deuteronomy 5:16 when Moses reminds the Israelites of their covenant responsibilities.[44] The Ten Commandments have been called commands of the covenant and can be split up into two parts.[45] This separation of commands enables the reader to focus on

43. C. J. H. Hingley, "Old Testament Ethics," in *New Dictionary of Christian Ethics & Pastoral Theology*, ed. David J. Atkinson and David H. Field (Downers Grove: InterVarsity, 1995), 55.

44. Deuteronomy 5:16 has the additional clause, "that it may be well with you."

45. Brevard S. Childs, *The Book of Exodus; A Critical, Theological Commentary* (Louisville: The Westminster Press, 1974), 371. Childs states that, "The Decalogue supplies the detailed content for the covenant obedience required in v. 5.

who is the primary subject in the command. The first four commands deal with the Israelites' relationship with God, and the last six focus on their relationships with each another.[46] In Exodus 20:12, the Fifth Commandment states, "Honor your father and your mother, so that you may live long in the land the Lord your God is giving you." This text is directly addressing respect due to parents, but it also has important implications regarding honoring the elderly in general. One reason is that this command, like the others in the Decalogue, has little reference to a specific historical period: "The commandments deal with issues which remain central to the life of the nation from the beginning to the end."[47] By definition, parents are older than their children. Children are to honor their parents who are older than they are. This is rooted in the word, "honor." "The command to honor is a command to demonstrate in tangible, empirical ways the respect people must have for their parents."[48] Proper application of the command to honor one's parents requires that it be a normative pattern of life. "This honoring, if we are to judge on the basis of the usage of the verb "to honor" in the Old Testament, involved: (1) highly prizing them (Prov 4:8); (2) caring and showing affection for them (Psalm 91:15); and (3) showing respect, fear, and reverence to them (Lev 19:3)."[49]

Filial responsibility entails respect for father and mother as well as care for them in their time of need. Indeed, the death penalty

---

It makes known the will of God which the people have agreed to accept." Thus, for the Israelites, their decision as whether to obey these commands carried the consequences of divine blessing or wrath.

46. Eugene H. Merrill, *Deuteronomy*, The New American Commentary: An Exegetical and Theological Exposition of the Holy Scripture, NIV Text (Nashville: Broadman & Holman, 1994), 143. Merrill presents a common method of looking at the Ten Commandments when he designates the first four as "The Commandments Pertaining to Humankind's Relationship to God" (143), and the next six as "The Commandments Pertaining to Humankind's Relationship to Others" (152).

47. Brevard S. Childs, *The Book of Exodus*, 396. Childs is hesitant to ascribe these commands as being only timeless principles, nevertheless he acknowledges that this is one aspect of their purpose.

48. Eugene H. Merrill, *Deuteronomy*, 153.

49. Walter C. Kaiser Jr., *Toward Old Testament Ethics* (Grand Rapids: Zondervan, 1983), 156.

could be pronounced upon a person who struck, cursed or dishonored his or her parents, (Exodus 21:15, 17; Deut 27:16). Respect was an important issue in the families of Israel, especially towards the father, but the Fifth Commandment includes the mother, as well as the issue of respect and care were seen as normative in order properly to honor one's parents. This normative care had a broad understanding and application as is seen in the comments of Gerald Bildstein,

> Our rabbis taught: What is reverence and what is honor? Reverence means that he (the son) must neither stand nor sit in his (father's) place, nor contradict his words, nor tip the scale against him. Honor means that he must give him food and drink, clothe and cover him, and lead him in and out.[50]

The Fifth Commandment expands upon what has already been presented in Genesis, which also presents an ethic where elderly parents deserve honor and respect. In contrast to QALY calculations that make age a negative assessment, in the Jewish culture age insured *more* care, not less. The extended family was responsible to care for their elderly parents, because in Israel "physical descent was the natural basis for a moral relationship."[51] Calvin also comments on the extent of the care inherent in the term, 'honor' when he writes that children should follow the example of storks who "supply food to their parents when they are feeble and worn out with old age."[52] But the application does not limit this command to just one's parents. The Fifth commandment was the first of the last six which "sets forth the principles guiding Israel's relationship with the covenant community, and more broadly, with the human family."[53] The admonition to "honor" parents is also seen to extend to "governmental

50. Gerald J. Bildstein, Honor Thy Father and Mother: Filial Responsibility in Jewish Law and Ethics, 38.

51. Benno Jacob, *The Second Book of the Bible: Exodus*, trans. Walter Jacob (Hoboken, NJ: KTAV Publishing House, Inc., 1992), 570.

52. John Calvin, "The First Commandment of which is the Fifth of the Law; The Fifth Commandment," *Christian Classic Ethereal Library* [on-line]; accessed 30 December 03, available from http://www.ccel.org/c/calvin/comment#/comm_vol05/htm/ ii.htm; Internet.

53. John Durham, *Exodus*, Word Biblical Commentary, vol. 3, gen. ed. (Waco: Word, 1987), 290.

surrogates" and apparently applied to society as well.[54] Regarding the breadth of the Fifth Commandment;

> The large number of references to the honoring of parents within wisdom literature would certainly point to this area of Israel's life as being equally influential in the formulation of this commandment (Prov 1:8; 15:5; 19:26, etc.). It seems most probable that the problem of the right of the parent was a concern which emerged out of a variety of different situations and was controlled through several means (court, cult, household). Lying at the heart of the original prohibition was a command which protected parents from being driven out of the home or abused after they could no longer work.[55]

The admonition to care for parents was familial, communal and non-negotiable for the people of ancient Israel. Later, Jewish tradition also understood this commandment to have far reaching application, and rabbis taught that it applied to the elderly in general. Thus, "Old age in the Bible signifies more than divine blessing; it also indicates a transition into a weakened social and physical condition which needs respect and protection to compensate for its losses (Prov 19:26; 28:24)."[56] Willingness to accept personal and social responsibility are revealed in willingness to assist in the care of the elderly.

> The relationship of children to their parents was the only one which was in accordance with creation; therefore, it represented a divine and natural dependence among men. Every other relationship represented a human creation and could, therefore, be reversed, but not that of parents, which was formed through birth. Masters might become

---

54. Terence E. Fretheim, *Exodus*, Interpretation: A Bible Commentary for Teaching and Preaching (Louisville: John Knox, 1991), 232.

55. Brevard S. Childs, *The Book of Exodus*, 418. A number of texts from the Torah support the position that children were to honor their parents regardless of the age of their parents. Childs notes that some of those texts, such as Exodus 21:15; 21:17; Lev 20:9; and Deut 27:16, warn of dire consequence for failing to honor one's parent(s).

56. J. Gordon Harris, "Old Age," *The Anchor Bible Dictionary*, vol 5, O-Sh (New York: Doubleday, 1992), 12.

servants, or the reverse, but every person remained the child of his parents.[57]

Both divine command and natural law point to the familial and social responsibility of honoring one's parents.

> The command (cf. also Lev 19:3a) is not about the obligation of (young) children to submit to parental authority, but is directed to adult persons, those who in the patriarchal society are family heads. They, the (oldest) sons, when their parents have relinquished authority and are no longer able to look after themselves, must provide them with food, clothing and shelter.[58]

The adult children were responsible for the totality of care for their elderly parents. One may argue that this is concerning parental care and not applicable to the issue of medical allocation. Yet in Israel for a person not to have a family to care for him or her was uncommon and was considered generally unacceptable. In the Decalogue the Fifth Commandment has added importance because, "The fifth commandment is thus both as foundational to commandments six through ten as the first commandment is to commandments two through four, and also is the logical link from the relationship of Israel to Yahweh to the relationship of Israel to humankind."[59] Thus the blessings associated with honoring parents included the elderly in a context that is social and religious, as well as familial. The extent of the social responsibility to care for the elderly is seen in the extent of its application.

> The command to honor one's parents is large and comprehensive—as can be demonstrated from the universality of Old Testament moral propositions or narratives and from the unusual grammatical form of using no finite verbs in which the Decalogue is cast. Thus it is not limited to the immediate superiors under view—one's

---

57. Benno Jacob, *The Second Book of the Bible: Exodus*, 570–71.

58. Cornelis Houtman, *Exodus*, Historical Commentary on the Old Testament, vol. 3, ch. 20–40, trans. Sierd Woudstra (Leuven, Belgium: Peeters, Bondgenotenlaan, 2000), 51–52. Caring for others, especially one's parents was considered one of Israel's fundamental principles of life.

59. John Durham, *Exodus*, 290.

parents, but it extends to all that are our superiors: governors, magistrates, teachers, leaders in the house of God, and all who are superior by virtue of the gifts of divine providence, whether of age, riches or knowledge.[60]

Thus the application of the Fifth commandment has broad social implications revealing a corporate responsibility of respect towards those in authority. The elderly, in general, fall into a category in which social responsibilities demand that they be "honored."

What has been established to this point is that in Israel, the elderly were placed in a special context wherein they were to be respected and cared for by their children. The care and respect for the elderly most often occurred in the context of the extended family. Families were not to neglect their filial responsibilities in Israel. However, when people, such as widows and orphans, were in need, and there were no families to support them, the community of Israel was required to assume responsibility to care for them. An example of the social services provided for those without familial support is found in the texts concerning the poor gleaning in the fields (Lev 19:9,10; Deut 24:17–22). The connection between the poor and the elderly is usually seen in the context of widows whose children have died and have left them destitute. This does not negate the possibility of older men being identified with those who are poor, but it was far more common for widows to find themselves in a position where they were without familial protection.[61] A typical situation is described in the book of Ruth where the widow Naomi and her wid-

---

60. Walter C. Kaiser Jr., *Toward Old Testament Ethics* (Grand Rapids: Zondervan, 1983), 159. Kaiser states that it is part of being a holy society that social responsibility extends to the elderly, widows, orphans, the poor and others who are oppressed or in need.

61. Elderly men and women both were in a position in which, if the need arose they could appeal to Scripture, or tradition, to obtain social services such as gleaning. In The Wisdom of Solomon 2:10, judgment is called down upon those who do not reverence the elderly men among them. Later, in the book of Sirach the idea of honoring was broadly developed; Sirach 3:1–16. Though widows are often identified as people who needed social assistance, they were not exclusive in their need. In 2 Kings 7, four men with leprosy are identified as being in danger of starvation during the siege of Samaria. Although they are not expressly identified as elderly, this text demonstrates that men, as well as women, could be sick, destitute and in need in Israel.

owed daughter-in-law try to obtain their daily bread in this manner (Ruth 2:2–3).[62] Briefly, the provisions for gleaning and the prophetic judgments directed against the people guilty of the neglecting of widows and orphans points to the moral and social requirements for the people of Israel to care for those in need. "The Mosaic law displayed particular compassion for the alien, the orphan, and the widow by prescribing that harvesters deliberately leave the grain in the corners of their fields for these economically vulnerable classes and not go back and gather ears of grain they might have dropped (Lev 19:9, 10; 23:22; Deut 24:19)."[63] In relation to the issue of "honor" as seen in the Fifth Commandment, the gleaning provision reveals that when circumstances occurred which prevented the family from carrying out its responsibilities the greater community of Israelites were responsible to care for people in need, which included the elderly.

The feelings and actions associated with "honoring," demonstrate an amazing interconnectedness in Israelite society. To fail to render the "honor" due to parents because they became burdensome would have been an unimaginable concept to the Israelites in light of the Fifth Commandment. Unfortunately, the present culture of American medicine as represented by the use of QALY calculations, is disenfranchising the elderly by making a clear separation between stages of life, and in so doing, they are denying the social responsibility that children have for parents.

Leviticus 19:32

In Leviticus 19:32, one finds another command concerning the elderly that is important for this discussion concerning the biblical care of the elderly because it seems to present the command in a

---

62. Meir Zlotowitz, *The Book of Ruth/Meggilas Ruth*, 2nd ed. (Brooklyn, NY: Mesorah Publications, Ltd., 1982), 86–87. "The verse stresses the noble character of their princess who offered to glean like a common pauper to spare her mother-in-law the indignity of *her* going out and being subject to the humiliating gaze of those who knew her in her former affluence." Thus Ruth did what Israelite society expected her mother-in-law, Naomi, to do for support. The point is that Israel had a type of social program for the poor, and that social net also provided for those without the help of relatives.

63. Daniel Block, *Judges, Ruth*, The New American Commentary, vol. 6, gen. ed. E. Ray Clendenen (Nashville: Broadman & Holman, 1999), 652.

broader context and strengthens the idea that to "honor" the elderly is more than simply a familial responsibility. Leviticus 19:32 states, "Rise in the presence of the aged, show respect for the elderly and revere your God, I am the Lord." This text occurs within the context of an extended list of laws designed to set Israel apart from its pagan neighbors by legislative distinctive religious and moral behavior. It is broader than the Fifth Commandment in that it addresses the elderly in general, not just parents, and designates them chronology. "Due to the experience that the years bring, such persons often stand in the same relation to younger persons that parents stand to children. And to show respect for aged persons is simultaneously to walk in the fear of God."[64] This type of respect finds dual expression. Within its original context, it has been surmised that its meaning may have involved making a space for an older man when he wanted to sit down somewhere.[65] This verse also presents the more courteous gesture of rising in respect. It is not enough to give the older person a seat, but it also commands the necessary ungrudgingly deferential attitude that should accompany the action. Respect and deference are identical responses by God to the Israelites in regard to Himself. "The blind and deaf (19:14) and the aged (19:23) cannot enforce the dignity they merit, but God will punish those who deny it."[66] It was out of awe toward Yahweh, the covenant God who revealed himself to Israel, and gave the Law by Moses, that the Israelite was to care for and respect those who were his elders, be they their parents or simply the unrelated elderly in their community. Commenting on Leviticus 19:32 Rabbi Yahuda Appel quotes the Talmud saying, "If the youth

---

64. Walter C. Kaiser Jr., *Leviticus*, The New Interpreter's Bible, vol 1 (Nashville: Abingdon, 1994), 1135. Holiness is equated with social justice. Lev 19:32 sees respect for the elderly as a part of the social fabric of a nation that reveals its relationship with God. In one sense it is an expansion of Lev 19:18, "Love your neighbor as yourself." Kaiser also sees parallels between the social justice of Lev 19 and the practical Christianity found in the book of James (1136). In both contexts holiness is demonstrated in social activism that serves those who are not necessarily able to repay, such as widows, foreigners, and the aged.

65. Martin Noth, *Leviticus; A Commentary*, Rev. ed. (Philadelphia: The Westminster Press, 1965), 144.

66. Jacob Milgrom, *Leviticus 17–22; A New Translation with Introduction and Commentary*, The Anchor Bible (New York: Doubleday, 2000), 1703.

tell you to build, and the elders tell you to destroy, you should destroy and not build, because the destruction of the elders is in itself destructive."[67] Thus the preeminence of the elderly in the life of Israel is seen in the responses of younger Israelites' to them. The priority of caring for the elderly in Israel was an uncontested given.

The fear or respect of the elderly in this text also relates to the Fifth Commandment in that it presents the "honor" due to parents as also being due to the elderly in general. The verses preceding Leviticus 19:32 had been primarily cultic, but with this text, there is an abrupt shift to address the social responsibilities of Jewish life. Nevertheless, there is a close connection between the religious life in Israel and its accompanying social responsibilities. "The first regulation is concerned with having respect for the elderly, for according to Proverbs 16:31 and 20:29, old age is a "crown of splendor" that is given by the grace of God. Because of his greater experience, one who bears this crown stands in the same position with respect to younger persons as parents to their children (Job 12:12). Showing honor to the aged was at the same time considered an expression of fear of God."[68] The connection between honoring parents and the aged is found in the "fear of God." The awesome respect due to the God of Israel was echoed in practical expression through deferential respect and care for the elderly. An interesting comment on this text certain Jewish Law Codes that state that this type of "honor" was not simply reserved for Jews, but even for pagans outside the nation of Israel.[69] This presents a principle of "honor" and respect for the elderly that is quite inclusive.

Leviticus 19:32 presents the issue of honoring the elderly through a broad based command.

> The inculcation of respect for the aged man is a fundamental commandment of a larger secondary society;

---

67. Yehuda Appel, "Kedoshim (Leviticus 19–20), Retirement," *Appel's Parsha Page* [on-line]; accessed 25 March 2004; available from http://www.aish.com/torahportion/appel/Retirement.asp; Internet.

68. A. Noordtzij, *Leviticus*, Bible Students Commentary, trans. Raymond Togtman (Grand Rapids: Zondervan, 1982), 207.

69. Yehuda Appel, "Kedoshim (Leviticus 19–20), Retirement" [on-line]. Referring to the Shulchan Aruch, the God of Jewish Law, Appel cites the requirement that Gentile elders are also to be honored and respected.

such a commandment is both unnecessary and impossible within the family circle, since the older men in the extended Israelite family unit quite naturally occupied the highest position in the familial hierarchy. The grandfather, father, and possibly the father's brother held power. By contrast, respect for other "graybeards" outside a young person's immediate family circle had to be inculcated.[70]

This command goes beyond the Fifth Commandment and provides a basis for the application of honoring the elderly within the larger community. There simply was not an option in ancient Israel to allow elderly people to be abandoned by their families or by the greater community.[71] This being said, the attitude of respect and honor as commanded in the these texts was clearly normative for the Old Testament period. These commands provided a basis for fair and just treatment of both parents and the elderly in general. They also provide principles of care and respect for the elderly which, when applied to the present health care context, provide strong Scriptural support for elder care.

Some may argue that these commands were culturally specific and often so broad in their appeal as to be nebulous in their application. In one sense this is correct. The commands *are* broad in their application, but the pervasiveness of these commands to respect the elderly are not isolated to Israel. In nearly every other culture there is an equally great emphasis on respect for the elderly. The stress on caring for the elderly is not embraced as enthusiastically by northern European and American culture, but as Hiebert points out, "The emphasis on youth [in the West] is the exception rather than the rule around the world. In most societies old people are viewed positively as wise and experienced. They are shown respect, given places

---

70. Erhard S. Gerstenberger, *Leviticus: A Commentary* (Louisville: Westminster John Knox Press, 1996), 278–79.

71. John E. Hartley, *Leviticus*, Word Biblical Commentary, vol. 4 (Dallas: Word, 1992), 322. "Showing proper honor to the elders is an expression of one's fear of God." Hartley goes on to comment that in the greater context of this text holiness for Israel included social justice. In Leviticus 19:32 that would include societal honoring of the elderly.

of honor and consulted about family and community decisions."[72] The West may be overly concerned with youth, but that does not exempt it from the responsibility of caring for the elderly in its midst. It seems disingenuous to relegate the elderly to a place in society where they are perceived as having little worth, as has happened in the utilitarian calculations found in the QALY model.[73] Thus while in one sense, these commands are not culturally specific, in another sense, their structure and emphasis are a unique part of the ethic of care found in the Bible.

The Testaments' Ethical Relationship

It is important to identify the ethical relationship between the Testaments when seeking a biblical ethic of elder care. Walter Kaiser has stated that, "The ethics of the Old Testament are an absolute necessity for formulating New Testament ethics or any kind of Christian ethics, for only in the Old Testament can the proper foundation be laid for all biblical, theological, or Christian ethical theory or action."[74] Although not everyone agrees to the extent of the Torah's influence on developing New Testament ethics it seems that there is a general agreement that there are similar moral principles embodied in the Mosaic legislation are expressed in the New Testament precepts for Christians.[75] These similar moral principles are the result of some measure of influence of the Old Testament Law on New Testament ethics.[76]

The implications of the Torah's influence on the New Testament means that although there may not be a direct command, such as the Fifth Commandment, regarding honoring parents, or Lev 19:32 regarding deference toward the elderly in general, the overall application of principles of elder care in the Old Testament can still be iden-

72. Paul G. Hiebert, *Anthropological Insights for Missionaries* (Grand Rapids: Baker, 1985), 132–33.

73. Ibid.

74. Walter C. Kaiser Jr, *Toward Old Testament Ethics* (Grand Rapids: Academie Books, 1983), 33.

75. Norman L. Geisler, *Christian Ethics: Options and Issues* (Grand Rapids: Baker, 1989), 204.

76. Ian S. Knox, *Older People and the Church* (London: T&T Clark, 2002), 129.

tified in the New Testament. Regarding the Fifth Commandment and the admonition to "honor" parents it can be acknowledged that while considerable evidence in the Gospels, Acts and the many of the Epistles points to the importance of age it is not addressed as a subject in its own right. "One may conclude that either there was no discrimination against age calling for special attention or that concern for the aged is implied in Jesus' concern for all people, especially for the disfranchised, the neglected, the disadvantaged, and the rejected. Many such are singled out for explicit attention, and probably more explicit attention was not given to older people because in Jewish piety there was great respect for age."[77] Though it is difficult to build an argument regarding the care of the elderly based upon an absence of propositions concerning elder care one does find that Jesus, as a rabbi, shows that there is continuity between the Jewish and Christian understanding of the social responsibilities appropriate for caring for the elderly.[78]

Continuity and Discontinuity

Even though there is a similarity, or continuity between the Testaments concerning social responsibilities for elder care that does not mean there is complete agreement on the relationship of the Torah to the New Testament. In light of the contentions concerning the Testaments' interrelationship it is important at least to address the issues surrounding the continuity, and discontinuity, that exists between the Testaments. As has been noted in one sense the ethics of the Old Testament can be seen in the New Testament, but the discussion does not end at that point.[79] There is much deliberation concerning the authority and relationship of the Old Testament to the New Testament. Although it is beyond the scope of this dissertation to address all of the conflicts involved in a discussion concerning the relationship between the Testaments what seems to be the focal

---

77. Frank Stagg, *The Bible Speaks on Aging* (Nashville: Broadman, 1981), 133.

78. J. Gordon Harris, *Biblical Perspectives on Aging: God and the Elderly* (Philadelphia: Fortress,1987), 81.

79. Cf. p. 150 in this dissertation.

point of the discussion regarding continuity and discontinuity is the identity of Israel and the Church.[80]

Some of Jesus' own statements in the Sermon on the Mount reveal the tension of His continuity and discontinuity with the Torah.[81] In the Sermon on the Mount Jesus affirmed a continuity with the Old Testament when he said, "Do not think that I have come to abolish the Law or the Prophets; I have not come to abolish them but to fulfill them. I tell you the truth, until heaven and earth disappear, not the smallest letter, not the least stroke of a pen, will by any means disappear from the Law until everything is accomplished" (Matt 5:17–19). The New Testament records no quarrels from Jesus over the authority of or ethical application of the Old Testament.[82]

The effect of Old Testament ethics, like that developed from the Fifth Commandment, on first century Judaism may be one reason why the Sermon on the Mount is considered as, "a series of interpretations of teachings in the Torah and the Prophets."[83] Nevertheless, there may be an objection that Jesus looks like He is modifying the Law in the Sermon on the Mount rather than simply interpreting it in a unique manner, when he continually states, "But I tell you," in contrast to a statement in the Law.[84] In one sense Jesus does ap-

---

80. For more developed discussions concerning Covenant and Dispensational understandings of the Testaments and their views of Israel and the church; for a Dispensational model see, Daniel Fuller, *Gospel and Law: Contrast or Continuum?* (Grand Rapids: Eerdmans, 1980); for a Covenant perspective see, John Murray, *The Covenant of Grace: A Biblico-Theological Study* (London: Tyndale, 1953). For a more general discussion see, John S. Feinberg, ed., *Continuity and Discontinuity: Perspectives on the Relationship Between the Old and New Testaments*, Essays in Honor of S. Lewis Johnson, Jr. (Wheaton: Crossway, 1988); and James D. G. Dunn, *The Parting of the Ways: Between Christianity and Judaism and their Significance for the Character of Christianity* (Philadelphia: Trinity Press International, 1991).

81. Richard B. Hays, *The Moral Vision of the New Testament: A Contemporary Introduction to New Testament Ethics* (San Francisco: HarperCollins, 1996), 95.

82. William Sanford LaSor, David Allan Hubbard and Fredric William Bush, ed. *Old Testament Survey: The Message, Form, and Background of the Old Testament*, 2nd ed. (Grand Rapids: Eerdmans, 1996), 585.

83. Glen H. Stassen & David P. Gushee, *Kingdom Ethics: Following Jesus in Contemporary Context* (Downers Grove: InterVarsity, 2003), 91.

84. Jesus makes this type of authoritative statement in numerous New Testament tests such as, Matt 5:22, 28, 32, 34, 39, 44; 10:23; 12:31; 17:12; 18:22; Luke 4:25; 6:26; 7:47; 9:27; John 6:32.

pear to be in contrast to Moses, but His statements may be more of an opposition to "an erroneous understanding of the original Mosaic writing," rather than to the Law itself since the writers of the Gospels quote Jesus as frequently affirming the authority of the Old Testament.[85] Additionally Jesus' statements could be a further development and application of the Law. In this way Jesus' statements show that the Law not only has a spiritual or internal dimension that should not be circumvented, but it also has ongoing demands, or a "more radical obedience."[86]

The writers of the New Testament also acknowledged a moral and ethical relationship between the two Testaments. This relationship is seen in shared themes, such as, "doing God's will is the highest moral good; immorality, idolatry, inhumanity, and spiritual rebellion are to be shunned; honesty, integrity, diligence are to be treasured; concern for the right and needs of others is valued as a sterling quality (2 Tim 3:16 ff; 1 Cor 10:1, 11)."[87] The ethical continuity between the Testaments is not only seen in shared themes. Even though there is agreement concerning ethical themes the writers of the New Testament applied ethical principles in the New Testament in ways that were not directly addressed in Old Testament texts, such as appropriate actions for God's people living under the control of a secular government (Rom 13:1–7).

The discussion concerning theological perspectives of the relationships between the Testaments often focuses on the application of eschatological issues such as the millennium and questions surrounding its literal or figurative relationship to the church. Although a study of the place of Israel is important, for this work the eschatological aspect that is most applicable centers around the identity of the kingdom of God. There are places in the Bible when

---

85. Thomas D. Lea, *The New Testament: Its Background and Message* (Nashville: Broadman & Holman, 1996), 196.

86. J. Knox Chamblin, "Matthew," in *Evangelical Commentary on the Bible* (Grand Rapids: Baker, 1989), 729.

87. Ibid., 588. Also, for a discussion concerning to what extent the apostle Paul used the Old Testament in his writings see, Brian Rosner, *Paul, Scripture and Ethics: A Study of 1 Corinthians 5–7*, Biblical Studies Library (Grand Rapids: Baker, 1999).

the Kingdom of God is described as a theocratic Kingdom.[88] The Song of Moses ends with the words, "The Lord will reign for ever and ever" (Exodus 15:18). Later, Isaiah the prophet sees a vision of God upon a heavenly throne ruling as the King of kings, and also as Israel's king.[89] The theocratic kingdom is seen in the present and enduring Kingship of God, the representative Kingdom of the nation of Israel, and an apocalyptic Kingdom. The apocalyptic Kingdom is that of the eternal theocratic rule of God as described in Dan 7. The theocratic kingdom of God was not only identified with the theocracy of Israel but also with God's universal sovereignty over all nations and people. The sovereign reign of God is found in both Testaments and it affirms God's rule over all things. Another aspect of the Kingdom of God can be seen in the idea of the immanency of the Kingdom in the life and ministry of Jesus. John the Baptist said, "Repent, for the Kingdom of heaven is at hand" (Matt 3:2). When Jesus arrived and proclaimed the nearness of the Kingdom it was already intruding on the world.[90] Even though there is disagreement on the extent of the Old Testament's theocratic Kingdom's applicability to the New Testament, there still seems to be an area of agreement concerning the Kingdom of God. The area of agreement centers around the idea that the Kingdom of God is "already but not yet."[91] This term means that the Kingdom "was already present in the

88. James Leo Garrett, *Systematic Theology: Biblical, Historical, and Evangelical*, vol. 2 (Grand Rapids: Eerdmans, 1995), 728.

89. Christopher R. Seitz, *Isaiah 1–39*, Interpretation: A Bible Commentary for Teaching and Preaching (Louisville: John Knox Press, 1989), 54.

90. Garrett, *Systematic Theology*, 731. This idea of the Kingdom having come is often objected to in Dispensationalism, which commonly sees the Old Testament kingdom age as separate from the present age.

91. Bruce K. Waltke, "Kingdom Promises as Spiritual," *Continuity and Discontinuity: Perspectives on the Relationship Between the Old and New Testaments*, Essays in Honor of S. Lewis Johnson, Jr., ed. John S. Feinberg (Wheaton: Crossway, 1988), 272. Regarding various interpretations of the Kingdom of God, Waltke states that "the increasing acceptance of understanding the Kingdom of God as "already but not yet" is tending both to solidify premillennialism into what Ladd called "historic Premillennialism" (i.e., OT kingdom promise are being spiritually realized in the church age and will be materially fulfilled in a millennium when national Israel will be restored), and to bridge partially the gap between premillennialism and amillennialism. Whereas historically dispensational premillennialism radically divorced in interpretation, though

person and work of Jesus (Matt 12:28). However, this kingdom also has an eschatological component, for it is an event to be experienced completely only in the future."[92] When Jesus referred to the "mystery of the kingdom" in Luke 17:20 He was referring to the fact that the Kingdom of God had already appeared on earth before its full manifestation. "The church represents those who have received the kingdom in Jesus and witness to its blessing."[93] The rule and reign of the King, Jesus, is envisioned as increasing in the work and witness of His followers while they look for his imminent return.

Kingdom of God

The Kingdom of God is an important theme for both Testaments. In the Old Testament it is God's sovereign rule over all His works as King. It has an eschatological element. An example of this eschatological element is seen in Zephaniah 2:11b where it states that one day, "The nations on every shore will worship him, every one in its own land." In the Old Testament the Kingdom of God also has its literal application in that Israel was originally to establish a theocracy, but the later kingdom of Israel where King David reigned became a type for the coming Messianic kingdom.[94]

The importance of the Kingdom of God in the New Testament is seen in its relationship to Jesus Christ. One finds the full revelation of God's divine rule in the person of Jesus Christ.[95] It is through Jesus Christ that the Bible provides a connection between the idea of

---

not necessarily in application, the OT promise of a restored Israel under an earthly Messiah from the advent of Christ to his church in the Holy Spirit, "modified dispensationalists" are granting in varying degrees that the NT regards the church as a partial fulfillment of those promises. At the same time, amillennialists are accenting more and more the future aspect of the kingdom, which they identify not with a supposed "Israelite" millennium but with the new cosmos (Revelation 21–22)."

92. Thomas D. Lea, *The New Testament: Its Background and Message* (Nashville: Broadman & Holman, 1996), 204.

93. Ibid.

94. Elton M. Eenigenburg, *Biblical Foundations and a Method for Doing Christian Ethics* (New York: University of America Press, 1994), 13.

95. George Eldon Ladd, *A Theology of the New Testament*, rev. ed. (Grand Rapids: Eerdmans, 2001), 65.

God's rule and reign in the Old Testament and the fulfillment and development of that Kingdom in the New Testament.

In order to understand the importance and applicability of the Kingdom of God to the issue of elder care it seems important to acknowledge some cultural realities that are presented in the Gospels. The first, and seemingly obvious cultural reality is that when one reads the Bible it seems clear that Jesus, as a Jew, was speaking primarily to Jews. The implications are that both He and the majority of His listeners followed the Torah. Also, the Israelites were looking forward to a Messiah. Some have seen at the heart of Jesus' conflict with the Jewish leaders their rejection of His proclamation of the Kingdom and its call to repentance, but Jesus' conflict with the Jewish leaders was more than a power struggle.[96] Jesus' detractors came to understand that Jesus was making a Messianic claim. Since Jesus' followers were Jews they too were looking forward to a type of Messianic kingdom, and that eschatological hope influenced their thinking. Although they were looking for a nationalistic revival Jesus led them into a broader understanding of what it would mean to be part of God's coming Kingdom. Jesus often proclaimed "the kingdom of God is near."[97] Although these points of clarity do not address the complex issues surrounding various interpretations of the Kingdom of God, they do demonstrate that Jesus and His followers took seriously the eschatological emphasis of the Old Testament Kingdom of God with its Messianic hope. Also, the New Testament does demonstrate that Jesus exercised his kingly authority in His ministry throughout His time on Earth as He cast out demons, preached with authority, healed the sick, raised the dead and confronted earthly authorities. Regarding the confrontation of earthly authorities Jesus' dialogue with Pilate the Roman Governor demonstrates his kingly authority. When Jesus is asked if He is the king of the Jews He answers Pilate in the affirmative (Matt 27:11; Luke 23:3). In the gospel of John more of this dialogue is recorded where Jesus talks to Pilate as one

---

96. Ibid., 105.

97. The importance of Jesus using this term, "the Kingdom of God," is most significantly seen in the Gospel of Matthew, and in particular in the Sermon on the Mount and the parables of the Kingdom, see Matt 5:3, 10, 19, 20; 7:21; 8:11; 10:7; 11:11, 12, 13:11, 24, 31, 33, 44, 45, 47, 52; 16:19; 18:1, 3, 4, 23; 19:12, 14, 23, 20:1, 2, 13; 25:1.

who has authority while explaining what it means that He is a king (John 19:33–38). After the resurrection Jesus assigned the Church its mission and purpose in Matt 28:18, where Jesus states, "All authority in heaven and on earth has been given to me."[98] Regarding this exercise of His kingly authority it is said that, "Jesus is not waiting passively in heaven for his glorious arrival as judge and king but is already exercising his Lordship as God's plentipotentiary Son."[99] The reason, among many, why Jesus could give the instructions that He gave to His disciples was that they saw Jesus as their King to whom their allegiance was due.

Jesus communicated various aspects of the Kingdom of God and in so doing it can be acknowledged that He affirmed the validity of the Old Testament, which can be found in Matt 5:17–18. Jesus considered the Torah the divine given rule of life. Jesus' mission in life fulfilled the intent of the Old Testament Law. The fulfillment of the Torah brought in a new understanding of the role of the Law.[100] The relationship between God and people was no longer to be mediated by the Law but through Jesus Christ and the incoming of the Kingdom of God.

> On his own authority alone, Jesus set aside the principles of ceremonial purity embodied in much of the Mosaic legislation. This is a corollary of the fact that the righteousness of the Kingdom is to be no longer mediated by the Law but by a new redemptive act of God, foreseen in the prophets but now in process of being realized in the event of his own mission.[101]

The Kingdom is unique in the sense that it does not involve the "ceremonial purity embodied in much of the Mosaic legislation," because Jesus fulfilled the demands of the Law regarding holiness through ceremonial purification, which is why it is said that

---

98. W. D. Davies and Dale C. Allison Jr., *A Critical and Exegetical Commentary on The Gospel According to Saint Matthew*, vol. III (Edinburgh: T&T Clark, 1997), 682.

99. Ibid.

100. George Eldon Ladd, *A Theology of the New Testament*, Rev. ed. (Grand Rapids: Eerdemans, 1974), 122–23.

101. Ibid., 123.

Christians are, "redeemed from the curse of the law" (Gal 3:13).[102] It can also be said that Jesus fulfilled the Law in that He accomplished all that the Law said concerning him. (Luke 24:44–6)

In light of Christ's fulfillment of the Law in His redemptive work the writer of Hebrews was able to state that because of Jesus' fulfillment of the sacrificial laws there is now direct access to God for the Christian. Christians were to now live in such a manner that the reality of Christ's atoning sacrifice was evident in their lives. In Heb 10:19–23 one finds a shift from the "cultic argument the writer has been developing to the response of faith it demands."[103] The recipients of the book of Hebrews are told to, "spur one another on toward love and good deeds" (Heb 10:24). Responding in obedience to Christ is considered a natural response to His redemptive work which fulfilled the requirements of the sacrificial system found in the Old Testament. It can be noted that the Torah was followed and affirmed by Christ while, and at the same time, being fulfilled and applied in a broader manner by His followers.

Jesus ushered in the Kingdom of God which was "at hand" in His presence and ministry, but which is yet to be fully realized. Involvement in His Kingdom means that one is involved in good works towards others. The application of "good works" to faith is seen in Israel regarding the Decalogue as well as in the New Testament where Christians "do good" because of what their King, Jesus, has done for them in their redemption.

New Testament Living

How followers of Christ were to live lives that reflected their relationship to their King, Jesus, is seen in how they applied certain foundational Scriptural principles. Among the most important are the concepts of *agape* and justice. When these principles are evaluated a foundation for living as Christ's followers develops. As Israel was instructed to love God singularly and holistically in Deut 6:4–9 so in a similar manner the followers of Christ are to live so that their

---

102. Leon Morris, *New Testament Theology* (Grand Rapids: Zondervan, 1990), 50.

103. William L. Lane, *Hebrews 9–13*, Word Biblical Commentary, vol. 47, gen. ed. David A. Hubbard and Glenn W. Baker (Dallas: Word, 1991), 282.

allegiance to Christ would be obvious to all by their devotion and righteous lifestyle.[104]

Agape

One of the biblical principles for people expressing the reality of the risen Christ in their lives is seen in the overarching biblical concept of love. Biblical love is said to be the Christian's responsibility toward God and toward others.[105]

When the Bible speaks about love in the New Testament, it is using the particular Greek word, *agape*. *Agape* involves sacrificial love without expectation of reciprocation. The model for Christians is God Himself, who allowed the Second Person of the Trinity in incarnate form to suffer and die at the hands of the ungrateful beings he had come to save from themselves. *Agape* involves the Christian concepts of God, Christ (the focal point of the Father's love), self-sacrifice (depicted in the death of Christ) and an obligation to imitate the example of Christ's model of self-sacrificial.[106] The concept of *agape* advances from principles found in Christian Scripture to practical application in the Christian's life, as was seen in the life of Mother Teresa and her work in the slums of Calcutta.[107]

When the Bible speaks about love, it is communicating a concept that goes far beyond mere emotions. This primary characteristic of God is also to be found in God's people. It is not surprising, then, to find the imperative to love God in Israel's theocratic declaration in Deuteronomy 6:4–5, the *Shema*, "Hear, O Israel: The Lord our

---

104. Stephen Charles Mott, *Biblical Ethics and Social Change* (New York: Oxford University Press, 1982), 29. In Mott's second chapter, *God's Grace and Our Actions*, he presents an analysis of the requirement given by many New Testament writers that Christians express their faith in a tangible way toward the myriad social problems that they face.

105. E. David Cook, "Shalom and Justice in Health Care," *The Southern Baptist Journal of Theology* 4 (2000): 64.

106. D. H. Field, "Love," in *New Dictionary of Christian Ethics & Pastoral Theology*, ed. David J. Atkinson and David H. Field (Downers Grove: InterVarsity, 1995), 9–10.

107. Clarke E. Cockran, "Health Policy and the Poverty Trap: Finding a Way Out," in *Toward a Just and Caring Society: Christian Responses to Poverty in America* (Grand Rapids: Baker, 1999), 235.

God, the Lord is one. Love the Lord your God with all your heart and with all your soul and with all your strength." This sentiment is repeated by Jesus in the New Testament where He summarizes this text and connects the ethical component. "Jesus replied: 'Love the Lord your God with all your heart and with all your soul and with all your mind.' This is the first and greatest commandment. And the second is like it: 'Love your neighbor as yourself.' All the Law and the Prophets hang on these two commandments."[108] Jesus summarizes the Law and connects it to *agape*. "Four centuries later, Augustine, the church's greatest theologian, caught the spirit of what Jesus was saying when he observed that everything written in Scripture is meant to teach us how to love either God or our neighbor. A millennium after him, a converted Augustinian monk named Martin Luther declared that the entire Christian life amounts to serving our neighbor."[109] It is not misleading to understand in Matt 22:37–40 a command for New Testament believers to express the Law's ethical component in their relationships with God and others.

One may rightly question to what extent Christian love is to be rendered to "others." When Jesus presented the story of the Good Samaritan he presented an application of the second greatest commandment, to love one's neighbor as oneself.[110] This ethic is more then a means of manipulating the affections of others. The *agape* ethic of neighbor love is expressed by selfless service to others *regardless* of their ability to reciprocate.

> If the Samaritan was neighbor to the distressed Jew, then the Jews, by a parity of reason, were neighbors to the Samaritans. If the Samaritan did well, in relieving a Jew that was his enemy, then the Jews would do well in relieving the Samaritans, their enemies.—What I particularly observe is that Christ here plainly teaches that our enemies, those that abuse and injure us, are our neighbors, and therefore come under the rule of loving our neighbors as ourselves.[111]

108. Matthew 22:37–40.

109. Michael E. Wittmer, *Heaven is a Place on Earth: Why Everything You Do Matters To God* (Grand Rapids: Zondervan, 2004), 102.

110. Luke 10:25–37.

111. Jonathan Edwards, *Christian Charity or The Duty of Charity to the Poor,*

Agape is seen as a theocentric concept describing God's character and the Son's redemptive example. Since *agape* is said to describe a primary divine characteristic its demands should cover every aspect of human experience, disposition, thought life, and behavior.[112] It relationship extends in and out of the religious community to "neighbors."

The indiscriminate *agape* of the Bible also has a social element that is important to the application of Kingdom principles. When the Bible discusses loving one's neighbor it is expressing an ethic that moves beyond the religious community.[113] Though there may be a claim that Jesus' ministry focused more on one's the vertical relationship with God that does not discount the prophetic and social application of God's love. Regarding the Christian's relationship to the world it has been said,

> Our relationships are far more complicated than just family and friends. We have relationships with the governments and with every level of society. Part of what it means to be a member of a society and a citizen is that we are inextricably involved in a web of social relationships ranging from the formal and legal to the informal and casual.[114]

These relationships ought to be affected by the King through His subjects, i.e., Christians, since Christians live in a social setting. An application needs to be expressed which puts this principle of the

---

Explained and Enforced [on-line]; accessed 25 Aug 2004; available from http://www.biblebb.com/files/edwards/charity.htm; Internet.

112. D. H. Field, "Love," in *New Dictionary of Christian Ethics & Pastoral Theology*, 11. Field goes on to say that *agape* is used in LXX as an umbrella term denoting physical attraction and delight in things like food and sleep as well as love in interpersonal and God-man relationships. The character of God sets *agape's* ethical parameters. 1 John 4:7–8 provides the biblical connection between the love of God for his people and their requisite responsibility also to love others. Thus *agape*, although perfectly exhibited only by God, is also to be a characteristic of God's people, to the extent that it is humanly possible.

113. Glen H. Stassen & David P. Gushee, *Kingdom Ethics: Following Jesus in Contemporary Context* (Downers Grove: InterVarsity, 2003), 339.

114. E. David Cook, *Living in the Kingdom: The Ethics of Jesus* (London: Hodder & Stoughton, 1992), 44.

Kingdom, *agape*, into practice regarding the elderly and their care. In one sense it is important to deal with the soteriological questions of the Kingdom, but it is also important to look at how social relationships are to be actualized by a Christian's unique relationship with God.

> The social aspect of morality cannot be ignored. An examination of nature and purpose might lead us to an ethic that is totally individualistic. Such an individualistic ethic would be totally unbiblical. An analysis of the personal aspect of morality revealed in the Bible leads to the goal of mutual love relationships. But the nature of love will not allow us to stop with isolated bi-polar relationships. Love creates community. A loving person seeks the good of any other human being that he or she might have contact with. From the social perspective, the goal of Christian ethics is a community—the Kingdom of God.[115]

Social morality then should be based upon a selfless love, *agape*. Christians live in the application of *agape*, a gracious and unconditional commitment to the good, and with such a commitment biblical love becomes applicable to a myriad of social issues. The application of *agape* to social issues should go beyond the any self-centered interests of any religious community.

Mott provides four reasons for the biblical requirements for Christians to reach out to those outside of their community of faith. 1. One cannot get to the social and economic roots of problems without community-wide efforts which affect all those in the community, Christian or not. 2. Jesus broke away from the traditional restrictions on love for one's neighbor in Matt 5:43–48, the parable of the Good Samaritan, cf. Matt 25; Rom 12:20; 1 John and 2 Cor 8 and 9. These texts show that there should be no qualitative difference in response for those in one's own group and those outside of one's own group. 3. A denial of love to non-Christians was never intended in 1 John and other passages used to argue against an enlarged sphere of social

---

115. Michael Hill, *The How and Why of Love: An Introduction to Evangelical Ethics* (Kingsford, Australia: Matthias Media, 2002), 118. The author states that he views the Bible as a single unit, and as such it comes out in his work that agape is to be applied by Christians in a social as well as religious manner.

responsibility. In many of the texts that use the terms, *brother* or *sister*, it could be replaced with *fellow man* or *fellow woman*. 4. Paul gives evidence of Scripture's universal application when he states in 2 Cor 9:13, "Obedience to the gospel of Christ and their liberality of sharing to them and to all." In that text "all" means all people, and not just the Christian community. Also, Paul ends his exhortation in Gal 6:10 with the words, "Therefore, as we have opportunity. Let us do good to all people, especially to those who belong to the family of believers."[116] The terminology "do good" refers to kind concrete acts of helping others, not merely having right relations, or not being bad.[117] Christians are to do good to "all people," which includes those outside of the religious community.

Some of the words of Jesus shed light on the importance of Christians living *agape* lives among non-Christians and applying Kingdom ethics to those who are not Christians are seen in Jesus admonitions concerning how Christians are to respond to an enemy and what their role is in the world. Both texts are found in the Sermon on the Mount.

Jesus told his disciples to be "salt" and "light" in such a way that people, "May see your good deeds and praise your Father in heaven." (Matt 5:16b) Salt and light are used as metaphors. The implication of this imagery is, "the disciples are vitally significant and necessary to the world in their witness to God and his kingdom."[118] They are said to be necessary to the world, not only to heaven in their Kingdom living. "When Jesus declares that the disciples are, "the light of the world," he means that they, as recipients of the kingdom, represent to the world the truth of the salvation that it has come."[119] The purpose of a lamp is to give light and the disciples were told that they were to be a shining example of hope to the world. In light of the eschatological implications of God's coming kingdom many Jews understood that they, the Israelites, were to be the "light of the world." This idea not only meant enlightening their surrounding culture religiously,

---

116. See 1 Thess 3:12; 5:15.

117. Mott, *Biblical Ethics and Social Change*, 35–37.

118. Donald A. Hagner, *Matthew 1–13*, Word Biblical Commentary, vol. 33A (Dallas: Word, 1993), 99.

119. Ibid., 100.

but it "clearly emphasizes ethics."[120] Being "salt and light" means that the social relationships in which Christians are involved should be influenced by the principles of the Kingdom of God.

The second text is also found in the Sermon on the Mount. Jesus tells his followers how they are to relate to their enemies. Jesus says, "You have heard that it was said, "Love your neighbor and hate your enemy," But I tell you: Love your enemies and pray for those who persecute you, that you may be sons of your Father in heaven" (Matt 5:43–5). Here Jesus expands on the Law when discussing treatment of one's enemies. "Jesus based his command to love on God's way and will. God as our loving heavenly Father provides for everyone through the creation order in nature. God's love is totally indiscriminate. So, too, is to be the love of the followers of Jesus."[121] The *agape* of Scripture is not only for other Christians, or for the friends of Christians, but it should extend even to enemies.[122] A loving lifestyle is demonstrated by prayer, however that is not all. "The love which is inculcated is not a matter of sentiment and emotion, but, as always in the OT and NT, of concrete action."[123] The application of this principle to the present point is that one who is part of the Kingdom of God ought to express a lifestyle that demonstrates social concern not only for other Christians, but also for those who are not Christians or who are even enemies.

Finally, a unique, but important text concerning the onus on Christians to extend their loving compassion socially is found in Matt 25:31–46 where Jesus is giving a parable about sheep and goats relating to the final judgment. In that parable Jesus describes the delineating factor in the judgment as the capacity to minister to those in deep need regardless of their social status. Those in deep need are described as, "the least of these brothers of mine," and they

---

120. Hans Dieter Betz, *The Sermon on the Mount: A Commentary on the Sermon on the Mount, including the Sermon on the Plain (Matthew 5:3—7:27 and Luke 6:20–49), Hermeneia—A Critical and Historical Commentary on the Bible* (Minneapolis: Fortress, 1995), 160–61.

121. Cook, *Living in the Kingdom,* 102.

122. Mott, *Biblical Ethics and Social Change,* 35–36.

123. D. A. Carson, *"Matthew," The Expositor's Bible Commentary with the New International Version of the Holy Bible,* vol. 8 (Grand Rapids: Zondervan, 1984), 158.

are described as those who are hungry, thirsty, a stranger, in need of clothes and in prison. (See Matt 25:40, 45) "It is the compassion or the failure in compassion to the hungry, the thirsty, the stranger, the sick and those in prison which is the deciding factor in judgment."[124] Although this parable is often seen in an eschatological manner, a present application of the future judgment is that being right with God means serving those people who may be outside of one's faith community.[125]

Objection to Agape

A twofold objection may be rendered at this point. The first is that the word "love," even *agape*, is a term so overused that it has come to be regarded as little more then a combination of beneficence and nonmaleficence. Nonmaleficence is based upon the Hippocratic dictum to, "do no harm," while beneficence speaks of positive acts which should be done to benefit the patient.[126] Beneficence is usually presented so that it is based upon a communitarian concept of what is beneficial to the patient. Unfortunately societal values are notoriously unstable, and if beneficence focuses on what, "ought" to be done and nonmaleficence focuses on what, "one ought not to do," then what is decided to "do" or "not do" is contingent upon the local value systems of the community which may opt to decide matters on a cost-benefit scale, in a way that best serves the interests of society.[127] Societal values, such as preferences, are unable to provide

---

124. Cook, *Living in the Kingdom*, 34.

125. A discussion of the differences between the biblical model under discussion that has social obligations and the Social Gospel is beyond the confines of this book. For further readings on the Social Gospel see, Shailer Mathews, *The Social Teaching of Jesus: An Essay in Christian Sociology* (New York: Macmillan, 1910); and Walter Rauschenbusch, *Christianity and the Social Crisis* (New York: Macmillan, 1907). Donald A. Hagner provides an alternative view which identifies the "brethren" as Jesus' disciples in *Matthew 14–28*, Word Biblical Commentary, vol. 33b (Dallas: Word), 745.

126. Beauchamp and Childress, ed., *Principles of Biomedical Ethics*, 114–15.

127. Ibid. Beauchamp and Childress are unable to provide an unchanging basis for nonmaleficence or beneficence. They are forced to rely on societal norms to define such important terms as, "good," "evil" and "harm." C.f. Ann Michele Holmes, "Uses and Abuses of QALY Analysis" (Ph.D. diss., The University of British Columbia, 1992), 1.

unchanging norms of nonmaleficence or beneficence. The instability of communitarian norms, both temporally and among community members, results in these virtues being impossible to define in an absolute manner. The biblical perspective of *agape*, as has been discussed, presents a stronger, more stable, practical love that it is directly expressed in identifying and meeting human care needs, and as such presents a distinct understanding of love.

The second objection is that love may be important in the Bible, but it that is not as foundational as it has been presented. Richard Hays sees love as not being universally emphasized as the primary ethical theme. He considers its "sporadic use" in the New Testament and its focus on the redemptive work of Christ a contraindication to its broader application.[128] Though this critique is appreciated, it falls quite short in light of Jesus' teaching on *agape* in parabolic form and in personal application (Cf. Matt 5:43, 22:39; Jn 12:25, 13:35). Indeed, even Hays admits that if his objections were taken individually, they would not be enough to disqualify love from being used as, "a synthetic lens."[129] He then goes on to note that because love has been "debased in popular discourse; it has lost its power of discrimination, having become a cover for all manner of vapid self-indulgence."[130] Even if love is often used in a manner that is self-indulgent that inappropriate use of love, however, does not mean that it is not foundational for how Christian's live out *agape* as subjects of their King, Jesus. As Shelp responds, "Love is not only the stimulus to community, but it is also the bond of community. Based upon the love of God and out of a desire to be obedient to God's command to love, man seeks to establish and maintain community. Admission to community life is contingent upon one's willingness to express a lifestyle of love."[131] In light of the broad application of

---

128. Richard B. Hays, *The Moral Vision of the New Testament: A Contemporary Introduction to New Testament Ethics* (San Francisco: Harper Collins, 1996), 202.

129. Ibid., 203.

130. Ibid., 202.

131. Earl Edward Shelp, "An Inquiry into Christian Ethical Sanctions for the 'Right To Health Care,'" (Ph.D. diss., The Southern Baptist Theological Seminary, 1976), 80.

agape, and its vital relationship to community life, it may be considered as foundational to biblical ethics.

It is noted then that God cares for his people generally, and that care includes the elderly. When the early church was confronted with a conflict over providing food for the Christian community's widows who were in need they assigned seven men of unique spiritual and practical character to correct the problem (Acts 6:1–6). The importance of caring for widows demonstrates the application of the *agape* principle that copies the love of God. *Agape* guides justice in that its application provides a moral confidence that actions made within the community are being made for the common good. To live practical lives of a*gape* means that Christians must care for others. As Cook explains,

> Those relationships with God, ourselves and our world are to be characterized by dependency on God and interdependency with each other. We realize that our worth and value depends upon our being made in the image of God. God calls us to exercise proper responsibility to God and to each other, by living in covenant relationships and by showing justice, mercy and love in all our dealings with each other. These are to be the standards shown and expected in all our relationships ranging from the family, to schools, neighborhoods and the global community.[132]

Relationships that lie at the heart of Christianity are characterized by an ethic that is based upon *agape*, and that *agape* should extend to the entire "global community."

Justice

It has been said that "love is the final action toward wholeness."[133] To obtain wholeness love requires justice, because justice expresses love, even though love is more than justice. In response one may question what is meant by "wholeness" and how it relates to the expression of justice. Wholeness can be summed up in understanding God's

---

132. E. David Cook, "Shalom and Justice in Health Care," *The Southern Baptist Journal of Theology* 4:64.

133. James Sellers, *Theological Ethics* (New York: Macmillian, 1966), 162.

creative purpose, which can be embodied in the word, "Shalom." Shalom is understood to be a state of wholeness or fulfillment. "It is the result of restored righteousness and cannot be achieved while one is persisting in sin or evil."[134] The reason why "restored righteousness" is important is because God desires humanity to experience the "Shalom" that existed in the Garden of Eden. In Genesis 3 humanity lost "Shalom" because sin negatively impacted their relationship with God. Thus God seeks a restored relationship with humanity, and He enabled that possibility through Jesus.

> Because peace in its religious sense can be seen only as God's blessing of a restored relationship, the NT can proclaim the fulfillment of the eschatological state of peace (Zech 9:10) in Jesus (Matt 5:9; 21:1; Luke 2:14). Through his death, reconciliation and peace with God are possible (Rom 5:1; Eph 2:14), and also between human beings (Eph 4:3; James 3:18). The NT, thus, continues the religious perception of ולמ and sees in the Messiah's triumph the concretization of ולמ (Luke 10:18; Rom 8:6; 16:20).[135]

The restored righteousness between God and human beings, the "Shalom," is expressed in one's relationship with God, and with others. The importance of seeking "Shalom" is seen in Jesus' discussion concerning divorce. In His discussion on divorce Jesus said that the original intent of marriage was to enable a oneness to occur between the man and woman. Jesus said that the restoration of the created order should be the focus of the Pharisee's inquiry into divorce, rather than its abuse use as an issue to engage in another religious conflict (Matt 19:1–12; Mark 10:1–12). Jesus guided the Pharisees back to the Garden of Eden to view God's original intent for marriage (Gen 1:24–25). Jesus wanted those involved in marriage to experience "Shalom."

The need to restore the righteousness of "Shalom" between God and humanity is also seen in the book of Revelation. According to the text, at the end of the events in Revelation restoration occurs be-

---

134. Philip J. Nel, "אולמ," in *New International Dictionary of Old Testament Theology & Exegisis*, vol. 4 (Grand Rapids: Zondervan 1997), 130.

135. Ibid., 134.

tween God and humanity. "And I heard a loud voice from the throne saying, "Now the dwelling of God is with men, and he will live with them. They will be his people, and God himself will be with them and be their God. He will wipe every tear from their eyes. There will be no more death or mourning or crying or pain, for the old order of things has passed away" (Rev 21:3–4). There was "Shalom" in the Garden of Eden between God and humanity and there will be "Shalom" at the end of the age. In the mean time, as Jesus demonstrated in his discussion concerning divorce, people should look back to the Garden of Eden, to creation, as a baseline example of how life should be if "Shalom" should prevail. "True justice resides in the restoring of relationships and the recreation of *shalom* (Rom 5:1)."[136] Justice restores *Shalom*.

Love requires justice and because justice is expressed in *agape* then they are inseparable norms. The connection between the Testaments is seen in how justice is used. In the Old Testament the prophet Micah contrasts the actions of Israelites who only offer sacrifices to what God really wants from an Israelite when he states, "He has showed you, O man, what is good. And what does the Lord require of you? To act justly and to love mercy and to walk humbly with your God" (Micah 6:8). Justice and mercy are common admonitions from Old Testament prophets. "This is the standard that marks our dealings in relationships with each other. We are to treat each other with justice and with mercy. We are to be fair with each other and to be merciful with each other. It seems that both qualities of justice and mercy are calls for us to regard and treat others properly."[137] Acting in a just manner provides a foundation for God's people to exercise responsible relationships with others.[138]

In the New Testament Jesus takes this principle of justice and uses it when He corrected His opponent.[139] Jesus is addressing, among many other things, the problem of distributive justice.[140] In

---

136. Christopher D. Marshall, *Beyond Retribution: A New Testament Vision for Justice, Crime, and Punishment* (Grand Rapids: Eerdmans, 2001), 68.

137. E. David Cook, "Shalom and Justice in Health Care," *The Southern Baptist Journal of Theology* 4:63.

138. Ibid., 64.

139. Cf. Matt 12:18, 20.

140. Matt 23:23; Luke 11:42.

this text justice "specifies a fair allocation of society's wealth, resources and power,"[141] and Jesus states, "Woe to you, teachers of the Law and Pharisees, you hypocrites! You give a tenth of your spices—mint, dill and cummin. But you have neglected the more important matters of the law—justice, mercy and faithfulness. You should have practiced the latter, without neglecting the former." The "more important matters of the Law," in this text, involve "bringing justice to those who are wronged, mercy to those who do wrong, and faithfulness to those who have departed from the faith."[142] In the parallel text in Luke 11:42 Jesus admonishes the Pharisees not to neglect, "justice and the love of God." When Jesus refers to justice as a foundational characteristic for God's people this does not mean it is more difficult, as if Jesus was adding requirements to the Torah.[143] He is clarifying and critiquing his opponents for not applying justice in, what should have been, a normative social manner. In His use of justice Jesus is, in part, also correcting the Pharisees for not seeking the restoration of "Shalom." One needs only to refer back to Micah 6:8 to see the parallel between the Testaments regarding the use of the application of justice to a restored relationship to God.[144] Consequently those who are committed to following Jesus as their Messiah and King are to lay a foundation of just interactions with others based upon *agape*. That interaction is universal in scope, and it should be directed even to those who are not part of their religious fellowship.

Principles in Elder Care

Those who claim to follow Jesus Christ are obligated to live in such a way that their religious commitment is evident, as was true of Israel

---

141. Stephen J. Mott and Ronald J. Sider, "Economic Justice: A Biblical Paradigm," in *Toward a Caring and Just Society: Christian Responses to Poverty in America* (Grand Rapids: Baker, 1999), 17.

142. Michael J. Wilkins, *Matthew*, The NIV Application Commentary (Grand Rapids: Zondervan, 2004), 753.

143. W. E. Davies and Dale C. Allison Jr., *A Critical and Exegetical Commentary on The Gospel According to Saint Matthew*, vol. III (Edinburgh: T&T Clark, 1997), 294.

144. Nicholas P. Wolterstorff, "Justice and Peace," in *New Dictionary of Christian Ethics & Pastoral Theology*, ed. David J. Adkinson and David H. Field (Downers Grove: InterVarsity, 1995), 20.

in obeying the Torah. Christians are to obey their Savior, Jesus. The changed life that Christians are said to enjoy is holistic. It is to affect all aspects of their lives (I Cor 5:17). As such, one should expect that in the New Testament when Christians were confronted with social issues they did so with an understanding of the Torah, since they were Jews, and with an understanding of those foundational characteristics of *agape* and justice. In light of these principles one may ask how the New Testament writers responded to the issue of the elderly care.

Care and Respect in the New Testament

Examples of how the followers of Christ, who trying to follow the commands of Jesus, applied *agape* and justice to their lives and to social situations involving the elderly can be found in the Gospel writings. At the onset of looking at the New Testament one can note the general positive nature in which some elderly are described reveals an attitude of general respect. As an example of this attitude of respect one can observe in the Gospel of Luke the elderly Simeon who is waiting for the Messiah, he is called, "righteous and devout." The prophetess Anna, who was at least eighty-four, is presented as a worshiper of God who frequented the Temple so much that she nearly lived there (Luke 2:25–26, 36–37). These old saints are seen as positive examples which are to be applauded and exemplified. Their righteous description refers to their character and roles. They proclaimed the arrival of the Messiah, Jesus. Although their task was to announce the presence and future work of the Christ child they were described in a particular manner, as righteous and elderly.[145] The primary emphasis in this text is that these two righteous, elderly people were announcing the coming of the Messiah. Luke may have pointed out their age to emphasize Israel's longing for the long awaited, promised Messiah. Nevertheless Luke description of this elderly pair reflects the Old Testament's pattern of seeing the elderly as people who deserve respect in the New Testament.[146] Respect toward

---

145. Richard B. Hays and Judith C. Hays, "The Christian Practice of Growing Old: The Witness of Scripture," in *Growing Old in Christ*, ed. Stanley Hauerwas, Carole Bailey Stoneking, Keith G. Meador and David Cloutier (Grand Rapids: Eerdmans, 2003), 7.

146. John Nolland, *Luke 1–9:20*, Word Biblical Commentary, vol. 35a

the elderly can also be seen in how they are expected to be treated by the religious community in other areas of the New Testament.[147]

Early Christian application of "Honor"

The author of the majority of the New Testament, the apostle Paul, elsewhere showed a relationship between the Fifth Commandment and its explicit application to Christians in light of their contemporary social application. In the New Testament Pauline letters to the Ephesians and Colossians one finds the Fifth Commandment quoted as the basis for his admonition for children to obey their parents. This use of the Fifth Commandment shows an understanding of the requirements of the community to show "honor" to their parents or to specific members of the community. Later the application of this principle will be seen in the actions taken in Acts 6.

Ephesians 6:1–2 states, "Children, obey your parents in the Lord, for this is right. "Honor you father and mother"—which is the first commandment with a promise."[148] The parallel with the Fifth Commandment of the Decalogue is clear, but the comment that this command is the first command with a promise is unique. Some believe that this may mean that it is the first commandment of the second table of commands found in the Ten Commandments.[149] Others disagree and state that the meaning of this section of the text is that this command is, "the first that has to be learned."[150]

(Dallas: Word, 1989), 119, 122. Nolland point out the Simeon and Anna were given a twofold positive description to which the early church could relate, they were righteous and elderly.

147. Richard B. Hays and Judith C. Hays, "The Christian Practice of Growing Old: The Witness of Scripture," in *Growing Old in Christ*, 9. "Respect due to older members of the community is emphasized in the Pastoral Epistles." Therein specific examples of the requirement of the community to provide assistance for the elderly are found. (See 1 Tim 5:1; 3–16; Titus 2:2–5; James 2:27).

148. Ephesians 6:1–2 has a parallel text in Colossians 3:20 which essentially covers the same material.

149. Oswald T. Allis, *God Spake By Moses, An Exposition of the Pentateuch* (Phillipsburg, NJ: Presbyterian and Reformed Publishing Company, 1951), 74.

150. T. K. Abbott, *The Epistles to the Ephesians and to the Colossians*, The International Critical commentary on the Holy Scriptures of the Old and New Testaments (Edinburgh: T. & T. Clark, 1979), 177.

Nevertheless, it does seem clear that honoring one's parents, from the apostle Paul's perspective then would be a basic social command.

Calvin follows the Apostle Paul's connection of the Fifth Commandment with children obeying their parents when he states, "For they [Parents] sit in that place to which they have been advanced by the Lord, who shares with them a part of his honor. Therefore, the submission paid to them ought to be a step toward honoring that highest Father."[151] Calvin follows the relationship which Paul says exists between the ethics of the Decalogue and the New Testament by stating that the Ephesians 6 passage reveals, among other things, that this admonition is one that is basic to society.

That the admonition to follow the Fifth Commandment is basic to social life as observed by the apostle Paul is seen in its application to the Christian community. "On the basis of his Christology and soteriology [Paul] emphasizes the practicability of his advice and wished to help his readers to find a good way of living."[152] As members of the Kingdom of God who were seeking to restore "Shalom" these acts of honor were a good way of living for the religious community as well as society in general. Calvin saw that the obedience rendered by children to parents was so clearly an expected act that God attached promise which is in place to motivate children to obey the command.[153] The promise attached to motivate children to obey is not a bribe, but a reminder of the positive consequences of obeying God's command. Though this text sets a limit, "in the Lord" as a boundary for the command, that limitation does not negate the command. Calvin states that children are to obey parents who are not violating their God given authority by abusing their kids, but he does not support obeying parents when they advocate acts that are contrary to God's commands. Calvin says this as a means of warning those parents who would use this command as a means of oppress-

---

151. John Calvin, *Institutes of the Christian Religion*, trans. Henry Beveridge, vol. one (Grand Rapids: Eerdmans, 1953), 346.

152. Markus Barth, *Ephesians: Translation and Commentary on Chapters 4–6*, The Anchor Bible (Garden City, NY: Doubleday & Company, Inc., 1960), 756.

153. John Calvin, *Commentaries on the Epistles of Paul to the Galatians and Ephesians*, trans. William Pringle (Grand Rapids: Baker, 1996), 328.

ing others.[154] The boundaries placed in the text by the apostle Paul for obeying parents is based upon the Fifth Commandment. In the text of Ephesians 6:1–2 one can see that the Fifth commandment is explicitly taught and applied in the writings of the apostle Paul.

That the writers of the New Testament understood the importance and breadth of the application of this command is seen in the book of Acts. The breadth of this command is seen in its general application. Just as in Leviticus 19:32 where the Covenant community is given a general requirement to respect the elderly through standing in their presence, so in the book of Acts those who desire to reflect the Kingdom express their respect in the form of food distribution for needy widows. In Acts 6:1–2 it states, "In those days when the number of disciples was increasing the Grecian Jews among them complained against the Hebraic Jews because their widows were being overlooked in the daily distribution of food." As will be noted in 1 Tim 5:9 and 16, there is a general principle of Christians caring for relatives, and the Church caring for its own elderly in need. In Acts 6:1–2 some widows were being neglected in the distribution of daily food. The issue here is not the conflict between the two groups, Jews and Greeks, but the tradition that formed the basis for daily care of these women. "There was an extended family concern for "their widows". Since girls could be married quite young, often to older husbands, it was inevitable that there should be a high proportion of widows in any community (cf. Acts 9:39–41; 1 Tim 5:9–16)."[155] Their extended family became the Christian community, and that community felt an explicit responsibility to care for widows who were in need. One reason why the Christian community cared for their widows, rather then the Jewish community, may have been because the Christian community was no longer regarded as part of the Jewish community. Though the Christian and Jewish communities may have developed distinct arrangement of relief for their widows their systems of relief were based upon the same underlining principles found in the Torah.[156] Others do not see a distinction

---

154. George Arthur Buttrick, ed., *The Interpreter's Bible*, vol. X (Nashville: Abingdon, 1992), 729–30.

155. James D. G. Dunn, *The Acts of the Apostles* (Valley Forge, PA: Trinity Press International, 1996), 82.

156. Ernst Haenchen, *The Acts of the Apostles: A Commentary* (Philadelphia:

The Biblical Basis for Elder Care

between the Jewish and Christian communities at this early period of the church, but rather see this as a racial issue where, "The fact that these widows belonged to the "Hellenists" means rather, that they belonged to a Jerusalem group of people which—in principle—was not included among the needy."[157] That the Hellenist widows in the church were denied this common distribution of food reveals the requirement of caring for those widows who were in need among the community of believers, because when it did not occur it was noticed as a significant social offense.[158] The caring for widows was a tradition in Jewish society. As has been noted the elderly occasionally fell into the category of being the widow and poor. When their families could not care for them then there was a direct responsibility for the community to care for them.[159] The responsibility not only came from the application of the Torah, but it also came from understanding what type of actions Jesus would want them to take in light of their relationship to Jesus and His Kingdom.

Guidelines for Elderly Widows

Another application of the biblical model, that has been developed through observing how the church dealt with the social issue of the elderly, is seen in the apostle Paul's use of it as a method of caring for elderly widows who were in need. The apostle Paul, who was quite familiar with the Torah having been trained as a Pharisee, applies the principles found in the Decalogue in one of his letter, while covering issues related to family and church responsibilities. In 1 Tim 5:8 the general principle of Christians caring for relatives is provided, but then Paul raises the specific issue of care for widows. "If anyone does

---

The Westminster Press, 1971), 262. Cf. Ajith Fernando, *Acts*, The NIV Application Commentary, gen. ed. Terry Much (Grand Rapids: Zondervan, 1998), 225–26.

157. Gerd Ludemann, *Early Christianity according to the Traditions in Acts: A Commentary*, trans. John Bowden (Minneapolis: Fortress Press, 1989), 75. See also, John Polhill, *Acts*, The New American Commentary, vol. 26 (Nashville: Broadman, 1992), 178–80.

158. Luke Timothy Johnson, *The Acts of the Apostles*, Sacra Pagina Series, vol. 5, ed. Daniel J. Harrington (Collegeville, MN: The Litergical Press, 1992), 105.

159. John MacArthur, *Acts 1–12*, The MacArthur New Testament Commentary (Chicago: Moody, 1994),178.

not provide for his relatives, and especially for his immediate family, he has denied the faith and is worse than an unbeliever" (I Tim 5:8). Paul makes this pronouncement concerning caring for relatives before discussing the problem of family-less widows. The admonition is that Christian families were to care for those in need within their own extended families.

In the Christian community, it is understood that, "A man is an interdependent being who needs relationship with other men (Gen 1:27; Rom 12:5). The value of the individual and the community is equally affirmed in the Bible. All men are bound to all other men in mutual responsibility."[160] The interdependence and mutual responsibility of human beings was addressed by Jesus when he was asked the question, "who is my neighbor?" Jesus responded by implying "everyone" (see Luke 10:29–37). 1 Tim 5:8 illustrates the interconnectedness that is to be a natural part of the Christian community, and exemplifies what ought to occur in the greater culture.

In the next verse the apostle Paul gives specific guidelines for widows who would be taken care of by the church. The requirements for a widow to be supported by the church were, age (1 Tim 5:9 states that she must be sixty years old), godliness and a servant's heart. Therefore, not all of the elderly would meet these requirements, but only those who were qualified, and who were in need, received the support. It is not insignificant that Paul limits the allocation of charity to widows who are part of the Christian community, lacking social support, and faithful followers of Christ. What Paul is doing is providing guidelines with which *to provide* for those widows who are in need. It is acknowledged that there are limitations to the allocation of social services in this text. Nevertheless in the context of the 1 Tim 5 those limitations are *to provide* for qualified widows rather than *not providing* those qualified widows with social services.

In 1 Tim 5:16, Paul is addressing Christians on the issue that the religious community should take responsibility for the care for qualified widows. It was the church's responsibility to care for those elderly who were without family, and it was the Christian family's responsibility to help those elderly who are part of its family. This

---

160. Earl Shelp, "An Inquiry Into Christian Ethical Sanctions for the "Right To Health Care" (Ph.D. diss., The Southern Baptist Theological Seminary, 1976), 64–65.

ethic of care and respect for the elderly by the church is also seen in the general epistle of James in which it is stated that true religion cares for widows, who often involve the elderly (James 1:27). The book of James follows the principles already set forth that reveal the greater responsibility of the Christian family, "in which we are accountable to one another without familiarity," and that is no more true than in the issue of caring for the elderly in need.[161] In each of these examples there were qualifications for widows who were cared for by the Christian community, but those qualifications included those who were truly in need.

Jesus Responds to Ageism

One of the more interesting examples of respecting and caring for the elderly comes from Jesus' discussion concerning the 'Corban' tradition in Matt 15:1–9 and Mark 7:1–13. These texts are of particular importance in light of the principles of *agape* and justice. The author of the first Gospel has Jesus confronting His opponents over the violation of these Kingdom principles. In Matt 15:1–9 Jesus criticized the Pharisees because they allowed an abuse of tradition to bring about a situation in which parental needs were neglected in favor of filial greed. In Corban people would swear to donate money to God, or the Temple of God, often after their own death, sometimes to avoid spending money to care for their ageing parents.[162] This implies a disrespect towards the elderly parent because the son was obligated to take over the duties of leading and caring for the family when the father could no longer fulfill his duties and the head of the family. If the son followed the Corban tradition as prescribed by the Pharisees then he would have violated the Fifth Commandment through this supposed act of "dedication."[163] It is then seen that this

---

161. Oliver O'Donovan, *Common Objects of Love: Moral Reflection and the Shaping of Community* (Grand Rapids: Eerdmans, 2002), 58.

162. William Barclay, *The Gospel of Mark*, Rev. ed. (Philadelphia: The Westminster Press, 1975), 170. Barclay comments that the Korban (Corban) oath is an example of law of the Scribes going beyond what the Law of God said and in effect made it impossible for a man to carry out the "law of the ten commandments" concerning his parents (171).

163. Rodney L. Cooper, *Mark*, Holman New Testament Commentary (Nashville: Holman Reference, 2000), 118. Cooper argues that Corban is a

abuse of Corban demonstrates a disrespect for one's parents and by implication the elderly.

> The scribes and Pharisees, as representatives of the Jerusalem rulers, attempt through their "traditions" to channel resources as well as loyalty to the central institutions of the Temple and high priesthood. Jesus, as the representative of the Galilean villagers, declares that their "traditions" in effect violate and void the fundamental Mosaic covenant and its principles of justice and mutual caring. Again he defends the Israelite popular tradition, particularly the Mosaic covenant that guided common life in the village communities, against the great tradition that had been developed in and for the interests of the ruling circles in Jerusalem.[164]

Resources were being channeled in another direction, against the support of parents in accordance with the Fifth Commandment, for the benefit of another group of individuals. In some cases, this redirecting of funds may have initially been for noble reasons; however, the text does not specify one way or the other. What it does state is that the Corban tradition violated the explicit responsibility that the children had in caring for their elderly parents. The Pharisees had taken a tradition and placed it over the principles of "justice and mutual caring" for parents, which were indicative of Jewish culture.

The culture of Judaism as well as the Mosaic covenant emphasized the responsibility of the family to care for those who were older.

> It is not perfectly clear whether, in the instance cited by Jesus, the son actually dedicated his property to God in haste, and was not allowed by the scribes to use it for

---

direct violation of the Fifth Commandment. Others argue that there is a conflict, or power struggle occurring in this passage as is seen in, J. Enoch Powell, *The Evolution of the Gospel* (New Haven: Yale University Press, 1994), 140, Donald A Hagner, "The *Sitz im Leben* of the Gospel of Matthew," in *Treasures New and Old: Recent Contributions to Matthean Studies*, ed. David R. Bauer & Mark Allan Powell, SBL Symposium Series, ed. Gail R. O'Day (Atlanta: Scholars Press, 1996), 55.

164. Richard A. Horsely, *Hearing the Whole Story: The Politics of Plot in Mark's Gospel* (Louisville: Westminster John Knox Press, 2001), 172.

the support of his needy parents, or whether he merely pretended to dedicate it while keeping it for his own use (a more flagrant act, to be sure). But in either case, the point in the illustration is, that the Pharisees and scribes justified the son in his evasion of responsibility for the support of his parents because he had taken advantage of one of the technicalities of the oral law. They cared more for the strict observance of their rules about 'Corban' than they did about the support and welfare of the son's father and mother.[165]

The "evasion of responsibility" is another offense found in this text. It was wrong for a son of the Covenant to disregard the welfare of his parents. There was also a direct connection between the issues of abdication of responsibility for one's parents and of resistance to participation in acts of kindness and sacrifice designed to help the elderly. "The Rabbis did not dispute that a man ought to honor his parents, and that the general duty of honoring them, implied the particular duty of supporting them."[166] The difficulty was that they thought that Temple obligations took precedence over this clear social responsibility. The redistribution of priorities which set the religious needs of the Temple over the social welfare of the parents were unequivocally rejected by Jesus.

> Jesus was attacking a system which put rules and regulations before the claim of human need. The command of God was that the claim of human love should come first; the command of the scribes was the claim of legal rules and regulations should come first. Jesus was quite sure that any regulation which prevented a man from giving help where help was needed was nothing less than a contradiction of the law of God.[167]

---

165. A. M. Fairbairn, *Studies in the Life of Christ*, 171 as quoted in Orville Ernest Daniel, "Corban," (Ph.D. Diss., Southern Baptist Theological Seminary, 1929), 79–80.

166. Allen Menzies, *The Earliest Gospel: A Historical Study of the Gospel According to Mark* (London: MacMillan, 1901), 152.

167. Barclay, *The Gospel of Mark*, 171.

Neither covert or overt neglect of parents is seen as acceptable for those who are following the Decalogue, as Jesus, who was Jewish, is clear to point out. The implications here are that the elderly parents were to be cared for, and the cultural demands of the religious leaders were not permitted to over rule that immutable principle. The principles concerning the family's and community's responsibilities for the elderly were not negated when Jesus arrived on the scene, for he came not to abolish the Law but to fulfill it (John 13:18).

In developing an understanding of how early Christians understood their obligations to the elderly the "Corban" episode is important. Jesus applies the Decalogue while admonishing the Pharisees to apply the more important aspects of the Law. Justice and agape are foundational for a Christian understanding of how the elderly should be treated. According to this story Jesus places the same requirement of honor on the Pharisees as is found in the Old Testament.

Jesus Himself took the Fifth Commandment seriously. His attitude toward the Fifth commandment, among many other things, can be observed in the passages describing how He assigned the apostle John to be the caretaker of his mother, just before his death in John 19:26–27. Jesus regarded it as His responsibility as eldest son to make sure that Mary, his mother, was adequately protected. At this point it is assumed that Joseph, Mary's husband, is dead. So, the apostle John was assigned the task of taking Mary into his household, and treating her as if she were his own biological mother. Although the text does not indicate why Jesus did not give this responsibility to his closer blood relatives, such as his brothers, it does indicate that caring for one's family members is a social as well as a familial responsibility[168]

---

168. A. T. Robertson, *Word Pictures in the New Testament*, Concise ed., James A. Swanson ed. (Nashville: Holman Reference, 2000), 252–53. Though this text is called a 'vivid and picturesque scene' no clear reason for this act is given without some use of allegory. Elwell disagrees with this view and takes the text to mean what it simply says, that Jesus provided for his mother's future. Walter Elwell, *Evangelical Commentary on the Bible* (Grand Rapids: Baker, 1989), 875. Tasker infers that this transfer of responsibility concerning Jesus' mother, Mary, included acceptance in his 'relations and friends.' It seems that Tasker sees the care of Mary, as an older woman, was familial and communal. This would mimic the principles of elder care already reviewed in the Old Testament. R. V. G. Tasker, *John*; Tyndale New Testament Commentaries (Grand Rapids: Eerdmans, 1960), 216.

Although Jesus' act of respect and responsibility toward his mother was in the context of first century AD Israel and the early Christian church the text has contemporary application. As the King who proclaimed the coming Kingdom, while in the midst of His redemptive work, Jesus understood the gravity of the situation for His elderly mother and as such fulfilled His filial responsibility to care for her through His disciple John, since He Himself could no longer do so. This example from Jesus shows that the principles of honor, along with the appropriate cultural responsibility towards the elderly, are part of the normative responsibility of a Christian community. The appropriate cultural responsibility is to honor the elderly and provide necessary care for the elderly when they are in need.

What the Bible then presents is an onus placed on both the children of the elderly, as well as the religious community in which the elderly reside, to provide care for them when they are in need, and to show them respect. The Mosaic covenant articulates the requirements of family and the religious community to show "honor" to the elderly. In the New Testament, Jesus upholds this teaching, and the book of Acts applies it as a community ethic. The apostle Paul provides admonitions and guidelines based upon this biblical ethic in a number of his epistles, as does James.[169] It has been seen that in light of God's original intent for His creation, "Shalom," and the Church's responsibility to live as participants in Christ's Kingdom, there is a clear responsibility that can be identified in Scripture, for Christians to show honor to the elderly, and care for those qualified elderly who are truly in need.[170]

Principles of Elder Care

It has been noted that the Bible presents the principles of honor and community as fundamental aspects of elder care. As was noted in the discussion concerning justice the original state of creation was that all of humanity was in a state of "Shalom." That state of wholeness and completeness included humanity functioning as individuals made in the image of God (Gen 1:27). The tenet of the *imago dei* is

---

169. Eph 6:1–2; Col 3:20; 1 Tim 5:3; James 1:27.

170. See, Matt 15:1–9; Mark 7:1–13; John 19: 26–27; 1 Tim 5:8–10, 16; and James 1:27.

crucial regarding how the elderly are treated in society, because it reveals a common connection between those who are in the Christian community and those who are not. That connection should result in just deeds of agape being expressed to all of humanity.

> God's love for us is unconditional. It calls the Church to become and act as a participatory and justice-generating community. In God's sight, all human beings have dignity and worth because they are made in His image. They have the freedom to relate to Him and the mandate to be in fellowship with others. The church should, therefore, continue to advocate the rights and responsibilities of older persons.[171]

Because humanity is made in the image of God and is responsible, in a general way, to care for others, it is not difficult to see how there is a development of that concept in the Fifth Commandment. The creation ethic, which encompasses the image of God, shows that each member of humanity has value and dignity because, in some mysterious way, human beings are image bearers of God.[172] Emil Brunner states the importance of the *imago dei* when he said, "the creation of all men in the image of God is the deepest foundation of the sense of right in the Bible."[173] Since human beings are created in the image of God, they have inherent value no matter what the stage of life. Rather, it becomes part of the normal stage of human life for every person who ages. Human worth and dignity then are inherent, not traits that dissipate with time. Certain conclusions can then be reached. The *imago dei* doctrine changes the basis of calculating human worth so that age no longer becomes a negative basis

---

171. Masamba ma Mpolo, *The Church and the Aging in a Changing World* (Geneva: Office of Family Education World Council of Churches, 1982), 1–2.

172. Anthony A. Hoekema, *Created in God's Image* (Grand Rapids: Eerdmans, 1986), 31. "We have noted that from the Old Testament passages cited and from James 3:9 it is clear that there is a very important sense in which man today, fallen man, is still a bearer of the image of God, and must therefore still be so viewed."

173. Emil Brunner, *Justice and the Social Order*, trans. Mary Hottinger (Cambridge: New York: Harper and Brothers, 1945, reprint: Lutterworth Press, 2003), 34.

for evaluating worth.[174] With the proviso that all human beings are of inherent value, then their age should not be regarded solely as a problem.

The equality of humanity also means that neither the elderly, nor the young should be discriminated against because of their age. If there exists a youth who is in need then their care ought to take precedence over an elderly person who is not in need. Though "honor" is due to the elderly their one finds in Scripture that it is the needy who are to receive care. It is the needy poor who are given "gleaning" as a method of receiving food. It is the needy widows who receive food in the early church and care in the instructions of the apostle Paul. As identified in the discussion in this chapter concerning justice as a means of bringing back "Shalom," there should be parity among human beings rather than preferences based upon such natural conditions as age, be that youth or old age. A decision making model which sets up a paradigm which uses age, like those which use other natural conditions, such as sex, or race, would find itself unjustly discriminating against those in need.

Community

As God's image bearers humans are given worth and dignity. Humans are also designed to function in dependence upon one another, because they cannot be truly human apart from their relationship with others.[175] Biblical admonitions concerning the elderly are within a religious community life that knew little of personal autonomy. When a person was destitute and without a family the Israelite com-

---

174. Not everyone agrees with the identity of the image of God concept of this type of application. Paul Simmons sees the image of God as, "capacities or characteristics that define the person as person and thus as bearers of the image of God." Paul Simmons, *Birth and Death: Bioethical Decision-Making* (Philadelphia: The Westminster Press, 1983), 86. The problem with Simmons' decision to interpret the *imago dei* in a functional manner is that human beings potentially lose their identity as image bearers of God the more they lose their physical and mental faculties. The implications of functionality in medical ethics is significant. If functionality defines personhood then the elderly, or any physically disabled person, would be likely to receive less medical care because of their natural loss of capacity would make them less of a person.

175. Anthony A. Hoekema, *Created in God's Image* (Grand Rapids: Eerdmanns, 1986), 77.

munity made provisions for him or her. In the New Testament the church took care to provide for selected widows.[176]

"By creating humanity social God revealed his intention for human being and the pattern of life that He desires. It is life in relationship."[177] In light of the "Shalom" which was established at creation the worth and dignity of the elderly, indeed of all human beings, are necessarily realized within the network of relationships that are common to humanity.

Honor, Respect and Old Age

It has already been noted that respect is be given to the elderly by those who are younger. This state of being old, of being 'elderly,' can bring about a number of responses from any given society. In some societies old age engenders respect, in others it produces contempt, and in still others it results in pressure to end one's life.

> Professor K. von Durckheim once asked some Japanese what was considered to be the supreme good of their country. 'Our old people,' was their reply. Alas! Our Western outlook is quite the opposite. It is not a matter only of the distress felt by the old among us, but of the effect on their behavior of this social contempt.[178]

Durckheim reveals that being old does not automatically bring about respect. What does need to be acknowledged is that, however the elderly are identified, they are a distinct group within a given society that attracts attention for good or ill.[179]

Scripture provides examples of the elderly being cared for and placed in positions of honor. Yet these are not the only ideas concerning the elderly that can be gleaned from Scripture.

---

176. Caring for widows was so significant for the church that one of the first controversies surrounded the issue of distributing food to widows of different races in a fair and just manner, see Acts 6:1–6.

177. E. David Cook, "Shalom and Justice in Health Care," *The Southern Baptist Journal of Theology* 4 (2000): 61.

178. Paul Tournier, *Learn to Grow Old* (Louisville, KY: Westminster John Knox Press, 1972), 37.

179. Beauchamp and Childress, *Principles of Biomedical Ethics*, 5th ed., 61–62.

Equally important, perhaps, are the things not said about older characters in the New Testament. Nowhere in the biblical cannon are they pitied, patronized, or treated with condescension. Nowhere is growing old itself described as a problem. Nowhere are elders described as pitiable, irrelevant, or behind the curve, as inactive or unproductive. Nowhere are they, as in so many Western dramas and narratives, lampooned as comic figures. On the contrary, they are seen as the bearers of wisdom by virtue of their age. Death is treated as an enemy to be conquered by Christ at the eschaton (e.g., 1 Cor 15:24–26), but it never seems to occur to the New Testament authors to characterize the aging process itself as an evil to be overcome. Thus, the New Testament offers us an alternative vision to which the modern, popular view of aging as a "problem" might appear puzzling and unhealthy.[180]

It is seen that the biblical principles surrounding the elderly are honor, which includes care and respect, and community, where they are always considered to be members and partakers. Although the needy elderly are acknowledged as the appropriate recipients of care the Bible does not characterize the elderly as people with problems simply because they are old. Though the principles developed in Scripture reveal a direct responsibility to care for the elderly it does not consider being "old" a problem. A survey of the Bible finds that living a long life is not considered a problem, but a blessing.[181] Old age is a blessing because of a number of reasons including the wisdom that the elderly bring to the community, their place as historians, their character contributions to the lives of those who are younger as well as a means of providing service opportunities to those who are younger. Old age is not seen as a problem to be cured, but the "old" are viewed in a positive light in both Testaments.[182]

180. Richard B. Hays and Judith C. Hays, "The Christian Practice of Growing Old: The Witness of Scripture," in *Growing Old in Christ*, ed. Stanley Hauerwas, Carole Bailey Stoneking, Keith G. Meador and David Cloutier (Grand Rapids: Eerdmans, 2003), 11.

181. See Gen 25:8; Judges 8:32; 2 Chron 24:15.

182. See Gen 15:15; 18:11; 21:2, 7; 24:1, 36; 25:8; 35:29; 37:3; 44:20; Judges 8:32; Ruth 4:15; 1 Kings 1; 1 Chron 29:28; 2 Chron 24:15; Ps 71:9; 92:14; Isa 3:5; 46:4; 65:20; Zech 8:4; Luke 1:36; 2:37; 1 Tim 5:9, 19; 1 Peter 5:1.

In the biblical model the care for the elderly exists, in part, because of an understanding that as followers of Christ there is a social responsibility to honor and care for them. That responsibility involves an understanding of the elderly person's place in the fabric of society, their connection to family and their status as members of humanity who bear God's image. These characteristics are not exclusive to the elderly, but are also common to all members of the community. What these characteristics demonstrate is that the general principle of distributive justice, that is to be applied to the each member of the community, is also applicable to the elderly, especially the qualified elderly who are in need. Consequently, just distribution is not according to maximization, but it is according to human dignity, rights and the common good. It looks at what society owes the elderly rather than what the elderly should do for society. "The principle of distributive justice implies that society has a duty to the individual in serious need and that all individuals have duties to others in serious need."[183] What this means for allocation is that triage should be based upon the seriousness of the health state. In the biblical model a person has inherent worth, and it is only "fair" to distribute resources according to need, rather then chronology.[184]

Responses to Community and Honor

In a perfect world, all families would be united and exist in harmony. Unfortunately the family unit—husband, wife, children and extended family, struggles to remain intact in American society. That some families are divided does not negate the familial nature of Christianity because Christians exist within the community of Christ, the church, however imperfectly it may be in a given secular setting. The first place, then, where Christians should demonstrate the principles of honor and community toward the elderly is in their individual homes. Even in a "less than perfect" home, these princi-

---

183. "Principles of Distributive Justice," Healthcare Issues, *Ascension Health* [on-line]; accessed 04 June 2004; available from http://www.ascensionhealth.org/ethics/public/ key_principles/distributive_justice.asp; Internet.

184. Ronald F. White, "The Principle of Justice," Ron White's Philosophy and Ethics Homepage, *College of Mount St. Joseph* [on-line]; accessed 04 June 2004; available from http://www.msj.edu/white/justice.htm; Internet.

ples can be applied. These principles can be applied to the advantage of respecting and caring for one's parent(s), and they may require as simple acts such checking on them to reassure them that they know that there is someone who cares available to help them should the need arise. On the other hand, it may become more involved, in such acts as checking blood sugars, preparing meals, or changing diapers. This is not to imply that every parent should move in with one of their adult children. What is being said is that Christians, above all others, should willingly produce acts of loving service that uphold their elderly parents. The reason for this is that the nation of Israel, as well as the Church, was commonly identified in familial terms.[185] The familial context assumed that within the nature of families, as identified in Scripture, a responsibility existed for children to fulfill their filial duties concerning their elderly relatives.

Some may protest that this type of burden would be too intrusive for the current American culture. Demonstrating honor by caring for the elderly in this manner could greatly effect the lifestyles of some people, but that discomfort does not discount the importance of community and honor for the elderly. Rather it reveals the extent of the Western culture's narcissism.[186] The notion that caring for the elderly is too intrusive is the product of an American culture that values youthful autonomy and denies or, at least minimizes, any substantive obligation to care for the elderly. This view disregards

---

185. Israel was called the house of David because the entire social order is viewed as an extension of a ruler's household, cf. J. David Schloen, *The House of the Father as Fact and Symbol: Patrimonialism in Ugart and the Ancient Near East* (Winona Lake, IN: Eisenbrauns, 2001), 51, 54. In the New Testament a common metaphor for the church is family. Cf. Wayne Grudem, "Metaphors for the Church," *Systematic Theology: An Introduction to Biblical Doctrine* (Grand Rapids: InterVarsity, 1994), 858.

186. Jan Narveson, "The right to be old and the right to have young: some conundrums about aging populations," *Respect For Persons, Tulane Studies in Philosophies* 31 (New Orleans: Tulane University, 1982), 193. Narveson objects to the idea that the old have a right to be cared for by those who are young because the right to be old is a negative argument and the right to receive care is a positive one. Also, she rejects this ethics because the requirement to care for others is coercive. It seems strange that Naveson's discussion of being old is under the umbrella of "rights." It may be better to acknowledge that there is a freedom in be old, or a natural state of being or becoming old, which has implications for the young as well as old.

society's interconnectedness, as well as the obvious point that most people, including those who comprise the younger generations, given sufficient time, will become old.

The biblical model calls the Christian community to care for the elderly, as has been shown in selected passages of Scripture, and from an understanding of the Kingdom which is "coming but is not yet" that shall usher in "Shalom." In light of the responsibility that the church has to help instill "Shalom" into a world that is lacking wholeness and peace, the church should seek to bring some aspects of "Shalom" into secular culture. An aspect of that effort to bring about "Shalom" is for the Christian community to follow God's call to honor the elderly and to care intelligently for them in their time of need.[187]

One of the ways that the church is to demonstrate care and respect is to deal with the elderly as persons worthy of receiving needed medical treatment.[188] In light of arguments concerning age based health care rationing, this is an important distinction from the QALY model's result of basing rationing on age. To honor the elderly means, at least from a biblical perspective, to include them in the social fabric of the community and care for them in their time of need. This, of course, includes medical care.

Conclusion

What has been attempted is an overview of the biblical principles which form a basis for elder care. At the onset of the discussion an understanding of the challenges of reading the Bible were evaluated. After coming to the point that there was a possibility of having a common reading of Scripture the Old Testament was evaluated for principles of elder care. Two texts were appraised for their specificity and general applicability. In the Decalogue, because of its place of importance, the Fifth Commandment was noted as a basis for honoring parents. Next, Leviticus 19:32 was looked at as a text that established "honor" as a principle that applied to the elderly in general.

187. Ibid., 179.
188. Edmund D. Pellegrino and David C. Thomasma, *Helping and Healing: Religious Commitment in Health Care* (Washington, D.C.: Georgetown University Press, 1997), 96.

In order to understand how the biblical model could use the New Testament it was noted that there are foundational principles which provide a basis for Kingdom living.

It was also noted that the coming Kingdom of heaven was a practical and eschatological event that had a present application as well as a future fulfillment. The contemporary application would be seen in how Christians applied the principles of *agape* and justice to cultural issues and in so doing seek to establish a sense of "Shalom." A*gape* and justice were explained as foundational if Christians were to live as "salt and light" toward secular society.

The principles of *agape* and justice were seen to apply to all of humanity and not just to the Christian community. It was noted that Jesus said that the *agape* that His followers were to display ought to be expressed toward fellow believers, neighbors, and enemies. Since the selfless *agape* had a category where every person could fit it meant that Christians could not fully apply the principles of the Kingdom in seeking "Shalom" if they insisted upon acting as an isolated religious community.

In the New Testament it was noted that the elderly were treated with honor, but only qualified elderly, as discussed concerning authorized widows, received special care. Not all elderly qualified as being in need. Although the gospel of Luke presented a generally positive view of the elderly in the story of Anna and Simeon, their piety and ministry purpose placed them into a position where they were not looked at as elderly in need, simply elderly who were to be looked at with honor.

The apostle Paul followed the general pattern found in the Fifth Commandment of honoring parents in his instructions to children in Ephesians 6:1–3. When he gave instructions concerning the care of widows in 1 Tim 5, it was with the same general principle of honoring the elderly, but the widows who were to be cared for were to have particular qualifications. The widows who were to be served were seen to have particular qualifications, which were age, need, and a positive relationship to the Church community as well as personal piety. It was observed that these resource limitations were designed to provide *for* those in need rather than keep needy widows from receiving care. Additionally, in Acts 6 widows who were in need received care from the church. In James 1:27 the limitation was to care for "widows in their distress." Though there are qualifications for these elderly to receive care those stipulations were designed to establish who were to be included.

The result of an inquiry into the biblical principles of elder care has revealed a responsibility to honor the elderly generally, and when the elderly are in need, such as the widows in the New Testament, then to enable them to receive needed provisions. That the Bible presents these principles towards humanity in general was also supported by the doctrine of the *imago dei*, which also places a responsibility on the "Christian" community to reach out to the wider culture, because all people are made in the image of God.

> Disinterestedness and lack of involvement cannot be the position of the church. When this happens churches lose their witness and, in some measure, their right to be called Christ's church. This was exactly the situation of some of the churches of Asia Minor (Rev 1–3). In such instances Jesus Himself threatened to remove the candle from the candlestick. Churches inevitably have sociological, cultural, and contextual dimensions. But to be a church, a called and chosen people of God—a church must be responsible. This means that we are responsible before God on behalf of the world.[189]

The church has a social responsibility that includes the care of the elderly. The social teachings of the church directly influence its response to needy elderly who are being discriminated against solely based upon age.

One may argue that this biblical model of elder care is beyond the religious community's areas of responsibility and involvement, and that the Bible's emphasis is more on spirituality, compassion and pastoral care than on medical care. However, the church has not been ignorant of the need for medical care. Pope John XXIII stated that the requirement for individual dignity included the right to

---

189. William L. Hendericks, *A Theology of Aging* (Nashville: Broadman, 1986), 84.

health care.[190] In 1995 the National Conference of Catholic Bishops reaffirmed the requirement of the Christian communities to "care for the old."[191] While these are Catholic writers, this responsibility has not been overlooked by Protestants.[192] Christian doctrines, such as the *imago dei*, the dominion mandate, (to be stewards of God's creation), and the commandment to establish "Shalom" require the church's involvement in caring for people in need, which often includes the elderly. Genuine Christian *agape* must start back at the thought of proclaiming the love of Christ which includes its accompanying just human actions.[193] This connection between *agape* and just human actions which support the principles of honor and community makes the biblical ethic worth examining. It is the basis for an ethic of care which includes care for needy elderly. Though this work has presented a model of elder care that model does not discriminate against those younger persons who are also in need. It presents a model where the people are not evaluated based upon the natural state of life that is called, age, but upon need.

This work has demonstrated that the Bible provides a possible model of elder care that can be contrasted with that of the QALY model. When the utilitarianism of the QALY model and the biblical principles of community and honor are compared, stark differences are revealed. Both models seek have an ethic concerning

---

190. R. Andrew Lustig, "Reform and Rationing: Reflections of Health Care in Light of Catholic Social Teaching," in *On Moral Medicine: Theological Perspectives in Medical Ethics*, 2nd ed., ed Stephen E. Lammers and Allen Verhey (Grand Rapids: William B. Eerdmans Publishing Company, 1998), 961.

191. William H. Keeler, "A Catholic Appeal: Leadership for the Common Good," *Office for Social Justice: Catholic Social Teaching* [on-line]; accessed 29 March 2004; available from http://www.osjsp.org/cst/keeler.htm; Internet. Cardinal Keeler presented this statement at the National Conference of Catholic Bishops on November 15, 1995.

192. See, H. Richard Niebuhr, *Christ and Culture* (New York: Harper & Row, Publishers, 1951); Stanley Hauerwas, *Vision and Virtue* (Notre Dame: Fides, 1974); Allen Verhey, *Remembering Jesus: Christian Community, Scripture, and the Moral Life* (Grand Rapids: Eerdmans, 2002); and Ian S. Knox, *Older People and the Church* (London: T&T Clark, 2002).

193. Karl Barth, *Church Dogmatics: The Doctrine of the Word of God*, 2nd ed., vol. 1, part 1, trans. G. W. Bromiley, ed G. W. Bromiley and T. F. Torrance (Edinburgh: T&T Clark, 1975), 50.

caring for the elderly. It, therefore, remains for the two principles to be compared in order to assess the application and affect that the principles of honor and community could have if applied to the QALY model.

Chapter Five

Comparing the Models

In this work QALYs and a biblical model of elder care have been surveyed. Consequently the two principles can now be compared in order to assess the influence that the principles of honor and community could have if applied to the QALY model. This chapter will seek to identify certain areas of harmony and disparity in these models, and an analysis of the methods will also reveal their ethical outcomes regarding the allocation of limited medical resources. Since these models stem from different philosophical presuppositions, health care allocation decisions based upon these models' foundational ideologies will tend to have different results from one another.

Foundations

Philosophical Basis

A perception may exist that any comparison of QALYs and the biblical model of elder care is actually a veiled discussion of teleology and deontology. A discussion of objections of this type could be found by reading the philosophical discussions in this work.[1] There are some relationships between the respective models. Examining utilitarianism, teleology and the QALY model, one can see the connection when utilitarianism is understood. Singer states that "the classical

---

1. See chapter 3, pp. 97–101 and chapter 4, pp. 161–68 of this book.

utilitarian regards an action as right if it produces as much or more of an increase in happiness of all affected by it than any alternative action, and wrong if it does not."[2] McKie affirms the utilitarian basis of QALYs when he states that "the QALY method (or cost-utility analysis) is a special form of utilitarianism; it is utilitarianism applied to health."[3] As Nord explains, "The QALY approach assumes that the societal value of an intervention is proportional to the size of the health improvement. We may call this a utilitarian view."[4] QALY's maximizations are "defined in terms of life extension and/or improvements in the quality of life."[5] This defined measurement is the utilitarian component. Even the Von Neuman and Morganstern's game theory is based upon a utilitarian maximization of probabilities. Utilitarianism is the philosophical basis for the QALY model that guides QALY calculations.

In this work, utilitarianism has been seen as the weightiest philosophical basis for QALYs. The QALY model seeks maximization through decisions based on calculations which attempt to produce a maximization of societal good by distributing resources to those who are seen as the best recipients of the limited resources.[6] The teleology found in QALY calculations sets up a dynamic where the maximization of limited medical resources does not itself identify what is right or wrong, but it presents a utilitarianism based sum which can be used as a reference for health care allocation decisions.[7] The teleologic and utilitarian foundations of QALY allocation methods are inextricably linked.

---

2. Peter Singer, *Practical Ethics*, 2nd ed. (New York: Cambridge University Press, 1993), 3.

3. John McKie and others, *The Allocation of Health Care Resources: An Ethical Evaluation of the 'QALY' Approach* (Hampshire, UK: Dartmouth Publishing Company, 1998), 60–61.

4. Eric Nord, *Cost-Value Analysis in Health Care: Making Sense Out of QALYs* (Cambridge: Cambridge University Press, 1999), 38.

5. Ibid., 36.

6. See chapter 3, pp. 97–101 of this book.

7. Richard Brandt, "Toward a Credible Form of Utilitarianism," *Moral Philosophy: Selected Readings*, ed. George Sher (San Diego: Harcourt Brace Jovanovich, Publishers, 1987), 384–85.

Comparing the Models

The biblical model does have some common issues with deontology, but unlike the relationship between teleology and the QALY model the relationship between the biblical model and deontology are not as close. In chapter 4, in the section on Principles of Elder Care, it was noted that the creation ethic, based upon the *imago dei*, endows all of humanity as having value and dignity because in some way all human beings possess the image of God.[8] Inasmuch as all human beings, regardless of age, are seen as being created in the image of God, they all have inherent value no matter what the stage of life is in which they are presently living.[9] The implications of the *imago dei* doctrine include, at least, one principle similar to Kant's categorical imperative. Kant's categorical imperative states that people are never to be treated as a means to an end but as an end in and of themselves.[10] His underlying principle is that things are to be used, but that people are not because they are an end unto themselves. Kant also saw ethics as duties or obligations that are virtuous because of their method of construction. The construction is seen in Kant's formulation of a universal law, "Act only according to that maxim whereby you can at the same time will that it should be a universal law."[11] Kant's effort to universalize moral laws as well as his idea concerning people being ends in themselves rather than objects to be used as a means to an end are in some ways like the biblical model in that the biblical model presents some moral principles which are

8. See chapter 4, pp.189–91 of this book.

9. The Bible presents no distinction between the young and the old as having more or less God's image. Cf. Ps 139, the "days ordained" for humanity in verse 16 is set in the context of a complete life. Stages of life do not change God's interest in humanity.

10. Immanuel Kant, *Foundations of the Metaphysics of Morals and What is Enlightenment?* trans. by Lewis White Beck (New York: The Liberal Arts Press, 1959), 49. Kant states that rational beings, and by "rational beings" he means human beings, are an end to themselves. Although one might argue that this places a burden upon people to be functionally intelligent to fall into Kant's group of rational beings, this objection seems to go beyond the scope of Kant's discussion. He seems to identify all human beings as eminently rational creatures. As such they are not a means to an end, but they are seen as the ends themselves.

11. Immanuel Kant, *Grounding for the Metaphysics of Morals: with On a Supposed Right to Lie Because of Philanthropic Concerns* (Indianapolis, IN: Hackett Publishing Company, 1993), 30.

seen as universal to human nature and it presents humanity as being unique, and not an instrument of utility.[12] Nevertheless, the biblical ethic's emphasis not only affirms the worth of the individual human being and the community, but it also places an emphasis on caring for the aged, especially the elderly in need.

The extent to which the biblical model is different from deontology is seen in the Christian community's responsibility to help re-establish "Shalom." In its discussion concerning "Shalom," and Jesus' teachings on the Kingdom of God, the church was put into a position where it was responsible for those inside and outside of the religious community. Accordingly, as Christians sought to establish a climate of "Shalom" they found that out of the overflow of their appreciation and dedication to their King, Jesus, they served society. The society in which they live consists of people who are dependent and interdependent. Verhey observes that in the book of Acts the author, Luke, "identified the community created by the Spirit as a community of friends in an economic world of patrons and clients. And their community of goods illustrated a new economic order, an economic order of friends."[13]

The biblical model shows it is unique when compared to Kant's categorical imperative by identifying people as not only ends in themselves, but as protected beings whose worth is based upon their identity as human beings made by God. One may appreciate Kant's commitment to reason in his philosophical work, but the biblical model provides a broader ethic in that it includes foundational principles of *agape* and justice designed to re-establish a sense of "Shalom" in society as presented in the Bible. When the principles of Kingdom living are applied to elder care one finds that a more expansive ethic is developed than in the QALY model, which includes those who may use more money for medical care.[14] The moral

12. As Romans 1:14–5 attests there is, at least, a broad affirmation of natural law in Scripture which attests to some moral principles which are seen as universal to human nature, i.e., premeditated murder. See Scott B. Rae, *Moral Choices: An Introduction to Ethics*, 2nd ed. (Grand Rapids: Zondervan, 2000), 38–39.

13. Allen Verhey, *Remembering Jesus: Christian Community, Scripture, and the Moral Life* (Grand Rapids: Eerdmans, 2002), 283.

14. See chapter 4, p. 189–91 of this book. In discussing the principles of elder care it was noted that the biblical ethic identifies an equality inherent in humanity that does not sanction ageism.

standards of the Kingdom, based upon the foundational principles of the biblical model, produce guidelines that can "help us discern the moral good."[15] The moral "good" in the biblical model is an inclusive paradigm. In the QALY model, the moral good is based upon a perception that maximization equals moral propriety, an exclusive paradigm.

In light of the disparity between the two models it might be contended that the utilitarianism of QALYs and the biblical model are two extreme models which have little in common. This assertion of radical incompatibility cannot be justified. In both models, the paradigm is able to assist in directing medical decisions, in light of resource limitations, in what each considers the "best" way. The QALY model developed because it became necessary to choose where limited medical resources would be used. The biblical model also presents principles which can guide the use of limited medical resources. The difficulty is not in the acknowledgment that there is a problem, or that "good" choices need to be made concerning limited resources. The larger question is which ethics and values will be used to make these decisions. "While economics can help us to make choices more rationally and to use resources more efficiently, it cannot provide the ethics and the value judgments that must guide our decisions. In particular, economics cannot tell us how much equality or inequality we should have in our society."[16] It is not only the mathematics of QALYs that should be reexamined, but the morality of its possible outcomes, such as ageism, that should be assessed. While finding what is "best" is more than identifying which model is most beneficial economically, economics cannot be completely dismissed when decisions are made regarding limited medical resources. "Part of the creation mandate is to make life on Earth better,"[17] and identifying the morally "best" method of making allocation decisions is part of

15. Dennis P. Hollinger, *Choosing the Good: Christian Ethics in a Complex World* (Grand Rapids: Baker, 2002), 36–37.

16. Victor R. Fuchs, *Who Shall Live? Health, Economics, and Social Choice*, expanded edition, Economic Ideas Leading to the 21st Century, vol. 3 (Singapore: World Scientific), 7.

17. Charles W. Colson, "Can We Prevent the 'Abolition of Man'? C. S. Lewis's Challenge to the Twenty-first Century," in *Human Dignity in the Biotech Century: A Christian Vision for Public Policy*, ed. Charles W. Colson and Nigel M. de S. Cameron (Downers Grove: InterVarsity, 2004), 13.

making life on earth "better." Despite their disparity, neither of these models are malevolent in the sense that one or the other model's basis for moral judgment purposely seeks to negatively affect the lives of those involved in medical care.

The two models also agree that the patient is important in the decision making process. QALY are defined as, "an exchange rate between the quality and quantity of life."[18] In chapter 3, in the discussion covering Quality of Life it was noted that in QALYs, quality of life is determined by comparing preference-based measurements which are obtained through questionnaires given to a patient, potential patients, or a community, which provide a medical "value judgment."[19] Here patient involvement is seen as occurring in the QALY model through the use of preference-based measurements. The QALY model attempts to protect the greater community through the guided utilization of limited medical resources.[20] Its argument demonstrates a concern for patients through the desire to maximize limited medical resources. In the biblical model, patients in general, and the elderly in particular, are important because of the commands of God and humanity's place as God's image bearers.[21] The biblical model cannot be used to formulate a medical decision without considering patients, their physical condition, the patients' families, as well as accounting for the responsibility of the community to "be faithful to the example of Christ the healer as well as Christ the suffering servant."[22] As with the QALY model the biblical model takes into account how decisions will apply to the greater community.[23]

18. Ibid., 23.

19. See chapter 3, p. 71–75 of this book, and Wesley Smith, *Culture of Death: The Assault on Medical Ethics in America* (San Francisco: Encounter Books, 2000), 27.

20. John McKie and others, The Allocation of Health Care Resources: An Ethical Evaluation of the 'QALY' Approach (Hampshire, UK: Dartmouth Publishing Company, 1998), 60.

21. Anne E. Streaty Wimberly, "Caring as Honoring," *Christian Reflection: A Series in Faith and Ethics* (2003):10. Wimberly states that the image of God is "clearly" seen in the elderly.

22. Edmund D. Pellegrino and others, "Must the Church be Mute Lest Its Truths be Distorted? A Response to Engelhardt," *Christian Bioethics* 8:46.

23. Stanley Hauerwas, *A Community of Character: Toward a Constructive Christian Social Ethic* (Notre Dame: University of Notre Dame Press, 1981), 126. Hauerwas notes that communities become places of moral power. Therefore

For the biblical model the examples of Christ as healer and suffering servant moves the community of Christ to act as a support, especially with regard those elderly who are needy. "When we see clearly the image of God in our elders, we understand caring as honoring to be a journey of God's people, the young and old together. The journey of the young with the elders is in preparation for our own continuing journey."[24] Caring as honoring in the biblical model means that no patient is marginalized or looked upon as inconsequential. Caring for the patient in the QALY model means that limited resources are maximized for the benefit of the greater community. Both models consider the patient important in the decision making paradigm.

Despite the broad agreement that patients are an important aspect of decision making, there is a distinction in the extent of the individual's importance in that process. It has been noted in the discussion concerning preference-based measurements that there is a danger that a system which seeks to maximize access to limited medical resources may deny care to some people who need it most.[25] The example that was given in chapter 3 was that of the elderly who are seemingly denied care based upon their age.[26] Another danger is that the consequentialist utilitarian use of the data in its effort to find the mean score could negate the preferences of the vast majority of those who have taken the multi-attributed utility measurement. Thus the extent of how individual patients are used in the two models is quite different. The difference in the two models is that the QALY model reduces certain patients' value and can refocus its preferences if, and when, they hinder resource maximization.

Moral Basis

There is a necessary starting point for both models which overtly or covertly express a common morality which seeks to provide the dis-

---

what impacts one member of the community impacts the whole community. Other examples of communities that have moral power are law and medical schools.

24. Anne E. Streaty Wimberly, "Caring as Honoring," *Christian Reflection*: 11.

25. See chapter 3, p. 86–97 of this book.

26. See Mark Siegler, "Should Age Be a Criterion in Health Care?" *Hastings Center Report* 14: 24.

tribution of medical care in a manner that the philosophical foundations present as "best." Simply, because the ideas presented from the biblical model are religious that, in and of itself, should not disqualify them from consideration. In the discussion concerning a Common Reading of Scripture it was noted that Western culture has been positively influenced by Christianity.[27] Even though the Christian Scriptures have influenced Western culture it was noted that the Bible is not universally accepted as a basis for ethics in America.[28] Since American society, along with its secular state, does not hold to the Bible as authoritative this discussion may be adequate for religious people, but not for those who reject the biblical position. There are two responses to this issue. The first addresses the propriety of the biblical model to be presented in a secular environment. As noted in the discussion concerning secular society's response to Christianity, "It is at the heart of the biblical vision of the human situation that the believer is a witness who gives his testimony in a trial where it is contested."[29] In light of its moral and ethical impact on American culture, the influence of the broader Christian church on society and the appropriateness of the biblical vision to be contested it ought not to be a voice that is quickly dismissed. Because a secular state provides the opportunity for its citizens to address moral concerns based upon utility or cost-value, it is only appropriate that the biblical position be afforded a hearing. Though the secular state does not need to follow the biblical model that model does present moral principles that are of interest to the beneficial functioning of the state.

There can be fundamental agreement between the biblical model and secular society when it comes to what is best for the secular culture. It has been said that there are *prima facie* obligations which should be followed unless there are compelling reasons

---

27. Cf. chapter 4, p. 119 of this book. Much of Western culture is based on Christian values and it can be argued that much of the economic force of the free-market economy is derived from the Puritan's positive understanding of work and commerce. See chapter 1, Sources of capitalism's remarkable productivity," in Graig M. Gay, *Cash Values: Money and the Erosion of Meaning in Today's Society* (Grand Rapids: Eerdmans, 2003), 21–46.

28. See chapter 4, pp. 120–21 of this book.

29. Leslie Newbigin, *Foolishness to the Greeks: The Gospel and Western Culture* (Grand Rapids: Eerdmanns, 1986), 63–64.

to override those obligations.[30] Though utilitarianism frames these social obligations differently than the biblical model, because there are two different foundations in use, it is not outside of the realm of agreement that both groups desire to live a good and peaceful life. There is a compelling interest to provide appropriate health care in light of limited medical resources. Because both groups seek to be as morally good as possible, in light of the need to provide people with health care, there can be meaningful dialogue, even though they may define "good" differently. The challenge is to provide a position that is morally good for as many people as possible without violating their personal rights. Though society is not obligated to listen to the biblical position, in light of their own levels of disagreement concerning the propriety and method of allocating health care resources, it seems unwise to disallow the biblical model simply because it is religious.[31]

Economic Strategies

Both models seek to have an effect on the medical community as decisions are made concerning limited resource allocation, but the economic effect that results from each model is different. The economic application of the QALY model is the commodification of persons in order to maximize resources and save limited financial resources. The economic outcome of the biblical model is a trade-off that will infuse values into free market economics but will most likely not markedly economize limited financial resources. The effect is different because, even though they are trying to accomplish similar tasks, the similar task is that of triage. Both models seek to influence those making health care decisions regarding the limited resource in the "best" manner. In looking at their common goals, what one apprehends are the moral implications of each model.

There are moral burdens that can be contrasted. A consequentialist utilitarian method of calculation, while seeking to produce as

---

30. Tom L Beauchamp and James F. Childress, *Principles of Biomedical Ethics*, 5th ed. (Oxford: Oxford University Press, 2001), 14–15.

31. Kilner, Age-Based Rationing," in *Aging, Death, and the Quest for Immortality*, 67–69. Kilner discusses utilitarian as well as non-utilitarian options for medical distribution.

great as possible a benefit through limited resource allocation, will naturally discriminate against those who are outside the maximization point of the calculation. The neglect is seen in the mathematics of QALYs which developed out of the von Neumann-Morgenstern hypothesis.

> Consider a situation with two outcomes, either $10 or $0. Obviously, people prefer $10 to $0. Now, consider two lotteries: in lottery A, you receive $10 with 90% probability and $0 with 10% probability; in lottery B, you receive $10 with 40% probability and $0 with 60% probability. Obviously, the first lottery A is better than lottery B, thus we say that *over* the set of outcomes X = ($10, 0), the distribution p = (90%, 10%) is *preferred to* distribution q = (40%, 60%). What if the two lotteries are not over exactly the same outcomes? Well, we make them so by assigning probability 0 to those outcomes which are not listed in that lottery. For instance, lotteries p and q have different outcomes. However, letting the full set of outcomes be (0, 1, 2, 3), then the distribution implied by lottery p is (0.5, 0.3, 0.2, 0) whereas the distribution implied by lottery q is (0, 0, 0.6, 0.4). Thus our preference between lotteries with different outcomes can be restated in terms of preferences between probability distributions over the *same* set of outcomes by adjusting the set of outcomes accordingly.[32]

What the above discussion concerning lotteries means is that in von Neumann and Morgenstern's theory, preferences over lotteries logically *precede* preferences over outcomes. The implication is that one may determine before the lottery is held what outcomes the preferences should produce. The desired outcome chosen beforehand through the game preferences then becomes the controlling variable in the above theory. In a practical sense, what this utilitarian mathematics means is that when there are opposing participants in any given arrangement, lottery or "game," there are limited choices depending upon the preferred goal. If, in a zero sum game, the goal

---

32. *The von Neuman-Morgenstern Expected Utility Theory* [on-line]; accessed 10 December 2003; available from http://cepa.newschool.edu/het/essays/uncert/vnmaxioms.htm; Internet.

Comparing the Models

is the optimal point, or the maximization of the possible outcomes, then one will pick a "Mixed Strategy." This strategy functions in such a manner that it is identified as the utilitarian method in von Neumann and Morgenstern's theory because it guarantees a maximization of the outcome.[33] This outcome can be seen by envisioning a saddle with the maximization or optimum point in the center of the saddle, and that is the inflection point of the curve. The optimal point of the Mixed Strategy maximizes the outcome. Though the Mixed Strategy maximizes outcomes, one may question whether that is enough when dealing with resource allocation decisions. Economics, by itself, struggles to clearly identify how much equality or inequality there should be in a given society.[34] The Mixed Strategy may maximize the outcome, but that does not identify that outcome as a "just" outcome. It may be argued that utilitarianism is a moral stance in that it identifies the maximum point, and that moral stance comes to reality through the calculations of QALYs. It may be true that the QALY method does present a moral position based on utilitarianism, but that does not imply that it is able justly to distribute resources across the American population landscape.[35] The emphasis on maximization does, as has been presented in chapter 3, QALYs and the Elderly, sets up a paradigm in which the elderly are blamed for not being healthy enough so as not to get sick, and not being

---

33. Eric W. Weisstein, "Mixed Strategy," from *MathWorld*—A Wolfram Web Resource [on-line]; accessed 23 February 2004; available from http://mathworld.wolfram.com/MixedStrategy.html; Internet. A Mixed Strategy is defined as, "a collection of moves together with a corresponding set of weights which are followed probabilistically in the playing of a game. The minimax theorem of game theory states that every finite, zero-sum, two-person game has optimal mixed strategies." The implication is that there is a prior commitment to utilitarian maximization before the theory is employed. It does not have to occur in that manner because there is a different option, the Mixed Strategy. The Mixed Strategy produces an inclusive outcome, but not a utilitarian outcome. For the QALY model to function as it currently is designed, there must be a prior commitment to this utilitarian, Mixed Strategy.

34. Victor R. Fuchs, *Who Shall Live? Health, Economics, and Social Choice*, expanded edition, Economic Ideas Leading to the 21st Century, vol. 3 (Singapore: World Scientific), 7.

35. See chapter 3, pp. 105–11 of this book.

progressive enough to end their lives before the high cost of dying uses more than their utility of medical resources.[36]

The difficulties with the Mixed Strategy, especially the utilitarian calculations derived from it, highlight the difference between the QALY model and the biblical model. In one sense, the differences between the two models are indicative of the differences between Mixed Strategy and another theory using a different strategy which can be identified as, "Pure Strategy." The Pure Strategy model of decision making has more options than the optimal strategy point. When used in game theory, there is a decrease in maximization, but an increase in choices.[37] It increases the choices because it is not front loaded by a pre-desired utilitarian preference. The nature of the Pure Strategy allows for greater neutrality in the game, because it allows for more choices. The implications of the two strategies are observed when it is understood that, "the morality of an act is a function of the state of the system at the time it is performed."[38] "Virtue" then is determined before the strategy is employed. If the system is set up with utilitarian preferences then that is what will determine the outcome. If the system is set up with a wider probability of outcomes then maximization will decrease but options will increase, because the nature of Pure Strategy is to provide every strategy option in a given game.[39] It is the Pure Strategy, not the Mixed Strategy with its preference for utility, which would provide more health care options. Since the elderly are not set near the optimum strategy point because

---

36. Fuchs, *Who Shall Live? Health, Economics, and Social Choice*, 26–27.

37. "Strategy," *PlanetMath.Org* [on-line]; accessed 23 February 2004; available from http://planetmath.org/encyclopedia/Strategy2.html, Internet. "A pure strategy provides a complete definition for a way a player can play a game. In particular, it defines, for every possible choice a player might have to make, which option the player picks. A player's strategy space is the set of pure strategies available to that player." A model of decision making using pure strategy has more options than the optimal strategy point. When used in game theory there is a decrease in maximization, but an increase in choices which shows different values. For a beneficial analysis of Von Neuman and Morgenstern's game theory see, William Poundstone, *Prisoner's Dilemma* (New York: Doubleday, 1992).

38. *No Pure Strategy Is Stable* [on-line]; accessed 07 April 2004; available from http://www.urticator.net/essay/4/427/html; Internet.

39. "Strategy," *PlanetMath.Org* [on-line].

of the amount of money that they use at the end of life, they have a decreased chance of receiving care when the Mixed Strategy is used.

An objection could be that the von Neumann-Morgenstern hypothesis problems are known, but that its potential weakness is an "irrelevant consideration."[40] The reason that some feel that the problems of the Mixed Strategy of the von Neumann-Morgenstern axioms are irrelevant is because there is always a tension between the number of patients medically treated and the funding for that treatment. That is, in light of the calculations, X% of patients are treated when Y$ are able to be spent, as noted in the prior expanded discussion of The von Neuman-Morgenstern Expected Utility Theory in this section. When there is a prior commitment to utility then, depending upon the amount of funding, a certain fraction of patients receive medical care. The objection continues by stating that the function of the hypothesis is the patient trade-off and "not necessarily a description of the real alternatives facing policy makers."[41] One may appreciate the complexities of the philosophical nuances of the von Neumann-Morgenstern hypothesis with its Mixed Strategy option, but the hypothetical strategy option does present more than a philosophical concept: It provides a basis for the "real alternatives facing policy makers." The difficulty at this juncture seems to be that the calculations presented are set as an alternative moral guideline, and that alternative moral guideline is discriminatory against the needy elderly.

One protest against employing the Pure Strategy might be that the Pure Strategy would not produce the most profitable outcome, and one outcome would be that the medical system would have more options. In this sense, the increased number of choices would allow the needy elderly a greater opportunity to receive limited resources. Utilitarianism, on the other hand, is unable to "protect the rights of minorities, and sometimes it can even justify obvious injustices when the greater good is served."[42] QALYs follow the Mixed Strategy in

40. John McKie and others, *The Allocation of Health Care Resources: An Ethical Evaluation of the "QALY" Approach* (Brookfield, VT: Ashgate Publishing Company, 1998), 28.

41. Ibid., 29.

42. Scott B. Rae, *Moral Choices: An Introduction to Ethics*, 2nd ed. (Grand Rapids: Zondervan, 1995), 86.

seeking the optimal point in the economic saddle through preference-based measurements and HLY calculations, and with that preference the maximization of limited resources occurs at the expense of those outside the parameters of its calculations.

The second area of deficiency in QALY calculations can be noted when QALY decision making processes are compared. With a goal of maximizing one could question whether the limitations of health care through QALY calculations are worth the consequences of greater distribution. This can be summed up in the idea that, "the end justifies the means," or simply that some would rather have the consequences of a maximization of limited resources, all the while ignoring the QALY model's ageism. Simply, because the medical community can limit the care given to the greatest consumers of medical resources does not meant that it should, even if maximization of resources occurs. The economic benefits of the QALY model need to be assessed in relation to the overall outcome that they will have on the medical community and patient care. One may desire actively to work "to understand what consumers will need and expect from an interconnected health care information system."[43] This ability to deal with patients solely as consumers is tempting in that they are easily identified in a cost-benefit paradigm, but that does not mean that patients should be solely dealt with as consumers.[44] Maximization can view the medical system in purely economic terms to the exclusion and detriment of some of those that the medical system was designed to serve.

Another possible concern of the economic strategies of these models is that the QALY computation can be said directly to relate to the potential economic issues, while the biblical model seems to disregard the ugly economic realities of limited resources. When addressing economics there is the temptation to look at money as a value rather than at the results of its use as honorable or dishonor-

---

43. Markle Foundation, "Connecting for Health . . . A Public–Private Collaborative Convened by the Markle Foundation," *Connection for Health* [online]; accessed 02 March 2004; available from http://www.connectingforhealth.org/aboutus/; Internet.

44. Mark R. Wicclair, *Ethics and the Elderly* (Oxford: Oxford University Press, 1993), 85. Wicclair argues that identifying the elderly as an economic burden because of the presuppositions of elderly persons are unproductive or diseased and in poor overall health are based upon ageist assumptions.

able. The result is that saving money is seen as a greater virtue than caring for the needy.[45] Though the biblical model does not reject fiscal responsibility it does place it within a context where it ought not to limit care for the needy.

At this juncture it should be noted that the biblical model does not have an exact computational method of prioritizing patients as do QALYs. Nevertheless, while there are no calculations, there are the general principles of *agape* and justice, along with the specific principles of honoring the elderly and community that can guide medical decision makers in where to direct limited resources. The biblical model, while having the potential to be less economically beneficial, provides a basis of care for those who may not count as much within the confines of QALY calculations, such as the elderly. The biblical model may also been seen as attempting to maximize the limited medical resources through the implementation of an ethos which acknowledges the restrictions of the needy elderly who are seen as being in a significant state of transition. The principles of honor and inclusion into community can be used to provide an alternative method of guiding decisions concerning the distribution of limited medical resources. A possible application of the biblical principles can be seen in the use of hospice care. Hospice care is cost intensive and it acts in a similar way to that of a biblical community in that it uses the community to meet the health needs of the individual.[46] Hospice deals with those patients who are terminally ill, but many elderly, though existing with chronic illnesses, are not in that state of physical decline. Through the use of a multi-optional method of allocation, that provides options for care which do not deny the clinical situation but which apply the biblical principles, medical resources

---

45. Graig M. Gay, *Cash Values: Money and the Erosion of Meaning in Today's Society* (Grand Rapids: Eerdmans, 2003), 97.

46. "What Is Hospice & Palliative Care?" *National Hospice and Palliative Care Organization* [on-line]; accessed 06 April 2004; available from http://www.nhpco.org/i4a/ pages/index.cfm?pageid=3281; Internet. Hospice has long been considered to be the model for quality, compassionate care for people facing a life-limiting illness or injury. Hospice involves a team-oriented approach to expert medical care, pain management, and emotional and spiritual support expressly tailored to the patient's needs and wishes. At the center of hospice and palliative care is the belief that every human being has the right to die pain-free and with dignity.

can be used to their fullest potential. To act in their fullest potential there may be a realization that the final months of a person's life will be economically cumbersome. That burden should not override the necessity for the medical community, families as well as society in general to care for those who are in medical need.

The QALY model does relate to economic forces, but the relationship of the QALY model to economic interests through computations does not protect it against the unstable nature of the economic market. It is not uncommon for preferences, even economic preferences, which may be seen as a priority today, to be less significant tomorrow. "In a world where we rely on market forces to determine the value of things, but in which health care is curiously insulated from all efficiencies that unfettered markets allow these forces, it is difficult to develop proper metrics for deciding what any particular task or service is really worth."[47] The movement of economic forces can make preference based prioritizing fluid, and QALYs, and the results then may become unpredictable even while the method is not. QALYs could be as reliable as possible in light of the movement of economic forces, but one may desire a more stable and just basis for making allocation choices.[48]

A further objection may be that the above mentioned utilitarian dependence is what is desired in QALYs, and that some groups will have to receive less in order that others may benefit. The difficulty is that the choosing of a particular group is often discriminatory. Selection criteria based on community choice may result in maximizing economic benefits, but these benefits may be at the expense of human lives among disfavored groups.[49] The response could be that the general welfare of the community is the greatest good and that individual groups should not be allowed to stand in the way

---

47. John Lantos, "RVUs Blues: How Should Docs Get Paid," *Hastings Center Report* 33 (2003): 39.

48. McKie, *The Allocation of Health Care Resources*, 59.

49. Ibid. McKie agrees that once utilitarianism is compromised so that there is an exemption, other groups can appeal for an exemption. These may include individuals at the peak of their earning power, people of high social standing, or those who are considered to possess some cultural value such as actors, musicians and artists.

Comparing the Models

of that chosen goal.[50] This choice does produce a society that has determined its priorities, but it only presents a morality that assesses worth as it relates to benefitting the community economically and economics is not the only method of defining what is good. Even worse, it presents the possibility of a "domino effect" of increasingly reducing various groups of people to consumer commodities and denying them resources, ostensibly for the benefit of others.[51] The difficulty with this utilitarian ethic is that it is patently unjust. The objection here is not that everyone would not be treated in the same way, but rather that the method of distributing care is not just. As has been noted in chapter 4, the Bible presents the minimum principles for elder care as involvement in community and applying all that it means to "honor" them.[52] These principles include providing justice for the elderly, especially the elderly in need. The utilitarian model characterizes all elderly as sick and especially the terminally ill.[53] The utilitarian model sees youth as the stage of life that is best able to benefit society. This decision making process commodifies the elderly, and since they are reduced to that status there becomes a perceived societal freedom to treat them as commodities, rather than as human beings that have worth and value to family and society. One alternative idea sees the only reason for rationing medical care to the elderly is that of "medical futility."[54] The use of "futility" as a criterion presents its own difficulties, but it does provide an alternative to treating the elderly population as a commodity to be regulated.

The biblical model develops an altogether different ethic when it presents the principle of "honor" by defining it as care and re-

50. Ibid., 60.

51. Verhey, *Reading the Bible in the Strange World of Medicine*, 280.

52. See chapter 4, pp. 216–21 of this book.

53. The biblical model presents an equitable medical ethic where any needy individual should receive care. It does not prefer the healthy elderly over a younger patient who was in need.

54. Gregory W. Rutecki, "Rationing Medial Care to the Elderly Revisited: Futility as a Just Criterion," *Journal of Biblical Ethics in Medicine* 7:71. Rutecki argues that utilitarian rationing toward the elderly is unjust. There must be a "sole foundation" for a rationing program directed at the elderly. Rutecki sees the concept of "futility" as a viable option, even though there is the constant danger that societal pressure may be used in the future to expand what "futility" means in order to justify voluntary or involuntary euthanasia.

spect. In the Old Testament God sets forth the Decalogue which, in the Law the Fifth Commandment demands that families care for their parents, but other texts reveal that "caring as honoring" applies to non-familial elders as well.[55] The command included all aspects of care for parents, including when they are elderly.[56] In the New Testament one finds that *agape* and justice are expressed in the virtues of the Kingdom that Jesus preached, and they are expressed by Jesus' followers who creatively apply the principle of honoring the needy elderly within local community. When the biblical principles of honor and inclusion in community are used in health care allocation decisions, a different perspective toward the elderly is produced than in the QALY model. Discriminating against the elderly solely based upon age is functional as a computational model but it also seems unfair, disrespectful towards the elderly as well as foreign to the biblical paradigm of elder care although it may be acceptable by utilitarian standards.[57]

While the biblical model presents an alternative paradigm of elder care this does not necessarily imply that utilitarian morality is unacceptable to the American culture. Presupposed foundations for medical ethics exist in American culture without foundational clarity. The medical community has not escaped a cultural perception that their profession is a vocation, which includes the technological ability to fix medical problems.[58] Health care allocation decisions will have to strike a balance between the patient's moral claim on the physician and the actual ability of the physician to help the patient. One

---

55. Anne E. Streaty Wimberly, "Caring as Honoring," *Christian Reflection*: 10. Scripture calls believers to honor their elders, especially their parents (Exodus 20:12; Deut 5:16; Eph 6:1–3). Respect and care for widows, family members and all elderly are seen in other texts (Acts 6:1–6; 1 Tim 5:1–8). Older adults are seen as assets to the community, gifts of God, and witnesses of God's blessing through their presence and participation in community (Ps 92:12–15; Luke 2:36–38).

56. Gerald J. Bildstein, *Honor Thy Father and Mother: Filial Responsibility in Jewish Law and Ethics*, 38.

57. Mark Siegler, "Should Age Be a Criterion in Health Care?" *Hastings Center Report* 14:24.

58. Edmund D. Pellegrino and David C. Thomasma, *Helping and Healing: Religious Commitment in Health Care* (Washington D.C.: Georgetown University Press, 1997), 92.

thing that may assist in striking such a balance is for physicians to communicate the reality of limited medical resources. Unfortunately, without Tort law reforms this level of medical honesty may prove to be difficult. The implications of limited resources may mean that the entire community will have to revise its view of medicine and illness radically.[59]

Certain aspects of American culture furthermore regard the medical community as a business. This consumerist perspective results in a view of the medical professional, as well as medical facilities, as "morally neutral." Neutrality seems to be impossible because someone's ethics must always guide the direction of economic decisions. Determining medical allocation solely on the basis of economic motives will not free anyone from their responsibility for the moral outcomes of decisions. Maximization of resources and an increased profit are part of medicine's business but they are not amoral. Medical decisions carry moral weight by the very nature of the act of making a particular medical choice.[60] Economic strategies and their implications point to the need for a better system of allocation than profit, because consumerism in isolation does not provide a fair and just method of resource distribution.[61]

Justice

A foundational difference between the two models may be observed in how the term "justice" is applied. In the discussion in chapter 4, there is an analysis of justice as the practical expression of *agape* and as an integral aspect of bringing a sense of "Shalom" into society.[62] It was noted that, in both Testaments, justice is a feature of relation-

---

59. Verhey, *Reading the Bible in the Strange World of Medicine*, 136. Verhey challenges the community not to follow the Baconian idea that the goal of medicine is to do away with pain, but, rather the goal is to help people live full lives even though pain is a constant companion.

60. Claire Andre and Manuel Velasquez, "System Overload: Pondering the Ethics of American's Health Care System," *Issues in Ethics* 3 (1990): 3 [on-line]; accessed 04 June 2004; available from http://www.scu.edu/ethics/publications/iie/v3n3/system.html; Internet.

61. John Harris, "QALYfying the value of life," *Journal of Medical Ethics* 13 (1987): 117.

62. See chapter 4, pp. 172–76 of this book.

ships within community which include obligations. Justice was seen as a feature of broader social relationships and the structures that mediate and maintain them.[63]

The importance of "Shalom" and justice was seen in the understanding that "Shalom is restored righteousness which cannot be achieved while people "persist in their sin or evil."[64] Righteousness existed at the beginning of creation in the Garden of Eden. When humanity acted in a self-serving, sinful, manner then "Shalom" was lost. (Gen 3) God now seeks a restored relationship with humanity, and He enabled that possibility through Jesus. "Shalom" means a restored relationship, not only with God, but with the rest of humanity. For Christians to seek "Shalom" they must be reconciled with God and seek the re-establishment of "Shalom" in the societies in which they live. For this reason, the restored righteousness between God and human beings, "Shalom," is expressed in one's relationship with both God and other people.

Regarding elder care, for the Christian community seeking to bring about a sense of "Shalom" there is not only a general duty to care, but a responsibility of the entire community to care for the needy elderly. The Christian model, unlike its utilitarian counterpart, does not pressure the elderly to justify their existence if they do not die "on schedule." "Shalom" rejects the premise that the elderly are "useless eaters,"[65] or, in the current discussion, "useless consumers." The impetus is on the Christian community to serve others sacrificially as Jesus, who endured suffering, served those around him.[66]

---

63. Sonda Ely Wheeler, "Broadening Our View of Justice in Health Care," in *The Changing Face of Health Care: A Christian Appraisal of Managed Care, Resource Allocation, and Patient-Caregiver Relationships*, ed. John F. Kilner, Robert D. Orr and Judith Allen Shelly (Grand Rapids: Eerdmans, 1998), 69.

64. See chapter 4, pp. 172–74 of this book, and Philip J. Nel, "mlv," in *New International Dictionary of Old Testament Theology & Exegisis*, vol. 4, gen. ed. Willem A. VanGemeren (Grand Rapids: Zondervan, 1997), 130.

65. Charles W. Colson, "Can We Prevent the "Abolition of Man"? C. S. Lewis's Challenge to the Twenty-first Century," in *Human Dignity in the Biotech Century: A Christian Vision for Public Policy*, ed. Charles W. Colson and Nigel M. de S. Cameron (Downers Grove: InterVarsity, 2004), 15.

66. Verhey, *Reading the Bible in the Strange World of Medicine*, 335. Verhey argues that care will do more to demonstrate the hollowness of utilitarian medicine than any verbal argument.

The conclusion of that section was that *agape* and justice were basic foundational principles which guided the community in their practical expressions of Kingdom living.[67]

Some may counter that the biblical view of justice ignores the reality that age usually brings increasingly debilitation. It would be wishful thinking to believe that every family will care for their elderly. Unfortunately that requirement would place an undue burden on the young. The "caring" thing to do in order not to "burden" others, especially when technology has enabled many people to live to the point by which they have become demented or severely debilitated, is to limit medical care. It is not a crass economic computation to limit medical resources and to "allow" the elderly to die, rather then to continue to burden the community, when they are severely ill.[68]

In responding to the objection that caring for the needy elderly can become an unacceptable burden, one's view of justice is important. In the biblical model it is seen that justice takes into account the burden of those who are potentially marginalized and through *agape* applies the principle of honor towards the elderly. What the application of honor means in this case is that there is a higher duty toward the preservation of life in the biblical model that negates the obligation to die. That the needy elderly have an obligation, because of their age, to die or an obligation to forgo needed treatment for the benefit of those younger infringes on human dignity. Clearly asking the elderly to die places more of the burden for care upon the needy elderly's overtaxed shoulders.[69] The "burden" of the needy elderly, in the biblical model, is not a "burden" as if it is a task too heavy to bear, but it is seen as part of the moral duty that a society should have a desire to care for its elderly in need. Most people would not want to be neglected in their time of need. Jesus statement is not a selfish ethic, as if doing to others as one would want done to oneself is a malevolent motivation born out of selfishness. The selfless *agape* that forms the foundation of the biblical ethic prohibits selfishness. Rather, Jesus' statement is a reminder of how compassion is a common aspect of humanity, even when that compassion requires effort.

67. Wheeler, "Broadening Our View of Justice in Health Care," *The Changing Face of Health Care: A Christian Appraisal of Managed Care,* 69.
68. John Harwig, "Is There a Duty to Die?" *Hastings Center Report* 27: 35–36.
69. Ibid., 37.

In response to the idea that it is unfair to care for the needy elderly because of the magnitude of the task, the "fairness" doctrine of utilitarianism stresses the need to promote an optimal balance of "good over bad." The purpose of the QALY model is to provide a computation by which "good" and "bad" sums identify the level of the consumption of resources. In the utilitarian sense, justice denies that there is a general duty to care for minorities at the expense of the majority.[70] Justice has only the duty to distribute equally because it seeks to present a, "fair, equitable, and appropriate distribution determined by justified norms that structure the terms of social cooperation."[71] When QALY calculations use the concept of "justified norms that structure the terms of social cooperation" the risks and burdens of limited resources cause society to make "tragic choices," such as curtailing care to needy elderly based solely on their age.[72]

Utilitarian is seen as the ability to place resources where they can "do the most good."[73] The difficulty for the American medical community, which uses the QALY model, is to define what is the "most good" for their patients while not promoting ageism.[74] The ageism that is inherent in QALYs sees the needy elderly as a "problem" and, as such, they are marginalized through the conclusions of the calculations and are, in one sense, discarded in favor of the young.[75] When utilitarianism is reduced to principles of maximum freedom and presumptive equality, it is unable to generate choices other than those that would be agreeable to an enlightened and self-interested consumer.[76] A prejudice against the needy elderly necessarily results.

70. Nigel Dower, "World Poverty," in *A Companion to Ethics*, Blackwell Companions to Philosophy (Oxford: Blackwell Reference, 1991), 281.

71. Beauchamp and Childress, *Principles of Biomedical Ethics*, 226–27.

72. Ibid., 227.

73. Ibid. Goodness here is seen as the maximization of limited resources.

74. Ibid., 52. "The QALY approach therefore cannot be defended against the charge of unfairly discriminating against the aged by eliminating the relevance of age altogether."

75. Ian S. Knox, *Older People and the Church* (London: T&T Clark, 2002), 48–55. Knox presents an in-depth definition of ageism using these qualities as starting points.

76. Allen Verhey, *Remembering Jesus: Christian Community, Scripture, and the Moral Life*, 250–250. Cf. John Rawls, *A Theory of Justice* (Cambridge: Harvard University Press, 1971).

Such value judgments cannot be disassociated from QALY allocation computations.[77]

It may be questioned as to whether the average American consumer would be agreeable to the results of the QALY calculations if their utilitarian implications were revealed on the nightly news. For the QALY model to sustain its objection that caring for the needy elderly is an unacceptable burden it must demonstrate that caring for those younger will bring about the greatest happiness to society. But, living in such a culture would make the prospect of getting sick while growing old a frightening prospect, and would undermine the implementation of decisions based upon the QALY model. It is also questionable as to whether passive or active neglect of the needy elderly is culturally acceptable, even in a free market society like America.

In the biblical model, age is not seen as a problem, but as a natural stage of life. Disavowal of the specific duty to care for the elderly is not an option.[78] Biblical justice does not sideline the elderly. It has a dynamic, restorative character that seeks through the application of *agape* to establish a sense of "Shalom" in the community. That sense of "Shalom" cannot occur when the elderly in need are discriminated against because of their age. "Scripture moves beyond a concern for unbiased procedures. Restoration to community—including the benefit rights that dignified participation in community requires—is a central feature of biblical thinking about justice."[79]

Agape and Justice

How medicine can "do the most 'good'" is a utilitarian goal of the QALY model. One response to the QALY model is seen in Gene Outka's comments on the need for universal access to medical care.

---

77. Wesley J. Smith, *Culture of Death: The Assault on Medical Ethics in America* (San Francisco: Encounter Books, 2000), 126–27.

78. Anne E. Streaty Wimberly, "Caring as Honoring," *Christian Reflection*: 9.

79. Stephen Mott and Ronald J. Sider, "Economic Justice: A Biblical Paradigm," in *Toward a Just and Caring Society: Christian Responses to Poverty in America*, ed. David P. Gushee (Grand Rapids: Baker, 1999), 26. Mott and Sider argue that defining justice in a minimal, procedural way does not represent an acceptable and broad biblical concept of distributive justice where distributive justice demands some reasonable standard of material well-being for all.

While it is true that Outka argues for universal access to health care some of his ideas relate to issues regarding the prioritization of health care. Outka bases much of his position on an *apape* model. He critiques five competing models of social justice using an agapeistic method of analysis.[80]

In his analysis of the first concept, *To each according to his merit or desert,* Outka points out that this idea goes beyond effort or achievement. Justice is seen as not being "exhaustively characterized by the notion of desert."[81] Merit alone is seen as unsuitable for determining the just distribution of health care. Medical treatment in the event of illness based on agape falls under the rubric of need. *Agape* allows for egalitarian distribution and allocation of health care. In contrast Outka argues that some social inequalities cannot, in the "real world" be entirely eliminated, but that medical need remains the best method for just distribution of health care.

The second concept, *To each according to his social contribution,* states that the common good or society's interests become the basis for medical distribution. In reviewing the principle of agape Outka concurs with the Kantian fundamental of opposing the use of human beings as means or instruments to an end. *Agape,* and part of its relationship to justice, is seen as prohibiting the reduction of a person's intrinsic value in response to issues of social productivity.[82] Outka sees *agape's* relationship to justice as the optimal basis for fair access to health care.

The third concept, *To each according to his contribution,* in satisfying whatever is freely desired by others in the open marketplace of supply and demand, reveals the problems of medical consumerism and patient commodification. Outka states the obvious. When someone is in a medical crisis much of the discussion concerning

---

80. Gene Outka, "Social Justice and Equal Access to Health Care," in *On Moral Medicine: Theological Perspectives in Medical Ethics,* ed. Stephen E. Lammers and Allen Verhey, 2nd ed. (Grand Rapids: Eerdmans, 1998), 947–60. The five concepts are; To each according to his merit or desert, To each according to his social contribution, To each according to his contribution in satisfying whatever is freely desired by others in the open marketplace of supply and demand, To each according to his needs, and Similar treatment for similar cases.

81. Ibid., 949.

82. Ibid., 952.

resource distribution seems "out of place."[83] The allocation of medical care to people experiencing a medical crisis seems to be the just and loving thing to do.

In the fourth concept of social justice, *To each according to his needs*, Outka criticizes this idea of justice based on need as excessively broad. He clarifies the definition of need by confining the term to *essential* medical need. Essential needs are those needs that are "distinguishable from felt needs or wants."[84] Outka regards the application of *agape* as a method of guiding the idea of equal access even when the potential inequality is present. While the *agape* model defines medical need more narrowly than the need model it is more generous in the scope of its inclusion of potential recipients. The inclusive nature of *agape* undergirds Outka's support of equal access to health care.

Outka's final concept is, *Similar treatment for similar cases*. He sees this concept as a method of impartially setting a standard for medical access. For Outka the *receipt* of medical treatment is as important as the *distribution* of medical treatment.[85] Inequality will always exist, but that should not hinder equal access to treatment, all things being equal.

Although Outka's assertion that there should be universal access to medical care is beyond the scope of this dissertation, he makes some important points concerning health care distribution that relate to this dissertation. Outka states that *agape* is a material principle for the just distribution of medical care. Neither merit nor a broad based understanding of need provide an adequate principle for allocating medical resources. Poorly informed patients are incapable of making wise allocation decisions in most cases due to the intrinsic complexity of medical allocation. The QALY model attempts to provide accurate preference based measurements to overcome the lack of clinical and practical knowledge that most people have about medical states. A final, and important, issue that Outka addresses is that of the distribution of health care according to need. In light of the primarily utilitarian basis for the QALY model, it seems that limited medical resources would hinder the distribution of treatment according to

83. Ibid., 953.
84. Ibid., 954.
85. Ibid., 955.

need. Although the QALY model does seek to meet medical needs its method of weighing age hinders it from using need as a sufficient basis for discerning the appropriate distribution of medical resources between equal parties. Outka sees the *agape* model as a better basis medical social justice, because it is more inclusive in determining eligibility for receipt of allocated resources.

Priorities in Health Care Distribution

The biblical and QALY models seek what they perceive to be the appropriate distribution of limited medical resources. However, they differ radically in their system of determining what is appropriate, and hence in their conclusions. In chapter 2, QALYs as a Basis for Allocation, it was stated that the purpose of QALYs is to facilitate resource allocation using cost-benefit analysis, by providing a single measure of the value of any medical intervention."[86] QALYs are seen as, "a quantitative measure, in terms of years of good-quality life, of the value of a medical procedure or service to a group of patients with similar medical conditions."[87] Thus the priorities of the QALY model are bringing together economic, clinical, and patient needs and considerations in order to maximize the utilization of the medical resources available. The objective of bringing together these considerations is to derive as much benefit as possible from resources devoted to health care. However, the prioritization of economic interests over clinical and patient needs in the QALY model is pure utilitarianism.[88] Allocating health care using a utilitarian precedence

---

86. See chapter 3, p. 51–53 of this book, and "Quality Adjusted Life Years," *A Dictionary of Sociology*, ed, Gordon Marshall (Oxford: Oxford University Press, 1998). *Oxford Reference Online*, Oxford University Press [on-line]; accessed 08 August 2003: http://www. oxfordreference.com/ views/ENTRY. html?subview=Main&entry=t88. 001836; Internet.

87. "Quality-adjusted life years," *A Dictionary of Nursing* (Oxford: Oxford University Press, 2003), *Oxford Reference Online*, Oxford University Press [on-line]; accessed 08 August 2003; available from http://www.oxfordreference.com/ views/ ENTRY.html? subview=Main&entry=t62.007626; Internet.

88. "Section 6: Principles of Justice," *Continuing Education for Case Managers, Social Workers, Rehab Nurses, and Life Care Planners* [on-line]; accessed 15 April 2004; available from http://www.ceus4casemanagers.com/ET1007_Section6.html; Internet.

Comparing the Models

makes cost-benefit computations the basis for determining priority in the QALY model.

One might accuse the QALY method of worrying as much about the utilitarian computations, or the economic well-being of society as that of the patient.[89] In response, defenders of the QALY model would explain that the technique attempts to maximize the medical welfare of the greatest possible number of patients and, as such, the QALY model is just and beneficent.[90] The QALY model looks at society as a whole and through preference-based measurements produces scores which empower decision makers to assess the most cost-beneficial place to apply scarce resources.[91] The objectivity of the calculations represents a triage in which those whose QALY scores are not cost-beneficial are given lower marks. The priorities of the QALY model are set in a utility format that presents various patient and medical treatment states. In so doing, QALYs "disadvantage the already disadvantaged" as has been demonstrated in the case of the elderly.[92] Their chronology gives them a QALY score which places them in a position in which certain kinds of therapy are adjudged unlikely to be cost-beneficial and denied to them.

The biblical model presents a different priority in elder care. The biblical model presents the elderly as ends in their own right with value that is not diminished because of chronology or economic considerations. For the Christian community one of the goals of the principles of honor and community is the maintenance of interconnection and inter-mutuality of the elderly with their communities. In chapter 4 in the discussion of the Principles of Elder Care, it was noted that because human beings are made in the image of God they should not be denied care for economic reasons.[93] Rather than denying care due to scarce resources, the principles provided in the Fifth Commandment and inclusion in community affirm a priority to

---

89. Ibid.

90. Beauchamp and Childress, *Principles of Biomedical Ethics*, 266.

91. See, chapter 3, pp. 75–86 of this book.

92. Sue Chetwynd, "Priorities in Healthcare: An Ethical and Legal Framework," *Warwick & Keele Universities* [on-line]; accessed 15 April 2004; available from http:// www.le.ac.uk/sm.LWMS/resources/ethics/Priori-5.doc; Internet.

93. See, chapter 4, pp. 175–92 of this book.

care for the elderly as exhibited by numerous examples of Christians in history, including Christ Himself, and as conveyed through the concepts of fairness, justice, and *agape*. It is the foundation of *agape* that motivates the community to realize its role in elder care. In the Bible the appropriate human and Christian response to the tragedy of limited resources has always been compassion and care.[94] Regarding the current state of limited medical resources the biblical model also means that more resources will be expended for the medical community to be sensitive to the needs of the needy elderly.

The compassion that *agape* expresses does not well guarantee the cessation of pain and suffering. Neither is it sympathy that provides a benign neglect without providing caring service. It is incarnational, and accompanies the elderly throughout their lives.[95] God's perfect care is the model. "The caring posture of Jesus is an extension of the loving concern of the Father (John 3:16)."[96] As is stated in the discussion in chapter 4 on *agape*, it goes beyond beneficence which seeks to find justification for acts that contribute to the welfare of others.[97] *Agape* is seen in the character of God and in the self-sacrificial redemptive work of the Son which provides an example for the community of Faith to follow.[98] The concept of *agape* moves from the principles found in Christian Scripture to an incarnational application of *agape*.[99] The church is called to follow Jesus' example of loving care, however much personal sacrifice may be required to do so.

---

94. Verhey, *Reading the Bible in the Strange World of Medicine*, 362.

95. J. Darly Charles, "Articulating a Distinctly Christian Approach to Suffering," *The Center for Bioethics and Human Dignity*, Commentary, 10 February 2004 [on-line]; accessed 24 February 2004; available from http:// www.cbhd.com/resources/endoflife/ charles_2004-02-10_Print.htm; Internet.

96. William Hendricks, *A Theology of Aging* (Nashville: Broadman, 1986), 97–98.

97. See, Beauchamp and Childress, *Principles of Biomedical Ethics*, 166.

98. D. H. Field, "Love," in *New Dictionary of Christian Ethics & Pastoral Theology*, ed. David J. Atkinson and David H. Field (Downers Grove: InterVarsity, 1995), 9–10.

99. Clarke E. Cockran, "Health Policy and the Poverty Trap: Finding a Way Out," in *Toward a Just and Caring Society: Christian Responses to Poverty in America* (Grand Rapids: Baker, 1999), 235.

Comparing the Models

While there are some similarities between these two models, the priorities displayed in each model set a different tone for allocating limited health care resources. For the QALY model, the "philosophy of rationing by age is not only based on dollars and cents but more significantly on the equitable and empirical search for the medical "value" of dollars spent."[100] The limitation of human value to consumer based considerations disregards what it means to be a human being. If the elderly are devalued solely based on their age in QALY calculations because there is a presumption that denying them care will give a better value in return for the medical dollar spent, then personhood has been reduced to a fiduciary or economic value, and there may even be an implied duty for the elderly to die to avoid becoming such an economic burden to their younger neighbors.[101] Within the implied duty to save funding through the denial of care is the presumption that the greatest good for society is saving health care dollars through limiting medical care. One may question fiduciary discipline in light of many questionable lifestyle choices of Americans, which if stopped and the funds were redirected, would provide significant financial resources.[102] What happens in the QALY model is that issues of funding can define personal and corporate value. Money, or the lack of it, can obscure what it means for humanity to be of intrinsic value.[103]

100. Gregory W. Rutecki and John D. Geib, "Teach Us to Number Our Days: Age and the Rationing of Medical Care: Use of a Biblical Valuation of Personhood," *Journal of Biblical Ethics in Medicine* 6 (1992); 95.

101. A developed discussion of the growing pressure on the elderly to die is beyond the scope of this work. For a perspective on opposing the notion of a "duty to die" see, David Cloutier, "The Pressures to Die: Preconceiving the Shape of Christian Life in the Face of Physician-Assisted Suicide," in *Growing Old in Christ*, ed. Stanley Hauerwas and others (Grand Rapids: Eerdmans, 2003) and Wesley J. Smith, *Culture of Death: The Assault on Medical Ethics in America* (San Francisco: Encounter Books, 2000).

102. John R. Kilner, "Age-Based Rationing of Life-Sustaining Health Care," in *Aging, Death, and the Quest for Immortality*, ed., C. Ben Mitchell, Robert D. Orr, and Susan A. Salladay (Grand Rapids: Eerdmans, 2004), 62. As an example of American spending choices that are questionable Kilner notes that $3 billion is spent annually for potato chips. If cost savings is the issue then perhaps other avenues of cost reduction can be approached rather than limiting care for the elderly.

103. Graig M. Gay, *Cash Value: Money and the Erosion of Meaning in Today's*

Another problem with the QALY model's priority in health care is found in the difficulty QALYs have in dealing with people holistically. Both models would agree that the goal is to enable patients to be as healthy as possible given the reality of limited medical resources. However, the extent to which QALY calculations, including multi-attributed utility measurements are able to measure health is limited. There may also be a question as to whether limiting care to the needy elderly will actually reduce the problems associated with limited medical resources. If this is the case then the QALY model is set up with a presumption that reducing the probability of care based upon age that is suspect. The biblical model does not have the calculation issues of QALYs, but the biblical model does attempt to deal with the elderly in community to address their physical, emotional, mental and spiritual needs.

It has already been noted that the World Health Organization's definition of health is quite broad. Its holistic definition is a reminder that health encompasses more than just physical parameters.[104] An objection may be raised that the perception of health as related to preferences allows for a clearer, socially chosen identity of "health."[105] One may question who are making the choices which identify health. In the QALY model is does not seem to be the needy elderly who are making those choices. Preference choices are then limited in that they respects individual choice, but not universal choice. Preferences are insufficient as a sole basis for determining health issues, although they may have an important contribution in identifying, in part, social partiality and discrimination. Respect for a patient's health cannot be reduced to respect for certain people's perception of physical health care states as identified by their choices made when they are

---

Society (Grand Rapids: Eerdmans, 2003), 17. Gay states that, "money has become on of the most important 'measures' in the determination of 'value' in the contemporary world." As such price signals have come to determine what things are desirable, but economics is unable to determine values, such as beauty, except that it imposes value based upon potential economic benefits.

104. "WHO definition of Health," *2003 World Health Organization* [online]; accessed 02 March 2004; available from http://www.who.int/about/definition/en/; Internet. "Health is a state of complete physical, mental and social well-being and not merely the absence of disease or infirmity." This definition was adopted in 1948 and has not be amended since that time.

105. Verhey, *Reading the Bible in the Strange World of Medicine*, 76.

healthy at the expense of those whose choices would be different.[106] Health is certainly desirable, but that it entails more than physical wholeness, both models would agree. The necessity of QALYs to calculate post-treatment perceptions and to establish a benchmark for the worth of a person regardless of health state leaves its calculations in an ethically precarious position. A person who is seventy years old who has had a stroke finds that her quality of life measurements are incapable of reflecting the value of non-material factors, such as love, dignity and justice, or inclusion in the life of the family and community which may make her life of value in spite of its physical limitations. The biblical model can better address the complexities of dealing with human beings in a holistic manner than can utilitarian methods, because it acknowledges the limitations of age, but it does not assume that the elderly are burdensome or debilitated. In QALY calculations, the individual is asked preference based questions, but if an elderly person were ill he or she might still have a number of support options, such as family, or other social groups, which could enable them to live a high quality of life despite their deteriorating health. Individual choice regarding health states are made at a time when people have a perception that their health is better because of, among a variety of reasons, they are younger and therefore healthier. The biblical model seems to provide a basis for addressing health in broader terms than QALYs that include non-material factors than QALYs. Although it may be harder to measure non-material factors, and in so doing it can make the biblical model more complex, it provides the community with a more holistic approach to health. Unfortunately, this does not mean that the community always appropriately expresses itself in a manner that meets those needs, but it does mean that the principle of inclusion in community should substantially increase the QofL values which are used in QALY calculations. In this way, some of the stress regarding resource allocation would be assumed by the community, thereby reducing the problem of ageism identified in the QALY model. While this method may not address comprehensively the economic issues, it does provide a basis for ameliorating the crisis in health care resource allocation expected to occur when the "Baby Boom" generation reaches retirement age.

106. Ibid.

There may be an objection that the biblical model also has problems. There are a number of difficulties with the biblical model. It may not present as clear a guideline for the distribution of limited resources as does the QALY model. The biblical model may need as much, or more, financial commitment to accomplish its goal of caring for the elderly in need. The biblical model does make demands of the community and those demands would cause people to come into direct contact with needy elderly persons. The burden of care is diffused among the general community, but there is still a burden of caring for the needy elderly. The biblical model does not emphasize health productivity as a means of assessing value and in so doing it can become difficult to discern those who are truly in medical need from those who may not want to work hard enough to meet their own needs. Though these economic, social and allocation issues are problematic they are not ageist. The biblical model does present a more equitable context for all people needing medical care, and that is an advantage when it comes to triage because it precludes unjust discrimination.

The two models have different priorities. The utilitarian QALY model defines what is best for society in terms of cost-benefit analysis. When utility is applied to a perception of health then the sums can present a clear calculation, even if the results are problematic. The biblical model is more inclusive and attempts to define health in a more holistic manner which includes non-physical factors. When addressing allocation it does not focus on the perception of health states, but it must address the present health states of patients. If the QALY model's calculations are straightforward the biblical model's results are not as clear because it is more inclusive, and therefore potentially more expensive. Although fiscal responsibility is important in assessing the allocation of resources it need not be the determinate value concerning the directing of resources. Also, there are other areas of American culture that can be addressed, such as the amount of money spent on fast food, which if redirected could provide substantial monetary support for health care.

Age

In the biblical model there are texts that indirectly address palliative care, as well as the level of care appropriate for the elderly as their health deteriorates.[107] One may wonder what the biblical model does with the elderly if medical resources are unable to heal. When these situations occur, exceedingly challenging decisions concerning how to care properly for those who are ill may become necessary.

The following examples demonstrate that the biblical model is practical when it comes to addressing the needs of the elderly when they are sick or limited by age. They also present a truthful view of the relative benefits and liabilities of intervention in the care that the elderly could receive in their later years.

While it is easy to consider elderly Isaac only as an example of someone who was deceived by his son, Jacob, he may also be viewed as one who was taken care of appropriately. The elderly Isaac, who was blind because of age, was cared for by his wife and sons until the deceptive trick that his son Jacob played on him in order to steal his brother Esau's birthright. Isaac's family met his basic needs providing the daily activities of living.[108] The deception does not negate the point that he was cared for within the community, even though he was limited by a condition caused by age.

That the elderly were cared for in community is also seen in the life of Jacob.[109] When Jacob was old, after Joseph his son was sold into slavery, he was cared for within his family. The respect and care that his sons afforded him is seen when Judah tells the Joseph, whom they did not recognize, that Jacob, his "aged father," would die if his youngest son, Benjamin, were not returned to him.[110] The empathy that is displayed by Judah throughout his plea for Benjamin's release from potential slavery exhibits a level of compassion that is commen-

---

107. Proverbs 31:6 simply describes alcohol has a medicinal method of comforting those who are dying. 1 Kings 1:1–4 relates the story of King David receiving a new wife in his old age whose purpose was to keep him warm as his health declined. This story may raise certain objections concerning the place of women in David's Israelite, but it does point to an effort to care for the elderly King. See Frank Stagg, *The Bible Speaks on Aging*, 60.

108. Genesis 27:1–17.

109. Genesis 42–47.

110. Genesis 44:20.

surate with the biblical model of elder care.[111] After Joseph revealed himself to his family, he took great pains to care for his family, even the brothers who had arranged to have him enslaved. He particularly cared for his father Jacob in Egypt for seventeen years. Jacob was cared for by his immediate family, and by Joseph in particular, in his old age, and was afforded respect and dignity, although he was limited in his mobility and abilities.

In the New Testament there are several examples of elderly Christians receiving care. It has already been noted that the principle of honoring the elderly within the family and greater community also finds a place in the New Testament.[112] Examples given included the elderly Simeon and Anna (Luke 2:25–26, 36–37), older saints presented as people who should be applauded and exemplified by believers. They are depicted as having been treated with honor and respect within the community of Israel.[113] They are also prototypes of how the elderly are perceived in the New Testament.[114] Another example of how the elderly should be treated when they are older, ill or physically limited is seen in the events surrounding the final days of the Apostle Paul. The aged Apostle Paul wrote 2 Timothy 4:9–13 while in prison facing a death sentence. In his letter, he asks for fellowship, his cloak (which he had left at Troas), and reading material. The Apostle Paul showed an awareness of those simple things that were familiar and could improve his QofL, as he understood it, although they would hardly improve his physical health or commute his capital sentence. Timothy's intervention through the bringing of these items would have had some minor economic significance regarding procurement and travel, but the greater benefit

---

111. Genesis 44:18–34.

112. See chapter 4, pp. 176–77 of this book.

113. Richard B. Hays and Judith C. Hays, "The Christian Practice of Growing Old: The Witness of Scripture," in *Growing Old in Christ*, ed. Stanley Hauerwas and others (Grand Rapids: Eerdmans, 2003), 7. Another example of how the elderly are viewed with respect can be seen in Luke 1:5–80. There, Zechariah and Elizabeth, are described in a positive manner, including their elderly status.

114. Ibid., 9. "Respect due to older members of the community is emphasized in the Pastoral Epistles."

would have presumably been to make the Apostle Paul's remaining life more enjoyable.

Some may counter that caring is not the primary purpose of the QALY model; instead, economic considerations dominate its agenda. The inability of QALYs to look beyond the economic and utility ventures of the QofL and HLYs calculations is a weakness, because it removes care from consideration as an important element in just health care resource allocation decisions. Although decisions regarding allocation may seek in some way to provide adequate medical care it seems to seek to benefit the medical system itself rather than the community it is designed to serve in its decisions. It is difficult to call the QALY model's maximization virtuous if it shifts its focus from serving patients' needs which are the primary focus of health care allocation. The QALY model's method of decision making is counterproductive to generating a compassionate and just health care system. But, if the goal of health care allocation is to take limited resources and distribute them in the "best" way, then developing a priority of care, which includes the community's taking responsibility for the needy elderly in their midst, provides a basis for the use of the biblical model as a corrective agent against the ageism in the QALY model.

The Limitations of the Elderly

The reason why the treatment of the elderly has become the focal point of this discussion is because they, among the many patient populations who are assessed for treatment, receive QALY scores that are lower based on their age regardless of health. The elderly also need the most care and consume the most medical resources.[115] As has been noted, both models acknowledge the limited physical status of the elderly.[116]

In the discussion concerning HLYs in chapter 3, it was noted that the very nature of being elderly places a patient at a disadvan-

115. Victor R. Fuchs, *Who Shall Live? Health, Economics and Social Choice*, Economic Ideas Leading to the 21st Century—vol. 3, Expanded edition (Singapore: World Scientific, 1998), 215. Fuchs states that one-fourth to one-third of a person's lifetime total medical costs for care will typically be spent during the last years of life.

116. See chapter 3, pp. 101–11 and chapter 4, 127–35 of this book.

tage.[117] Certainly, it is true that the elderly usually have fewer healthy years left to live and a potential for increased medical liability than their younger counterparts. A decreased QALY score is simply a reflection of the natural processes of life. The method of computation used in QALYs has already been discussed and the potential ageism found in its computations is not the issue at this juncture. Rather, it is that the elderly have limitations that influence their ability to function and also increase the amount of medical care that they may need during their declining years.

The acknowledgment that the elderly have decreased function has not escaped the biblical writers. If the discussion of the QALY model has revealed that the elderly use a lion's share of medical resources and dollars during their declining years, the biblical model also realistically acknowledges the limitations of the elderly. In the biblical model the discussion of the Leviticus 19:32 text, along with Jesus' comments concerning the Corban problem, describe the limitations of the elderly. This acknowledgment goes beyond simply stating that deference is due to the elderly. Scripture includes stories of older people who are suffering the common maladies associated with aging. The history of the Christian community also demonstrates an awareness of the physical and social needs of the elderly that produced social services that extended beyond mere sympathy.[118]

Both the QALY model and the biblical model attempt to deal with the elderly with the knowledge that they are in a limited state. QALY calculations try to be objective through the use of preference based assessments, acknowledging the reality of the physical limitations of the elderly through its definitions of QofL and its use of HLYs. The Bible also presents the situation of the elderly objectively without attempting to minimize their potential limitations. Instead, it readily acknowledges that the limitations of the elderly are aspects of humanity that have the potential to take up other people's time, energy and resources.[119]

The issue is not whether there is complete agreement as to the limitations of the elderly, but it is the *extent* to which age plays a factor in deciding whether an individual should receive care or not.

117. See chapter 3, pp. 101–11 of this book.
118. See chapter 4, pp. 191–92 of this book.
119. See chapter 4, pp. 146–50 of this book.

The biblical model does acknowledge that age brings limitations and debilitations which may be important aspects of medical assessment, but the biblical model is also interested in confronting the reasons offered for denying care.[120] John Kilner understands the nuances involved in using old age as an aspect of health care rationing, but correctly notes the impropriety of using age solely as a determinate aspect of the allocation calculation when he states, "age criterion *per se* is unjustified, though age may play a carefully defined role in medical assessment relevant to patient selection."[121] The limitations of the elderly can place their age in a position to be *part* of the computation concerning the distribution of limited health care resources if that particular *part* necessarily involves their health state, e.g., certain chemotherapy regimens and surgical procedures are relatively contraindicated in the elderly whose diminished pulmonary, renal and/or cardiac capacities may be unable to tolerate them. The agreement is on the involvement and limitations of age; the disagreement surrounds how the elderly should be valued in the allocation of limited health care resources.[122]

Conclusion

Other areas of agreement and conflict between these two models could have been addressed in this chapter. For instance, both models have a somewhat arbitrary nature in that they seek an objective manner of dealing with health care distribution, but rely on methods that are inherently fluid.[123] This chapter could have dealt with the issue that each model demonstrates a striking preference for a particular

---

120. Paul D. Simmons, *Birth and Death: Bioethical Decision-Making* (Philadelphia: Westminster Press, 1983), 53.

121. John F. Kilner, "The Ethical Legitimacy of Excluding the Elderly When Medical Resources are Limited," in *On Moral Medicine: Theological Perspectives in Medical Ethics*, 2nd ed., Stephen E. Lammers and Allen Verhey, ed. (Grand Rapids: Eerdmans, 1998), 980.

122. Sondra Ely Wheeler, "Broadening Our View of Justice in Health Care," in *The Changing Face of Health Care: A Christian Appraisal of Managed Care, Resource Allocation, and Patient-Caregiver Relationships*, ed. John F. Kilner, Robert D. Orr and Judith Allen Shelly (Grand Rapids: Eerdmans,1998), 72.

123. Cf. chapter 3, pp. 86–97 of this book.

age group.[124] Both models demonstrate a propensity to risk the lives and livelihood of selected patients under certain circumstances. The partiality towards the young in the QALY model and toward the needy elderly in the biblical model demonstrates intentions that could redirect limited resources. Instead, this chapter has sought to identify areas of harmony and disparity in these two systems. In so doing, their differing ethical perspectives, and the consequences of employing them, have been examined.

An area of analysis was the philosophical foundations of the two models. A close similarity was found between the QALY model and teleology. While the biblical model is closely associated with deontology, it was noted that the biblical had a different focus which based its view of humanity on the *imago dei* doctrine. That provided a context where the importance of the individual was seen as a consequence of creation itself rather than any functionality. The ethical conclusion of the QALY model sees the "best" way to care for patients is the provision of a utilitarian value judgment that enables excluding those who would use up more than their perceived common share of medical resources. The increase in benefit is towards those who are young and healthy, but that maximization comes at the expense of excluding care for needy elderly, and in so doing turns being old into a medical liability rather than having a medical illness as a medical liability. The ethical conclusion of the biblical model sees the "best" way to care for patients as the provision of a value judgment that sought to use limited resources in such a way that those who were in the greatest need were included in medical allocation. The distinction found in the two models concerning excluding and including also influenced how they dealt with economic issues.

In the discussion concerning economic issues, an effort was made to contrast how each model sought to identify what was the "best" manner of guiding decisions concerning the distribution of limited health care resources in light of current economic priorities. It was demonstrated that the *Mixed Strategy* of the *Von Neuman and Morgenstern Game Theory* front loads the calculation to be utilitarian. Following a purely utilitarian economic model turns QofL decisions into an economic analysis of the cost-benefit of elderly patients' lives. In that paradigm, the elderly were seen consistently to earn a lower

---

124. Cf. chapter 3, pp. 101–11, and chapter 4, pp. 135–60 of this book.

QALY score than younger people. QALY calculations were seen to be at risk of minimizing health care allocations to some people in order to maximize benefits to favored others.[125]

The biblical model presented an allocation strategy based upon principles of honor and inclusion into community, which are expressions of "Shalom" and the coming Kingdom of God. The biblical model was found to be different from the QALY model in that it offered a more holistic paradigm for dealing with the elderly. In the biblical model, economic decisions would have to be formulated on factors beyond merely the latest economic formulae. The goal of the biblical model was not necessarily to "fix" the patient, as if the elderly were machines to be repaired and not serviced again until their next scheduled date. The holistic nature of the biblical model calls for medical care that includes the family and other members of the society, not just medical professionals. The biblical model's foundation for care goes beyond determining the maximum benefit or happiness afforded to society by its decisions, as compared to utilitarianism. The agape and justice of the biblical model is not dependent upon societal preferences, as if determining medical allocation was based solely upon consumer popularity. From the biblical perspective, a decision that holistic elder care is too costly, time consuming, or distasteful is unjust, and it reveals a selfish narcissism that violates the heart and soul of God's will for humanity to experience "Shalom."[126]

When the economic conclusions are examined the ethical outcomes of the two models are again in contrast. When the Von Neuman and Morganstern game theory is guided by a desire for utilitarian maximization, then those who do not fit into the computational mean will tend to get a lower score. The purpose of the QALY model is to identify those who are outside of the normal scoring range and flag them as being potentially problematic. The passing over of patients identified as abnormal is discriminatory when the basis for the exclusion is a normal stage of life. Advocates of the QALY method argue that it is fair because the discrimination is based upon computations that include people of all ages in the service population.

125. Verhey, *Reading the Bible in the Strange World of Medicine*, 280.

126. Wheeler, "Broadening Our View of Justice in Health Care," in *The Changing Face of Health Care: A Christian Appraisal of Managed Care*, 69.

The basic priorities of the two models are seen to be quite different. The biblical model seeks "Shalom" through family and community involvement in solving the problems associated with limited health care resources. In so doing it seeks to include the needy elderly in innovative and holistic methods of caring. The QALY model seeks to exclude the elderly primarily because of their age state. Being elderly is seen in the QALY model as economically burdensome. When elderly patients are seen as of inherent value, medical necessity rather than economic desirability can become the deciding factor in continued care. Old age is seen as a normal state of life, and as such the limitations of the elderly are to be part of the computation concerning the propriety of their care, but not a primary aspect of the medical decision.

Chapter Six

Conclusion and Applications

THE PRIMARY purpose of this book was to investigate the impact or application of the biblical principles of community and honor on the ageism found in the QALY model. Secondary to this objective was the comparison of two patterns of elder care based upon either biblical principles or utilitarian presuppositions. This chapter will bring many of the summary conclusions of this dissertation together in a discussion of the effects of the application of the biblical model on the issue of ageism intrinsic in the QALY model.

Review of Conclusions

At the onset of this book, it was noted that the development of the American health care industry has produced some unique problems. Technological developments have curbed diseases and increased the life span of the average American. Unfortunately, along with an increase in the benefits of medical technology, a change in how medicine is perceived has developed. The American medical system moved from a more altruistic focus, that saw medicine primarily as a vocation, to a profit based industry, as discussed in chapter 2, Allocation's Modern Development.[1] As noted in chapter 2, the emerging financial market surrounding health care practices promoted business moves that made fiscal sense.[2] The medical community attempted to promote an organization that was able to make responsible eco-

1. See chapter 2, pp. 21–24 of this book.
2. See chapter 2, pp. 24–25 of this book.

nomic decisions The continued rise in medical costs coupled with the organizational development of health care associations resulted in new needs. Medical administrators came to play an increasing role in making healthcare decisions.[3] The purpose of the rise of healthcare managers is seen in their task. They were, and continue to be, tasked with the responsibility to hold down costs. Healthcare managers became responsible for allocating resources in directions that they, or those to whom they were accountable, decided were appropriate for the accomplishment of the company's mission. What made their decisions to allocate resources more complex was that medical and economic resources were limited. Thus, there was not only the issue of maximization, but also the problem of insufficient resources to offer optimal medical care to everyone.

Through the years, the medical industry has made incredible advances, but as early as the 1960's it was noted that resources could not keep up with consumer demand. The tension generated by resource limitation has continued to plague medicine to the present day. Resource limitation is particularly problematic as one reviews the demographics concerning the elderly, who continue to use up most of the available medical resources. At the current rate of longevity, it is projected that, "By the year 2050, one in five Americans will be 65 or older."[4] Thus, barring nearly miraculous medical breakthroughs in the treatment of degenerative diseases, the tension of resource limitation along with the desire for increased profit makes the portent of a better future with more available medical resources exceedingly improbable.

It was further noted that the limited medical resources included human resource shortages in medical staffing. Already, there are shortages of physicians in specialty fields, as well as of nurses, and of other ancillary medical workers. Not only are limited staff resources a problem, but various attempts at controlling the costs of health care have proven to be inadequate for such a herculean task as the fair and equitable distribution of limited medical resources. HMOs, the Clinton Health Care Reform Initiative, the Oregon Plan, Medicare

3. Beth Witrongen McLeod, "Relationship—Centered Care," *Noetic Sciences Review* 48 (1999): 36.

4. Hillary Rodham Clinton, ""Commonsense" reform for health care," *The Courier-Journal*, 25 April 2004, sec. D.

and the VA medical system were considered as representative programs that tried to control the spiraling costs of health care, all with, at best, limited success.[5]

Directing Funds

As the increased recognition of the need for guidance in resource allocation became apparent, the QALY model was developed. QALYs were introduced to help those who made the decisions concerning where the limited medical resources should be directed. It was noted in chapter 2 that, as the QALY model became a basis for allocation health care, economists attempted to find a computational model that could assist in prioritizing health care needs. QALY calculations were seen as a means of comparing cost effectiveness, cost benefit, and the risks involved in a given medical procedure.[6] Because QALYs focus primarily on economic issues, they have been considered by some to be fair and therefore desirable, as was noted in chapter 3.[7] Those who adhere to this position acknowledge the utilitarian basis for QALYs, but feel that having this particular utilitarian basis for the QALY model is preferable to other more subjective options in the struggle to prioritize health care needs in light of resource limitations because it limits the issue of allocation to that of cost-benefit analysis.[8]

As well documented as the economic and prioritizing benefits of the QALY model are, the ability of QALYs to help determine health care allocation has not eliminated ethically problematic issues.[9] Some of the problems of the QALY model that have been identified are its over-simplification of complex healthcare issues, an inability to show the variables in quality of life, and the question of whose values are

---

5. See chapter 2, 42–56 of this book.

6. See chapter 2, pp. 57–59 of this book, and Joshua Cohen, "Preferences, Need and QALYs," *Journal of Medical Ethics* 22 (1996): 267–72.

7. See chapter 3, pp. 63–64 of this book.

8. Victor R. Fuchs, *Who Shall Live? Health, Economics, and Social Choice*, expanded edition, *Economic Ideas Leading to the 21st Century*, vol. 3, ed. Lawrence R. Klein and Vincent Su (Singapore: World Scientific, 1998), 164.

9. See chapter 3, pp. 86–96 of this book.

to be used in determining the QALY.[10] In 1992, these problems in QALYs were being discussed in addition to charges of discrimination against certain populations.[11] The type of discrimination that became the focus of concern did not address who would receive limited resources based on medical need, but rather upon the dynamics which resulted from QALY's computations. An overt ageism was found to be the result of QofL and HLYs computation.[12]

Within the computational model of QALYs, it was noted that the particular utilitarian foundation of QofL and HLYs sought to provide the most economically efficient sum for those who are tasked to decide where limited resources are to be directed. The problem was that, in the effort to obtain an economically efficient model through QofL and HLY computations, the care of the needy came to be regarded as less important than the maximization of resources and profit. Thus, the QofL and HLY computations of the QALY model resulted in discrimination against the elderly.

A Different Focus

In contrast to the QALY model's ageism, the biblical model was shown to have a more inclusive perspective on elder care. In light of the biblical admonitions concerning the elderly found in the Fifth Commandment, Leviticus 19:32, Mark 7:1–13, 1 Tim 5:8, and James 1:27, and, the importance of community relationships the biblical model revealed a charge, a duty to care for the needy elderly in their old age, even when caring for the elderly might not be economically efficient or physically convenient.[13] The ethics of care found in Scripture goes beyond what is the most economically efficient treatment and focuses on holistic elder care. The biblical model does not count a universal quality such as age as a liability, but as a reminder that those who are limited by age are dependent

---

10. Mo Malek, "Implementing QALYs," *Hayward Medical Communications* (March 2001) vol. 2, no. 1 [on-line]; accessed 02 August 2002; available from http://www.evidence-based-medicine.co.uk; Internet.

11. Ann Michele Holmes, "Uses and Abuses of QALY Analysis" (Ph.D. diss., University of British Columbia, 1992).

12. See chapter 3, pp. 105–12 of this book.

13. See chapter 4, 172–75 of this book.

upon the community for sustenance, dignity and relationship. In the biblical model, limited funds and resources should be directed to those people that promote medical care, personal dignity and an honored place in society. The biblical model presents a foundational system in which allocation is based upon more than mere economic indicators.[14]

Justice

Another area where the biblical model can enlighten the QALY model is in the area of justice. Whether it is in an effort to obey the biblical Law or to re-establish "Shalom," when biblical justice is applied to the needy elderly they are not regarded as excessively burdensome because of their age.

Justice begins by recognizing that we are a community, members one of another, and where it demands, at a minimum, that an account be given, that a justification be offered, to the ones from whom we should be sundered, where it points to the simple fact that to reject such people is to reject part of ourselves.[15]

To consider the elderly excessively burdensome based upon their chronology, as in QALY calculations, fails adequately to address what it means to provide sufficient care to patients in need, and minimizes what it means to be a member of a community that has significant medical resources, even if those resources are limited. For Christians it violates the principles of the Kingdom of God that Jesus gave to His followers.

The biblical model's discussion of "honor" is based upon the principles of agape and justice. To honor the needy elderly goes beyond the economics of consumerism by establishing the significance of distributive justice in a health care system, as noted in the discussion in chapter 5.[16] The biblical model provides a context for social responsibility in which the community embraces accepted relationships, obligations and duties that exist between institutions and people.[17] Not only is it questionable whether it would be culturally, or

14. See chapter 4, p. 191–92 of this book.
15. Allen Verhey, Reading the Bible in the Strange World of Medicine, 357.
16. See chapter 5, pp. 224–39 of this book.
17. Donald P. Robin and R. Eric Reidenback, *Business Ethics: Where Profits Meet Value Systems* (Englewood, NJ: Prentice Hall, 1989), 39.

perhaps better, politically popular, but this denial of treatment to the elderly violates another aspect of biblical justice. In Deuteronomy 25:13–16, the Israelites are warned not to charge different rates for comparable goods. Shifting the health care burden from the young to the old is an injustice in today's health care system that violates the principles of Deuteronomy 25:13–16, placing an undue burden on the elderly by potentially limiting their care because it values them less than other patients with the same medical conditions. The objection to treating the elderly in an unjust manner is important to the Christian community because, as Stone and Day point out, "it violates the Golden Rule (Luke 6:31, 'Do unto others as you would have them do to you.'). No one in their right mind would want to be treated this way."[18] Another problem with the unjust distribution of resources is that it places an unfair financial burden on the needy elderly. Discussion of the financial burden of medicine is beyond the scope of this dissertation, but it can be agreed that when inequity occurs, those who are financially able are capable of receiving medical care regardless of allocation schedules.[19] The conclusion here is that the injustice of varied treatment and provision of health care toward the elderly is unacceptable in the biblical model, and ethically objectionable in all but the most utilitarian ethical systems.

Christianity not only calls for people to be just, but also to love their neighbors. "At its core, justice provides order to human relationships by laying out reciprocal sets of rights and duties for those living in the context of community."[20] The medical community is full of human interaction and it is therefore a place where real concern for justice ought to be present. One might object to this being a religious perspective, but society in general should be concerned with just distribution of resources and should not be hesitant to address the issue because it is raised by Christians. By calculation, the QALY model causes the needy elderly to take more of a burden upon

---

18. John E. Stone and Jackson H. Day, "Double Punch," *Christian Social Action* 17 (2004): 14.

19. Ibid., 13–14. Though Stone and Day are focusing on uninsured patients, the principles of justice also can be applied in a discussion of different levels of medical distribution for the elderly.

20. Alexander Hill, *Just Business: Christian Ethics for the Marketplace* (Downers Grove: InterVarsity, 1997), 34.

themselves than those younger. The biblical model rejects this indiscriminate discrimination based upon maximization and presents a more balanced approach.[21] The biblical model approach does not by necessity shift funds away from the elderly population who may have a diminished QofL because it is seen as unjust, as negligence of the society's basic duty towards those with whom community is shared. "If institutions of health care have a social character and if Christians hold to the view that the common good is the focus of public action, then justice in the distribution of health care means distribution primarily according to the need for health care."[22]

Commodification

Caring for the needy elderly as a social responsibility is in stark contrast to perceiving health care as a market commodity, a basic problem in the use of QALYs. The computational models of QALYs not only reveal a problem with overemphasizing health care as a market commodity, but they also run into difficulty when they have to deal with the variables involved in individual medical cases. The difficulty lies in the inflexibility of the QALY model when it comes to how people perceive QofL after a decline in health, and not in its ability to provide a prioritization of health care states. Its inflexibility stems from how multi-attributed utility instruments are employed in its calculations. As discussed in chapter 3, Defining Denominators, QofL is defined through multi-attributed utility instruments which ask people to identify health state preferences before health events occur. Although the definition of QofL is arbitrary in that it depends upon the preconceived notions or "value judgments" of what a "good" life is in each state of life, there clearly are benefits to the use of multi-attributed utility instruments.[23] It is certainly important to know how people feel about illness and disability and what their concerns are regarding future health states. However, it is disingenuous to assume that a prior preference will continue unaltered

21. Ibid.

22. Clarke E. Cockhran, "Health Policy and the Poverty Trap: Finding a Way Out," in *Toward a Just and Caring Society*, ed. David P. Gushee (Grand Rapids: Baker, 1999), 237.

23. Wesley Smith, *Culture of Death: The Assault on Medical Ethics in America* (San Francisco: Encounter Books, 2000), 27.

when a real event occurs. One may state, for instance, that life as a COPD patient might be an unfavorable condition.[24] However, that does not in and of itself deal with all of the variables involved in the disease process. Instead, it only deals with the perception of what one's desires are concerning a given health state before the health state occurs. The definition of QofL lacks a developed ethic of care, although it may fit readily into a commodification model of medical care. The health care due to those who become sick in their later years involves more than simple issues of technological resource distribution, and care is best considered as much more inclusive than the generally uninformed preferences that might be articulated when one is healthy. Care means that benevolence is extended to those in need, such as the elderly, even as their health status deteriorates. QofL preferences confuse health with the complete absence of pain, suffering discomfort or difficulty. Of course, if the goal of health care is solely the elimination of pain, suffering, discomfort or difficulty, then an individual's preference prior to a compromised health state might be appropriate.

There are two serious problems with this method of preferring prior perceived health states. The first is that it is narcissistic and the second is that it relies too heavily on autonomy. The problem of narcissism is found in the egoism inherent in identifying preconceived health states. Egoism posits that each individual "pursues her own interest as she conceives of it."[25] That pursuit then becomes, by necessity, beneficial to the rest of society. The problem with this pursuit is that conflict arises when there is a limitation of needed resources, such as in American medical care. When one person expresses a preference concerning a particular health state, it presupposes that the person's prior decision will be acknowledge and followed. But, as noted when discussing the problems with multi-attributed utility instruments in chapter 3, Defining Denominators, the effort to maximize resources through an utilitarian foundation means that most preferences will

---

24. COPD, Chronic Obstructive Pulmonary Disease, is a lung condition typically resulting from emphysema or asthma, that limits the flow of air through the airways.

25. Kurt Baier, "Egoism," *A Companion to Ethics*, Blackwell Companions to Philosophy (Oxford: Blackwell Reference, 1991), 200.

not be followed.[26] Rather, those whose preferences are closest to the mean will benefit more than those who are on the outer edges of the preference curve generated by the group taking the multi-attributed utility instrument.

The second problem with preferences is that of autonomy. Autonomy focuses too narrowly on a person as independent and rationally controlling. In the preference regarding QofL calculation, it is questionable whether those taking the test can be as objective as necessary to make the calculations beneficial. What it does is produce the preferences of those who are in particular health states, usually good health states. This overemphasis on autonomy neglects the complexities of human emotions when contemplating health issues, ignoring the issue of communal life, reciprocity, and the variable maturity of those surveyed.[27] While QofL calculations seem quite sterile, they do not lend themselves to an adequate treatment of the variables involved in individual medical cases, especially as health states develop.

The biblical model is inclusive in its ethic of care. One might object that the biblical model does not make good business sense. One's response probably depends upon what one means by "good business." If by "good business" one means the maximization of financial profits for shareholders even to the exclusion of caring for the elderly according to a predetermined mathematical health care computation, then the objection is sustained. If however, by "good business" one means mutual respect and an acceptance of fiscal responsibility as members of a connected community, then maximization does not produce "good business." One reason why is that it presents a dual morality, in which those who are young benefit from medical care but the elderly, because of their age, do not enjoy the benefits of the same opportunities for care. Thus, the principle of justice is undercut because financial gain takes precedence over the duty to care for the elderly. "The Christian model of justice is not so easily and unilaterally ignored. Reposed in the character of God, it demands that basic rights—dignity and free will being primary—not be ignored. It provides a moral trump care that supersedes common

26. See chapter 3, pp. 76–82 of this book.

27. Tom L. Beauchamp and James F. Childress, *Principles of Biomedical Ethics*, 5th ed. (New York: Oxford University Press, 2001), 60.

business practices."[28] Instead of a computational model that seems to be unjust, or at least unfair although economically sound, the Christian Scriptures present biblical love as the basis of elder care, as was noted in chapter 4, Principles in Elder Care.[29]

Moral Medicine

Agape, as presented in the biblical model of elder care undergirds most Scriptural principles pertaining to how the elderly are to be treated, thereby revealing how fundamental the Christian view of God's love to the biblical model truly is. As stated in chapter 4, Principles in Elder Care, God's *agape* is seen as unconditional, and that love is to become incarnational through the acts of the Christian community.[30] Incarnational acts are those acts that bring about the reality of Christ in society, and in so doing help to bring about "Shalom" and the Kingdom of God. The social expression of the gospel means that in the biblical model of elder care, the elderly cannot be marginalized in order to provide more resources for others, because it would violate the principle of *agape*.[31]

The contrast with the QALYs model is not only with the QofL denominator. HLYs represent a computation that discriminates against the elderly because their age becomes a direct factor in their ability to receive care when placed in the priority scale generated by QALYs. So rather than following the Golden Rule, "Do unto others as you would have them do unto you," HLYs sets up a "dog-eat-dog environment where authentic caring for others is inappropriate. All business players are expected to watch their own backs."[32] If the needy elderly have enough money to pay for needed services, then they have that option. However, in the QALY model, love is set aside as unsuitable, or regarded as "pie-in-the-sky" thinking. Instead, the utility of the computation makes age a deficit. Age, a factor that people cannot change, part of their physiological nature, becomes perceived as a

28. Hill, *Just Business*, 65.
29. See chapter 4, p. 161–68 of this book.
30. Ibid.
31. Masamba ma Mpolo, *The Church and the Aging in a Changing World* (Geneva: Office of Family Education World Council of Churches, 1982), 1–2.
32. Hill, *Just Business*, 65.

Conclusion and Applications

hardship to themselves and to society in general. HLY calculations assume that the elderly will become ill by a predetermined age, and that their survival past that predetermined age will excessively tax the economic system. If the issue is solely economic maximization then, once again, the utilitarian model takes precedence. Yet one must question whether the maximization of resources at the expense of the elderly is the morally right thing for the American medical system to do. The purpose of QALY calculations is to assist in the maximization of limited medical resources, but it seems that the sheer economic implications of the QALY model become intolerable since it is unable to permit the medical community's role as productive, socially responsible elements of society.[33] This is because it is unable to focus on people and instead focuses on utility. Nevertheless, utility does not provide a measurement for intrinsic value, but instead provides a measurement of cost-benefit, reducing social responsibility and societal happiness to an economic incentive.[34] U. S. Supreme Court Justice, Louis Brandeis stated, regarding the social purpose of business that, "In the field of business, so rich in opportunity for the exercise of man's finest and most varied mental faculties and moral qualities, mere money-making cannot be regarded as the legitimate end."[35] Brandeis' comments can be understood in the light of the free market's influence upon America's medical system, which among other things, is a business. As Justice Brandais stated, profit alone is not a legitimate end for a moral business.

Medicine has a natural or expected end. The traditional goals of medicine have been to restore the sick patient to health, (aiming to cure), to alleviate the patient's distressing symptoms (when health cannot be restored—aiming to comfort, to offer palliative care), and to promote health, (to prevent illness). These goals support the overall ends of the doctor-patient healing-caring relationship.[36] Yet it

33. Robin and Reidenback, *Business Ethics: Where Profits Meet Value Systems*, 40.

34. Gay, *Cash Values*, 83–84.

35. Hill, *Just Business*, 69.

36. Theresa Iglesias, "Medicine's Intrinsic Good," Commentary 09 September 2003, *The Center for Bioethics and Human Dignity* [on-line]; accessed 24 October 2003, available from http://www.cbhd.org/resources/bioethics/iglesias_2003-09-09_print.htm; Internet.

seems that when one looks at the foundations involved in the QALY calculations these goals and ends fade to be replaced by principles of utility. Those principles, as has been shown in chapter 3, QALYs and the Elderly, are ageist.[37] The promotion of utility and maximization does not directly promote health, and undermines the doctor-patient healing-caring relationship in that it places the physician's loyalties potentially at odds with the patient's health needs.

Medicine is not a morally-neutral activity.[38] It is not value free. Rather, any act involving the completion of a health care goal, be it based on a biblical or a QALY model, has moral aspects. The question is which values best support the overall goals and aims of medicine. Although the QALY model may effectively accomplish a utilitarian goal, utilitarianism is not the only medical allocation model that the medical system has discussed. Though these alternative models are not the focus of this discussion it does seem that utilitarianism reaches its goal at the expense of medicine's intrinsic goodness. The choice comes down to what type of values, be they based upon secular ideas or biblical norms, should be practiced in the American medical community to produce the best results with the fewest problems.

It seems, then, that if the commitment of medicine is to the cost-containment of needy elderly, or whatever other group may consume a disproportionate amount of resources, these selected groups will be at continual risk of having their medical care limited or even terminated. From a utilitarian perspective, they have become the cost-containment problem. If, however, the elderly, and similar needy populations, are part of the interconnected community wherein *agape* and justice form the basis for their place of "honor," as the biblical model presents, then a utility-based model is unacceptable and it must re-evaluate its suspect motives no matter how much its calculations may maximize resources. "While economics can help us to make choices more rationally and to use resources more efficiently, it cannot provide the ethics and the value judgments that must guide our decisions. In particular, economics cannot tell

37. See chapter 3, pp. 105–11 of this book.

38. Theresa Iglesias, "Medicine's Intrinsic Good," *The Center for Bioethics and Human Dignity* [on-line].

us how much equality or inequality we should have in our society."[39] The QALY model cannot adequately guide the moral choices for resource allocation because it lacks the ability to deal with patients holistically or the elderly justly.

Application

Given that the biblical model has shown that it provides a better moral basis with which to allocate health care, then the biblical model is able to make sense out of the conflicting demands in health care allocation. These demands include the conflict between the goal of obtaining maximal profit and that of optimally caring for patients. In the discussion in chapter 2, trends were revealed which showed that the profit motive in health care coupled with a desire for fiscal responsibility and limited resources placed increasing pressure on the American medical system to cut services.[40] The problem is not the allocation of limited resources, per se, but how allocation decisions will be made and in what way the available resources will distributed. In chapter 3 QALYs were seen as a way in which resources could be prioritized according to QofL and HLYs computations.[41] The QALY calculations are based upon a utilitarianism that seeks the maximization of limited resources. Unfortunately, the objectivity that QALYs sought through their calculations were identified as ageist. This ageism, along with a bent towards the maximization of profit, was identified as a motive in health care which set up an ethical conflict between the elderly, elder care providers and consumers. It set at odds the virtuous efforts to use limited resources in the best manner without limiting the medical care given to those who are in medical need, including the elderly.

Responding to Ethical Issues

As stated in chapter 2, Allocation's Modern Development, the increasing commercial focus of medicine was seen in the emergence of

39. Victor R. Fuchs, *Who Shall Live? Health, Economics, and Social Choice*, expanded edition, *Economic Ideas Leading to the 21ˢᵗ Century*, vol. 3, ed. Lawrence R. Klein and Vincent Su (Singapore: World Scientific, 1998), 7.
40. See chapter 2, pp. 24–42 of this book.
41. See chapter 3, pp. 75–86 of this book.

investor owned hospital companies in the 1970's which were, "more oriented toward economic performance."[42] A loss of profit became an undesirable issue for the hospitals, physicians, and stockholders. Physicians and the stockholders may have had different motivations for being involved in medicine, but they both had a vested interest in hospitals' economic solvency. Although physicians might have been concerned for the needs of their patients and their own economic security, the privately owned hospital ultimately had to be obligated to its stockholders. Thus medical decisions have come to be increasingly concerned with basic economic issues. Although in the QALY model a loss of profit is unwelcome and its utilitarian emphasis limits its breath of medical coverage these are used in an attempt to provide the best guidance for resource allocation decision in light of its calculations.

In the discussion concerning the biblical model in chapter 4, Honor, Respect and Old Age, though a similar desire to guide resource allocation decisions to their best end is in view it is accomplished with a different ethic regarding the elderly.[43] It can be noted that nowhere in the Old Testament is growing old itself described as a problem. Nowhere are elders described as pitiable, irrelevant, "behind the curve," inactive, or unproductive. The New Testament offers an alternative vision in contrast to which the contemporary, popular Western view of aging as a "problem" appears puzzling and unhealthy.[44] The biblical model of elder care presents the needy elderly in a position where care for them is preferential. This is in sharp contrast to QALY's calculations that put the elderly at a disadvantage because of their age. The Bible clearly imposes the duty to care for the needy elderly on the healthy young and on the community as a whole. This care goes beyond simple affirmation. It requires that "the community should provide assistance" to the elderly, whether

---

42. Cf. 21–23, and Bradford H. Gray, *The Profit Motive and Patient Care: The Changing Accountability of Doctors and Hospitals* (Cambridge: Harvard University Press, 1991), 6.

43. See chapter 4, pp. 175–91 of this book.

44. Richard B. Hays and Judith C. Hays, "The Christian Practice of Growing Old: The Witness of Scripture," in *Growing Old in Christ*, ed. Stanley Hauerwas and others (Grand Rapids: Eerdmans, 2003), 11.

widows or simply those who have had the benefit of chronology.[45] The emphasis in Scripture that the family, community and society in general are jointly responsible for the care of the elderly is one of the reasons why those who do not provide for their older family members are harshly condemned in the Bible.[46] Thus, a contrast is seen between an emphasis on economics which is a natural aspect of health care allocation in the QALY model and an emphasis on care, as a broadly applicable principle for the needy elderly in the biblical model.

The ageism found in QALYs was identified as part of the philosophy of the calculations. Since the elderly consume a disproportionate number of resources, an effort to maximize utilization of scarce resources would mean that the elderly would need to limit their consumption of medical resources. Therefore in the current system of health care allocation the elderly have been made to carry a greater burden than those younger, even if their health states were comparable.

The biblical principles of honor and inclusion in community were found to be in disagreement with the emphasis that the elderly, as a whole, should be marked for limitation of medical care. Society has come to view "growing old not as a part of the human condition but as a solvable problem."[47] Of course, the problem is that, barring an event which causes premature death, everyone eventually grows old and dies. Old age is a normal part of humanity's fallen condition, and as such, use of age as a determinant of resource allocation is problematic in QALY calculations. It is not a "solvable condition" in the sense that society can cure it or make it go away, i.e., society cannot "cure" old age without redefining what it means to "cure" someone. In the biblical model, since elderly people are seen as unique, and blessed by God, they are afforded honor, with all that it implies, and are included in the community. The biblical model finds agreement with Hippocratic medicine which sees medicine's primary

---

45. Ibid., 9.

46. Staggs, *The Bible Speaks on Aging*, 185. Also see, Isa 58:7; Matt 25:35–36; I Tim 5:8; James 1:27.

47. Carole Bailey Stoneking, "Modernitiy: The Social Construction of Aging," in *Growing Old In Christ*, Stanley Hauerwas and others (Grand Rapids: Eerdmans, 2003), 70.

purpose as serving humanity rather than seeking the maximization of limited resources at the expense of a particular group of humanity.[48] The biblical model seeks to acknowledge the complexities of caring for the elderly. Acknowledging the complexities of a world in which limited medical resources exist does not provide a license to violate the biblical principles which believers are obligated to follow. Through the effort of following what the biblical principles present as the appropriate responsibility of families, communities and society to care for the elderly, an ethic is presented which is more flexible than the QALY model in addressing the various ethical challenges involved in health care. These challenges extend beyond that of caring for chronic diseases, as if disease treatment were the sum total of growing old. Rather, the challenge to care expands to walking with the elderly so as to help them flourish in their declining years.

Minimum Biblical Standards

In the QALY model, one finds that the desire to maximize resources has a tendency to identify the elderly as a group that consumes a disproportionate share of medical resources. In the biblical model, the needy elderly are seen as a group that should be preferred even though they can, at times, require a greater expenditure of medical resources, human and economic, than other age groups. What the biblical model does is provide a minimum standard for treating the elderly. In the principles of honor and inclusion into community, the elderly are placed within a context where they can receive needed medical care. As stated in chapter 4, the Christian community has an inherent responsibility to care for the elderly, because the elderly population's involvement in community is seen in a covenant context.[49] Therefore, Christians are bound by their relationship with God to care for the elderly within community. For this reason, in chapter 4 emphasized that, in the Bible, people are not seen as autonomous beings, but rather individuals who are bound to a community. As such, members of the community have responsibilities as

---

48. C. Ben Mitchell, "Ethical Challenges," in *Cutting-Edge Bioethics: A Christian Explaration of Technologies and Trends*, John F. Kilner and others (Grand Rapids: Eerdmans, 2002), 192.

49. See chapter 4, pp. 175–91 of this book.

well as rights. One of those responsibilities is to care for the elderly. That care, which is part of honoring the elderly, means that the "least of these" are cared for even though they may require more medical resources.[50] The Christian community does not have the option of neglecting to care, even with limited medical resources, for the needy elderly. Loving their neighbors, including the needy elderly, is part of their sociological, cultural, and communal mandate.[51]

It has been noted in chapter 4 that the question raised in this work is whether age is a fair criterion for negating the requirement for equality.[52] In the Bible, justice is more than giving people their due. Justice is characterized by broad social relationships and structures that mediate and regulate those relationships.[53] Biblical distributive justice requires Christians to respond to others in and through community. To decide that elder care is too costly is unjust because it violates the biblical principles of association, of "honor," and of community. Biblical justice goes beyond the ability to choose preferences. The biblical model provides a context in which the value of the elderly is not only identified by their economic contributions, but by their status as respected members of society.

Identifying Ageist Trends

Since the Bible provides a better moral basis with which to address allocation in health care, unfair utilitarian trends can be identified and the public can be warned about policies which are identified as ageist. When the elderly are honored and included in community

50. Matthew 25:40. In this text, Jesus provides a parable concerning the Final Judgment. In his approving remarks, Jesus commends the righteous for caring for those who were undeserving or who could not care for themselves. He mentions those hungry, thirsty, strangers, those without clothes, the sick and imprisoned. This parable provides a contrast to the QALY model which would limit the elderly who, when in need, can easily be seen as fitting into at least one of these categorizes, from receiving needed medical care because of their age.

51. William L. Hendericks, *A Theology of Aging* (Nashville: Broadman, 1986), 84.

52. See chapter 4, pp. 192–95 of this book.

53. Sonda Ely Wheeler, "Broadening Our View of Justice in Health Care," in *The Changing Face of Health Care: A Christian Appraisal of Managed Care, Resource Allocation, and Patient-Caregiver Relationships*, ed. John F. Kilner and others (Grand Rapids: Eerdmans, 1998), 69.

then a context will be provided whereby ageist trends can be identified and minimized. The identification of such trends can make the public aware of potential dangers that certain policies present to ageing people's ability to receive needed medical care.

Some ageist trends are already identifiable in the American medical culture. Since the elderly population is expected to rise dramatically with the ageing of the Baby-Boomer generation, some are targeting the elderly as the cause of an impending health care financial crisis. The number of elderly will provide opportunities for the American culture to change, but it seems unfair to place on their shoulders the entire blame for societal difficulties, such as limited health care resources. The argument that the limitation of care to a particular group of people will solve the problems of resource allocation is fallacious and ethically problematic. One could conjecture that if the elderly were not identified as the "problem," then QALYs could be adjusted so that another group could be so identified. This type of "profiling" is dangerous in that it inspires a continual blaming of various groups for societal difficulties instead of specifically addressing the problems themselves. An example of this is seen in health care. Identifying the elderly as potentially exorbitant consumers does not seem to be an appropriate way of correcting the difficulties in health care allocation. This perspective is likely to result in a continual shift where during one crisis the needy elderly are identified as the "problem," and then another crisis will ensue causing a different population to be identified as the problem.

The impact of the biblical principles of honor and community on the ageism found in QALYs is that it shifts the problem from being one of pure economics to a more holistic computation. As it has been discussed in chapter 4, some economists believe that adjusting the utilitarian base of QALYs would, in effect, nullify its benefit; however, an adjustment could also provide a higher view of human beings as well as provide a basis for caring for the needy elderly.[54]

Lack of support from families and communities, in part, contributes to the rising costs of health care among the elderly.[55] One of

54. See chapter 4, pp. 195–97 of this book.

55 Martha Sullivan and others, "Stepping Out on Faith: Geriatric Mental Health in 2015," *The Future of Aging in New York State* [on-line]; accessed 24 May 2004; available from http://aging.state.ny.us/explore/project2015/artmentalhealth.htm; Internet.

the ways in which some health care costs can be addressed is through the promotion of a public policy which rewards families and communities which support the elderly. It is obvious that this suggestion would mean that there needs to be a reversal in the trend that the elderly are to live in separation and isolation from the rest of society.

Other undesirable trends that can be identified through the biblical model are the tendency to isolate and exclude the elderly based upon reasons other than age. The elderly are susceptible to discrimination based upon their race, gender or increased susceptibility to disease.[56] Susceptibility does not assure an older person of a disease. It simply is an indicator of the likelihood of developing age-related disabilities. One may also question whether there will be an increasingly hostile attitude toward the elderly because of the perception that they are no longer useful to society because they have lived "too long." The danger for a society that relies on a utilitarian calculation is that it comes to view people as of value based upon a pre-conceived or preferred state of health or livelihood. This type of segregation is unfair and unjust towards the elderly and future generations in that it sets up a paradigm in which there will be a perceived duty for the elderly to deny themselves resources and end their lives, e.g., through voluntary euthanasia. While more discussion concerning the implications of the elderly having a duty to the young to stop using resources that are perceived to be valuable would be helpful, this must await further research.

Honor and Inclusion in Community

In the comparison between the two models it has been noted that the biblical model provides an alternative moral basis with which to make health care allocation decisions. It is believed that as these principles are applied, the needy elderly will receive a greater measure of respect within the medical system, as well as in society in general. The elderly will not be viewed as a "problem" to be solved, but as individuals of inherent worth and valued members of society. The church has a social responsibility that includes efforts that enable just care of needy elderly.

---

56. Tom Kirkwood and others, *Healthcare and Ageing Population Panels*, 8–9.

In this work QofL, has been identified as the result of preference-based outcome measurements which rely on *a priori* preferences. It would be quite remarkable if enjoying livelihood was based only on youthful personal preferences. Unfortunately, these preferences weigh heavily against the elderly because of ageist presuppositions. The definition of a good QofL seems to be much broader than youthful preferences, encompassing metaphysical realities and relationships which make even compromised health states acceptable conditions in which to live and, perhaps even flourish. The biblical model sees the *agape* relationships that should exist within community as part of the holistic understanding of what QofL means.[57] This connection between doctrine and praxis is why a biblical ethic is better than one based upon the maximization of resources.

Respect for the elderly as valued members of society will only occur when the widespread prejudice against growing old is confronted. As the elderly continue to exceed the projected number of years of healthy life and live beyond eighty in positive health states, QALY calculations will become even more colored by ageism. As long as age is a primary criterion for the QALY, it will not be able to provide a just system of allocation.

The QALY model will need continuous adjustment if it is going to remain a helpful guideline for those who must decide where scarce medical resources are directed. As has been noted in chapter 5, in the discussion on Foundations, there are some who believe that a lack of a utilitarian base for QALYs would render them useless.[58] Although it would definitely change the calculation results, QALYs could still provide some measure of guidance for those allocating resources. What is needed as QALYs are adjusted is a foundation that is morally beneficial to all age groups. The biblical model provides such a foundation through the principles of honor and inclusion in community. It provides a minimum of care for the elderly by including them in familial and communal relationships while they are healthy and during times of compromised health states.

---

57. Karl Barth, *Church Dogmatics: The Doctrine of the Word of God*, 2nd ed., vol. 1, part 1, trans. G. W. Bromiley, ed. G. W. Bromiley and T. F. Torrance (Edinburgh: T&T Clark, 1975), 50.

58. See chapter 5, pp. 202–11 of this book.

Conclusion and Applications

In the current discussion, it has been noted that the impact of the biblical principles of honor and community on the ageism found in the QALY model can be significant if those using the QALY model shift its focus away from the utilitarian basis of maximizing resources, as well as profit. If utility and profit continue to be the dominant characteristic of the QALY model then the impact of the biblical principles will be minimal. Those who adhere to biblical principles will need to function outside of the system. It will be necessary to develop familial and communal relationships which shore-up what the medical system lacks.

Whether there will be significant legislation, cultural awareness or a philosophical shift before the system collapses under its escalating demands is unknown. The future presents an opportunity to distribute medical care as health states dictate, or it presents an opportunity to continue the distribution of medical resources as youthful preferences and predetermined mortality statistics. Providing medical resource for the all people, including the needy elderly, in light of their current health state, is the morally superior position.

Bibliography

Books

AARP. *Beyond 50, A Report to the Nation on Trends in Health Security*. Washington DC: AARP, 2002.

Abbott, T. K. *The Epistles to the Ephesians and to the Colossians*, The International Critical commentary on the Holy Scriptures of the Old and New Testaments. Edited by Samuel Rolles Drivers, Alfred Plummer, and Charles Augustus Briggs. Edinburgh: T. & T. Clark, 1979.

Allis, Oswald T. *God Spake By Moses, An Exposition of the Pentateuch*. Phillipsburg, NJ: Presbyterian and Reformed Publishing Company, 1951.

Arras, John and Robert Hunt eds. *Ethical Issues in Modern Medicine*. 2nd ed. Palo Alto, CA: Mayfield Publishing Company, 1983.

Barclay, William. *The Gospel of Mark*, Rev. ed. Philadelphia: The Westminster Press, 1975.

Barth, Karl. *Church Dogmatics: The Doctrine of the Word of God*. 2nd ed. Vol. 1. Part 1. Translated by G. W. Bromiley. Edited by G. W. Bromiley and T. F. Torrance. Edinburgh: T&T Clark, 1975.

Barth, Markus. *Ephesians: Translation and Commentary on Chapters 4–6*, The Anchor Bible. Edited by William F. Albright and David N. Freedman. Garden City, NY: Doubleday & Company, 1960.

Bayertz, Kurt, ed. *The Sanctity of Life and Human Dignity*. Norwell, MA: Kluwer Academic Publishers, 1996.

Beachamp, Tom L., and James F. Childress. *Principles of Biomedical Ethics*. 5th ed. New York: Oxford University Press, 2001.

Betz, Hans Dieter. *The Sermon on the Mount: A Commentary on the Sermon on the Mount, including the Sermon on the Plain (Matthew 5:3–7:27 and Luke 6:20–49)*, Hermeneia—A Critical and Historical Commentary on the Bible. Minneapolis: Fortress, 1995.

Bildstein, Gerald J. *Honor Thy Father and Mother: Filial Responsibility in Jewish Law and Ethics*. New York: KTAV Publishing House, 1976.

Block, Daniel I. *Judges, Ruth*, The New American Comentary. Vol. 6. Edited by E. Ray Clendenen. Nashville: Broadman & Holman Publishers, 1999.

Boskey, James B., Susan C. Hughes, Robert H. Manley and Donald H. Wimmer, *Teaching About Aging: Religion and Advocacy Perspectives.* Washington, DC: University Press of America, 1982.

Brunner, Emil *Justice and the Social Order.* Translated by Mary Hottinger. New York: Harper and Brothers, 1945; reprint, Cambridge: Lutterworth Press, 2003.

Buttrick, George Arthur, ed. *The Interpreter's Bible.* Vol. X. Nashville: Abingdon Press, 1992.

Callahan, James. *The Clarity of Scripture.* Grand Rapids: InterVarsity, 2001.

Calvin, John. *Institutes of the Christian Religion.* Translated by Henry Beveridge. Vol. one. Grand Rapids: Eerdmans, 1953.

_____. *Commentaries on the Epistles of Paul to the Galatians and Ephesians.* Translated by William Pringle. Grand Rapids: Baker, 1996.

Carson, D. A. "Matthew," *The Expositor's Bible Commentary with the New International Version of the Holy Bible.* Vol. 8. Grand Rapids: Zondervan, 1984.

Carson, D. A. and John Woodbridge, eds. *Scripture and Truth.* Grand Rapids: Baker,1992.

Childs, Brevard S. *The Book of Exodus; A Critical, Theological Commentary.* Louisville: The Westminster Press, 1974.

Coast, Joanna, Jenny Donovan, and Stephen Frankel, ed. *Priority Setting: The Health Care Debate.* New York: Wiley, 1996.

Cook, David. *The Moral Maze: A Way of Exploring Christian Ethics.* London: Spck, 1983.

_____. *Living in the Kingdom: The Ethics of Jesus.* London: Hodder & Stoughton, 1992.

Cooper, Rodney L. *Mark,* Holman New Testament Commentary. Nashville: Holman Reference, 2000.

Daniels, Norman. *Am I My Parents' Keeper?* New York: Oxford University Press, 1988.

Davies, W. D. and Dale C. Allison Jr. *A Critical and Exegetical Commentary on The Gospel According to Saint Matthew.* Vol. III. Edinburgh: T&T Clark, 1997.

Department of Health and Human Services, Centers for Disease Control and Prevention, and National Center for Health Statistics. *Chartbook on Trends in the Health of Americans, Excerpted from Health, United States, 2002.* Hyattsville, MD: Department of Health and Human Services, 2002.

Dunn, James D. G. *The Parting of the Ways: Between Christianity and Judaism and their Significance for the Character of Christianity.* Philadelphia: Trinity Press International, 1991.

_____. *The Acts of the Apostles.* Valley Forge, PA: Trinity Press International, 1996.

Durham, John. *Exodus,* Word Biblical Commentary. Vol. 3. General editors David A. Hubbard and Glenn W. Barker. Waco: Word, 1987.

Eenigenburg, Elton M. *Biblical Foundations and a Method for Doing Christian Ethics.* New York: University of America Press, 1994.

Bibliography

Elwell, Walter. *Evangelical Commentary on the Bible.* Grand Rapids: Baker, 1989.
Fernando, Ajith *Acts*, The NIV Application Commentary. Grand Rapids: Zondervan, 1998.
Fletcher, Joseph. *Morals and Medicine.* Boston: Beacon, 1954.
Forell, George Wolfgang. *History of Christian Ethics.* Vol. 1. Minneapolis, Augsburg Publishing House, 1979.
Fretheim, Terence E. *Exodus*, Interpretation: A Bible Commentary for Teaching and Preaching. Louisville: John Knox Press, 1991.
Friedan, Betty. *Fountain of Age.* New York: Touchstone Books, 1993.
Fuchs, Victor R. *Who Shall Live? Health, Economics, and Social Choice.* Expanded edition. Economic Ideas Leading to the 21st Century. Vol. 3. Edited by Lawrence R. Klein and Vincent Su. Singapore: World Scientific, 1998.
Fuller, Daniel. *Gospel and Law: Contrast or Continuum?* Grand Rapids: Eerdmans, 1980.
Gay, Graig M. *Cash Values: Money and the Erosion of Meaning in Today's Society.* Grand Rapids: Eerdmans, 2003.
Garrett, James Leo. *Systematic Theology: Biblical, Historical, and Evangelical.* Vol. 2. Grand Rapids: Eerdmans, 1995.
Geisler, Norman L. *Christian Ethics: Options and Issues.* Grand Rapids: Baker, 1989.
Gerstenberger, Erhard S. *Leviticus: A Commentary.* Louisville: Westminster John Knox Press, 1996.
Gray, Bradford H., ed. *For-Profit Enterprise in Health Care.* Washington, DC: National Academy Press, 1986.
_____. *The Profit Motive and Patient Care: The Changing Accountability of Doctors and Hospitals.* Cambridge: Harvard University Press, 1991.
Gushee, David and Glen Stassen. *Kingdom Ethics: Following Jesus in Contemporary Context.* Downers Grove: InterVarsity, 2003.
Haenchen, Ernst. *The Acts of the Apostles: A Commentary.* Philadelphia: The Westminster Press, 1971.
Hagner, Donald A. *Matthew 1–13*, Word Biblical Commentary, vol. 33A. Dallas: Word, 1993.
_____. *Matthew 14–28*, Word Biblical Commentary. Vol. 33B. Dallas: Word, 1995.
Hall, Mark A. *Making Medical Spending Decisions: The Law, Ethics, and Economics of Rationing Mechanisms.* Oxford: Oxford University Press, 1997.
Harris, J. Gordon. *Biblical Perspectives on Aging: God and the Elderly.* Philadelphia: Fortress, 1987.
Hartley, John E. *Leviticus*, Word Biblical Commentary. Vol. 4. Dallas: Word, 1992.
Hauerwas, Stanley. *Vision and Virtue.* Notre Dame: Fides, 1974.
_____. *A Community of Character: Toward a Constructive Christian Social Ethic.* Notre Dame: University of Notre Dame Press, 1981.
Hays, Richard B. *The Moral Vision of the New Testament: A Contemporary Introduction to New Testament Ethics.* San Francisco: Harper Collins, 1996.

Hendricks, William L. *A Theology of Aging.* Nashville: Broadman, 1986.
Hiebert, Paul G. *Anthropological Insights for Missionaries.* Grand Rapids: Baker, 1985.
Hightower, James Jr. *Caring for People from Birth to Death.* Binghamton, NY: The Haworth Pastoral Press, 1999.
Hill, Alexander. *Just Business: Christian Ethics for the Marketplace.* Downers Grove: InterVarsity, 1997.
Hill, Michael. *The How and Why of Love: An Introduction to Evangelical Ethics.* Kingsford, Australia: Matthias Media, 2002.
Hobbs, Herschel H. *The Baptist Faith and Message* Nashville: Convention Press, 1971.
Hoekema, Anthony A. *Created in God's Image.* Grand Rapids: Eerdmans, 1986.
Hollinger, Dennis P. *Choosing the Good: Christian Ethics in a Complex World.* Grand Rapids: Baker, 2002.
Hopkins, Charles Howard. *The Rise of the Social Gospel in American Protestantism, 1865–1915.* New Haven: Yale University Press, 1940; reprint, Brooklyn, NY: AMS Press, 1967.
Horsely, Richard A. *Hearing the Whole Story: The Politics of Plot in Mark's Gospel.* Louisville: Westminster John Knox, 2001.
Houtman, Cornelis. *Exodus,* Historical Commentary on the Old Testament. Vol. 3. Ch. 20–40. Translated by Sierd Woudstra. Leuven, Belgium: Peeters, Bondgenotenlaan, 2000.
Hunter, David J. *Desperately Seeking Solutions: Rationing Health Care.* Reading, MA: Addison-Wesley, 1998.
Jacob, Benno. *The Second Book of the Bible: Exodus.* Translated by Walter Jacob. Hoboken. NJ: KTAV Publishing House, Inc., 1992.
Johnson, Luke Timothy. *The Acts of the Apostles*, Sacra Pagina Series, vol. 5. Edited by Daniel J. Harrington. Collegeville, MN: The Litergical Press, 1992.
Kaiser, Walter C. Jr. *Toward Old Testament Ethics.* Grand Rapids: Zondervan, 1983.
_____. *Leviticus,* The New Interpreter's Bible, vol 1. Nashville: Abingdon, 1994.
Kant, Immanuel. *Foundations of the Metaphysics of Morals and What is Enlightenment?* Translated by Lewis White Beck. New York: The Liberal Arts Press, 1959.
_____. *Grounding for the Metaphysics of Morals: with On a Supposed Right to Lie Because of Philanthropic Concerns.* Indianapolis, IN: Hackett Publishing Company, 1993.
Kilner, John F. *Who Lives? Who Dies? Ethical Criteria in Patient Selection.* New Haven: Yale University Press, 1990.
_____. *Life on the Line: Ethics, Aging, Ending Patient's Lives, and Allocating Vital Resources.* Bannockburn, IL: Center for Bioethics and Human Dignity, 1992.

Bibliography

Kilner, John F., Robert D. Orr, and Judith Allen Shelly. *The Changing Face of Health Care: A Christian Appraisal of Managed Care, Resource Allocation, and Patient-Caregiver Relationships.* Grand Rapids: Eerdmans, 1998.

Kirkwood, Tom and others. *Healthcare and Ageing Population Panels.* Joint Taskforce on Older People. London: Department of Trade and Industry, 2000.

Knox, Ian S. *Older People and the Church.* London: T & T Clark Ltd., 2002.

Kramer, Mary K. *Faith and Justice.* Chicago: Loyola University Press, 1982.

Ladd, George Eldon. *A Theology of the New Testament.* Rev. ed. Grand Rapids: Eerdemans, 1974.

LaSor, William Sanford, David Allan Hubbard and Fredric William Bush, eds. *Old Testament Survey: The Message, Form, and Background of the Old Testament.* 2nd ed. Grand Rapids: Eerdmans, 1996.

Lammers, Stephen E., and Allen Verhey, eds. *On Moral Medicine.* 2nd ed. Grand Rapids: William B. Eerdmans Publishing Company, 1987.

Lane, William L. *Hebrews 9–13*, Word Biblical Commentary, vol. 47. Dallas: Word, 1991.

Lea, Thomas D. *The New Testament: Its Background and Message.* Nashville: Broadman & Holman, 1996.

Ludemann, Gerd. *Early Christianity according to the Traditions in Acts: A Commentary*, Translated by John Bowden. Minneapolis: Fortress, 1989.

May, William F. *The Physician's Covenant: Images of the Healer in Medical Ethics.* 2nd ed. Louisville, KY: Westminster John Knox, 2000.

MacArthur, John. *Acts 1–12*, The MacArthur New Testament Commentary. Chicago: Moody, 1994.

Marshall, Christopher D. *Beyond Retribution: A New Testament Vision for Justice, Crime, and Punishment.* Grand Rapids: Eerdmans, 2001.

Mathews, Shailer. *The Social Teaching of Jesus: An Essay in Christian Sociology.* New York: Macmillan, 1910.

McCarter, P. Kyle Jr. *II Samuel: A New Translation with Introduction, Notes and Commentary*, The Anchor Bible. Edited by William Albright and David Freedman. Garden City, NY: Doubleday & Company, 1984.

McKie, John, Peter Singer, and Helga Kuhse. *The Allocation of Health Care Resources: An Ethical Evaluation of the 'QALY' Approach.* Hampshire, UK: Dartmouth Publishing Company, 1998.

Menzies, Allen. *The Earliest Gospel: A Historical Study of the Gospel According to Mark.* London: MacMillan and Company, Limited, 1901.

Merrill, Eugene H. *Deuteronomy.* The New American Commentary: An Exegetical and Theological Exposition of the Holy Scripture, NIV Text. Nashville: Broadman & Holman, 1994.

Milgrom, Jacob. *Leviticus 17–22; A New Translation with Introduction and Commentary.* The Anchor Bible. New York: Doubleday, 2000.

Moltmann, Jurgen. *Man: Christian Anthropology in the Conflict of the Present.* Translated by John Sturdy. Philadelphia: Fortress, 1974.

Mooney, G. *Economics, Medicine and Health Care.* London: Harvest Wheatsheaf, 1992.

Morris, Leon. *New Testament Theology*. Grand Rapids: Zondervan, 1990.
Mott, Stephen Charles. *Biblical Ethics and Social Change*. New York: Oxford University Press, 1982.
Mowsesian, Richard. *Golden Goals, Rusted Realities, Work and Aging in America*. Far Hills, NJ: New Horizon, 1986.
Mpolo, Masamba ma. *The Church and the Aging in a Changing World*. Geneva: Office of Family Education World Council of Churches, 1982.
Murray, John. *The Covenant of Grace: A Biblico-Theological Perspective*. London: Tyndale House, 1953.
_____. *Principles of Conduct: Aspects of Biblical Ethics*. Grand Rapids: Eerdmans, 1957; reprint Grand Rapids: Eerdmans, 1999.
Niebuhr, H. Richard. *Christ and Culture*. New York: Harper & Row, 1951.
Newbigin, Leslie. *Foolishness to the Greeks: The Gospel and Western Culture*. Grand Rapids: Eerdmanns, 1986.
Nolland, John. *Luke 1–9:20*, Word Biblical Commentary. Vol. 35a. Dallas: Word, 1989.
Noordtzij, A. *Leviticus*, Bible Students Commentary. Translated by Raymond Togtman. Grand Rapids: Zondervan, 1982.
Nord, Eric. *Cost-Value Analysis in Health Care: Making Sense Out of QALYs*. Cambridge: Cambridge University Press, 1999.
Noth, Martin. *Leviticus; A Commentary*. Rev. ed. Philadelphia: The Westminster Press, 1965.
Oakes, Charles G. *Working the Gray Zone: A Call for Proactive Ministry by and with Older Adults*. Franklin, TN: Providence House, 2000.
O'Donovan, Oliver. *Common Objects of Love: Moral Reflection and the Shaping of Community*. Grand Rapids: Eerdmans, 2002.
Pellegrino, Edmund D., and David C. Thomasma. *A Philosophical Basis of Medical Practice: Toward A philosophy and Ethic of the Healing Professions*. Oxford: Oxford University, 1981.
_____. *Helping and Healing: Religious Commitment in Health Care*. Washington, D.C.: Georgetown University, 1997.
Pipher, Mary. *Another Country: Navigating the Emotional Terrain of our Elders*. New York: Riverhead, 1999.
Polhill, John. *Acts*, The New American Commentary. Vol. 26. Nashville: Broadman, 1992.
Poundstone, William. *Prisoner's Dilemma*. New York: Doubleday, 1992.
Pohl, Christine D. *Making Room: Recovering Hospitality as a Christian Tradition*. Grand Rapids: Eerdmans, 1999.
Powell, J. Enoch. *The Evolution of the Gospel*. New Haven: Yale University, 1994.
Rapoport, John, Robert L. Robertson and Bruce Stuart, *Understanding Health Economics*. Rockville, MD: Aspen Publication, 1982.
Rae, Scott B. *Moral Choices: An Introduction to Ethics*. 2nd ed. Grand Rapids: Zondervan, 1995.
Rauschenbusch, Walter. *Christianity and the Social Crisis*. New York: Macmillan, 1907.

Rawls, John. *A Theory of Justice.* Oxford: Oxford University Press, 1972.
Robertson, A. T. *Word Pictures in the New Testament.* Concise edition. Edited by James A. Swanson. Nashville: Holman Reference, 2000.
Robin, Donald P. and R. Eric Reidenback. *Business Ethics: Where Profits Meet Value Systems.* Englewood, NJ: Prentice Hall, 1989.
Rosner, Brian. *Paul, Scripture and Ethics: A Study of 1 Corinthians 5–7.* Biblical Studies Library. Grand Rapids: Baker, 1999.
Rosner, Fred. *Medicine in the Mishneh Torah of Maimonides.* New York: KTAV Publishing House, 1984.
Schenck, Kenneth. *Jesus is Lord: An Introduction to the New Testament.* Marion, IN: Trinity Publishing, 2002.
Schloen, J. David. *The House of the Father as Fact and Symbol: Patrimonialism in Ugart and the Ancient Near East.* Winona Lake, IN: Eisenbrauns, 2001.
Seitz, Christopher R. *Isaiah 1–39,* Interpretation: A Bible Commentary for Teaching and Preaching. Edited by James Luther Mays. Louisville: John Knox, 1989.
Sellers, James. *Theological Ethics.* New York: Macmillian, 1966.
Shelp, Earl, ed. *Justice and Health Care.* Dordrecht, Holland: Reidel, 1981.
Silva, Moises. *Biblical Words and their Meaning: An Introduction to Lexical Semantics.* Rev. and Expanded edition. Grand Rapids: Zondervan, 1994.
Simmons, Paul. *Birth and Death: Bioethical Decision-Making.* Philadelphia: The Westminster Press, 1983.
Singer, Peter. *Practical Ethics,* 2nd ed. NY: Cambridge University, 1993.
_____. *Rethinking Life and Death* New York: St. Martin's Press, 1994.
Smith, Wesley J. *Culture of Death: The Assault on Medical Ethics in America.* San Francisco: Encounter Books, 2000.
Stagg, Frank. *The Bible Speaks on Aging.* Nashville, TN: Broadman, 1981.
Stassen, Glen H. & David P. Gushee, *Kingdom Ethics: Following Jesus in Contemporary Context.* Downers Grove: InterVarsity, 2003.
Stein, Robert H. *Playing By the Rules: A Basic Guide to Interpreting the Bible.* Grand Rapids: Baker, 1994.
Tasker, R. V. G. *John,* Tyndale, New Testament Commentaries. Grand Rapids: Eerdmans, 1960.
Temkin, Owsei, William K. Frankena, and Sanford H. Kadish. *Respect for Life in Medicine, Philosophy, and the Law.* Baltimore: The Johns Hopkins University Press, 1976.
Tournier, Paul. *Learn to Grow Old.* Louisville: Westminster/John Knox Press, 1972.
Ubel, Peter A. *Pricing Life: Why It's Time for Health Care Rationing.* Cambridge, MA: MIT Press, 1999.
Vanhoozer, Kevin J. *Is there a Meaning in this Text?: the Bible, the Reader, and the Morality of Literary Knowledge.* Grand Rapids: Zondervan, 1998.
Velasquez, Manuel G. *Business Ethics: Concepts and Cases.* 2nd ed. EngleWood, NJ: Prentice Hall, 1988.

Verhey, Allen. *Remembering Jesus: Christian Community, Scripture, and the Moral Life*. Grand Rapids: William B. Eerdmans Publishing Company, 2002.

_____. *Reading the Bible in the Strange World of Medicine*. Grand Rapids: William B. Eerdmans Publishing Company, 2003.

White House Conference Reports: *Religion and Aging, Reports and Guidelines from the White House Conference on Aging*, U.S. Dept. of Health, Education and Welfare, 1961; and *Toward a National Policy on Aging*, U.S. Dept. of Health, Education and Welfare, 1971.

Wicclair, Mark R. *Ethics and the Elderly*. Oxford: Oxford University, 1993.

Wilkins, Michael J. *Matthew*. The NIV Application Commentary. Grand Rapids: Zondervan, 2004.

Williams, Alan. *Being Reasonable about the Economics of Health*. Edited by A.J. Culyer and Alan Maynard. Cheltenham, UK: Edward Elgar, 1997.

Williams, Bernard. *Ethics and the Limits of Philosophy*. London: Fontana Press, 1985.

Wing, A. J. *Quality-Adjusted Life Years*. London: Christian Medical Fellowship, n.d.

Wittmer, Michael E. *Heaven is a Place on Earth: Why Everything You Do Matters To God*. Grand Rapids: Zondervan, 2004.

Wolterstorff, Nicholas. *Reason within the Bounds of Religion*. 2^d ed. Grand Rapids: Eerdmans, 1984.

Wyatt, John. *Matters of Life and Death: Today's Healthcare Dilemmas in the Light of Christian Faith*. Leicester, UK: InterVarsity, 1998.

Yount, Lisa. *Patients' Rights in the Age of Managed Health Care*. New York: Facts on File, Inc., 2001.

Zlotowitz, Meir. *The Book of Ruth/Meggilas Ruth*. 2nd ed. Brooklyn, NY: Mesorah Publications, 1982.

Articles

Aers, David. "The Christian Practice of Growing Old in the Middle Ages." In *Growing Old in Christ*, ed. Stanley Hauerwas, Carole Bailey Stoneking, Keith G. Meador and David Cloutier, 38–62. Grand Rapids: Eerdmans, 2003.

"Aging." In *American Medical Association Complete Medical Encyclopedia*. New York: Random House Reference, 2003.

Baier, Kurt. "Egoism." In *A Companion to Ethics*, Blackwell Companions to Philosophy. Oxford: Blackwell Reference, 1991.

Benner, Patricia. "When Health Care Becomes a Commodity." In *The Changing Face of Health Care*, ed. John F. Kilner, Robert D. Orr and Judith Allen Shelly, 119–35. Grand Rapids: Eerdmans, 1998.

Blackburn, Simon. "Teleology." In *The Oxford Dictionary of Philosophy*. Oxford: Oxford University, 1994.

Brandt, Richard. "Toward a Credible Form of Utilitarianism." In *Moral Philosophy: Selected Readings*, ed. George Sher, 384–404. San Diego: Harcourt Brace Jovanovich, Publishers, 1987.

Bibliography

Brown, C. A. "Teleology." In *New Dictionary of Christian Ethics and Pastoral Theology*, ed. David J. Atkinson and David H. Field, 835. Downers Grove: InterVarsity, 1995.

Chamblin, J. Knox. "Matthew," In *Evangelical Commentary on the Bible*, ed. Walter A. Elwell, 719–60. Grand Rapids: Baker, 1989.

Cloutier, David. "The Pressures to Die: Reconceiving the Shape of Christian Life in the Face of Physician-Assisted Suicide." In *Growing Old in Christ*, ed. Stanley Hauerwas, Carole Bailey Stoneking, Keith G. Meador and David Cloutier, 247–66. Grand Rapids: Eerdmans, 2003.

Cockhran, Clarke E. "Health Policy and the Poverty Trap: Finding a Way Out." In *Toward a Just and Caring Society*, ed. David P. Gushee, 229–60. Grand Rapids: Baker, 1999.

Collins, Francis. "Human Genetics." In *Cutting-Edge Bioethics: A Christian Exploration of Technologies and Trends*, ed. John F. Kilner, C. Christopher Hook and Diann B. Uustal, 3–17. Grand Rapids: Eerdmans, 2002.

Colson, Charles W. "Can We Prevent the "Abolition of Man"? C. S. Lewis's Challenge to the Twenty-first Century." In *Human Dignity in the Biotech Century: A Christian Vision for Public Policy*, ed, Charles W. Colson and Nigel M. de S. Cameron, 11–20. Downers Grove: InterVarsity, 2004.

Cook, E. David. "Health and Health Care." In *New Dictionary of Christian Ethics & Pastoral Theology*, ed. David J. Atkinson and David H. Field, 435–37. Downers Grove: InterVarsity, 1995.

_____. "Quality of Life," In *New Dictionary of Christian Ethics & Pastoral Theology*, ed. David J. Atkinson and David H. Field, 715–16. Downers Grove: InterVarsity, 1995.

Daniels, Scott E. "Managed Care's Financial Incentives." In *The Changing Face of Health Care*, ed. John F. Kilner, Robert D. Orr and Judith Allen Shelly, 91–102. Grand Rapids: William B. Eerdmans Publishing Co., 1998.

Davies, Elizabeth. "How are thresholds used elsewhere?" In *Cost-Effectiveness Thresholds: Economic and Ethical Issues*, ed. Adrian Towse, Clive Pritchard and Nancy Devlin, 69–75. London: King's Fund, 2003.

Devlin, Nancy. "An introduction to the use of cost-effectiveness thresholds in decision making: what are the issues?" In *Cost-Effectiveness Thresholds: Economic and Ethical Issues*, ed. Adrian Towse, Clive Pritchard and Nancy Devlin, 16–24. London: King's Fund, 2003.

Dower, Nigel. "World Poverty." In *A Companion to Ethics*, Blackwell Companions to Philosophy. Oxford: Blackwell Reference, 1991.

Field, D. H. "Love." In *New Dictionary of Christian Ethics & Pastoral Theology*, ed. David J. Atkinson and David H. Field, 9–14. Downers Grove: InterVarsity, 1995.

Fried, Charles. "Health Care, Cost Containment, Liberty." In *Ethical Issues in Modern Medicine*, 2nd ed., ed. John Arras and Robert Hunt, 527–31. Palo Alto, CA: Mayfield Publishing Company, 1983.

Fryback, Dennis G. "Methodological Issues in Measuring Health Status and Health-related Quality of Life for Population Health Measures: A

Brief Overview of the "HALY" Family of Measures." Appendix C. In *Summarizing Population Health—Directions for the Development and Application of Population Metrics*, ed. M. J. Field and M. R. Gold, 7–14. Washington DC: National Academy Press, 1998.

Grudem, Wayne. "Metaphors for the Church." In *Systematic Theology: An Introduction to Biblical Doctrine*, 858–59. Grand Rapids: InterVarsity, 1994.

Hagner, Donald A. "The *Sitz im Leben* of the Gospel of Matthew." In *Treasures New and Old: Recent Contributions to Matthean Studies*. Edited by David R. Bauer & Mark Allan Powell. SBL Symposium Series, ed. Gail R. O'Day, 27–68. Atlanta: Scholars Press, 1996.

Harris, J. Gordon. "Old Age." In *The Anchor Bible Dictionary*, vol. 5, O–Sh. New York: Doubleday, 1992.

Hays, Richard B. and Judith C. Hays. "The Christian Practice of Growing Old: The Witness of Scripture." In *Growing Old in Christ*, ed. Stanley Hauerwas, Carole Bailey Stoneking, Keith G. Meador and David Cloutier, 3–18. Grand Rapids: Eerdmans, 2003.

Hingley, C. J. H. "Old Testament Ethics." In *New Dictionary of Christian Ethics & Pastoral Theology*, ed. David J. Atkinson and David H. Field, 48–55. Downers Grove: InterVarsity, 1995.

Horner, Stuart. "Conclusion: Change Health Care—A British Point of View." In *The Changing Face of Health Care*, ed. John F. Kilner, Robert D. Orr and Judith Allen Shelly, 480–98. Grand Rapids: Eerdmans, 1998.

"Justice, Distributive," In *Oxford Dictionary of Philosophy*. Oxford: Oxford University Press, 1994.

Kilner, John F. "Ethical Legitimacy of Excluding the Elderly When Medical Resources Are Limited." In *On Moral Medicine: Theological Perspectives in Medical Ethics*. 2nd ed., ed. Stephen E. Lammers and Allen Verhey, 979–95. Grand Rapids: Eerdmans, 1998.

_____. "Age-Based Rationing of Life-Sustaining Health Care." In *Aging, Death, and the Quest for Immortality*, ed. C. Ben Mitchell, Robert D. Orr and Susan A. Salladay, 58–74. Grand Rapids: Eerdmans, 2004.

Kelly, Brent R. and E. Ray Clendenen. "Family." In *Holman Illustrated Bible Dictionary*. Nashville: Holman Bible Publishers, 2003.

Littlejohns, Peter. "Does NICE have a threshold? A response." *Cost-Effectiveness Thresholds: Economic and Ethical Issues*, ed. Adrian Towse, Clive Pritchard and Nancy Devlin, 31–37. London: King's Fund, 2003.

Lustig, R. Andrew. "Reform and Rationing: Reflections of Health Care in Light of Catholic Social Teaching." *On Moral Medicine: Theological Perspectives in Medical Ethics*, 2nd ed., ed. Stephen E. Lammers and Allen Verhey, 960–73. Grand Rapids: Eerdmans, 1998.

Mitchell, C. Ben. "Ethical Challenges." In *Cutting-Edge Bioethics: A Christian Exploration of Technologies and Trends*, ed. John F. Kilner, C. Christopher Hook and Diann B. Uustal, 181–93. Grand Rapids: Eerdmans, 2002.

Bibliography

Moss, M. J. "Ageing." In *New Dictionary of Christian Ethics & Pastoral Theology*, ed. David J. Atkinson and David H. Field, 148–49. Downers Grove: InterVarsity, 1995.

Mott, Stephen and Ronald J. Sider. "Economic Justice: A Biblical Paradigm." In *Toward a Just and Caring Society: Christian Responses to Poverty in America*, ed. David P. Gushee, 15–45. Grand Rapids: Baker, 1999.

Narveson, Jan. "The right to be old and the right to have young: some conundrums about aging populations." In *Respect For Persons*, Tulane Studies in Philosophies 31, ed. O. H. Green, 183–217. New Orleans, Tulane University, 1982.

Nel, Philip J. "ולם." In *New International Dictionary of Old Testament Theology & Exegisis*, vol. 4. Grand Rapids: Zondervan, 1997.

"Old." In *Cyclopedia of Biblical Theological, and Ecclesiastical Literature*, vol. III, New–Pes. Grand Rapids: Baker, 1981.

Outka, Gene. "Social Justice and Equal Access to Health Care." In *On Moral Medicine: Theological Perspectives in Medical Ethics*, ed. Stephen E. Lammers and Allen Verhey, 2nd ed., 947–60. Grand Rapids: Eerdmans, 1998.

Petersen, Rodney. "Continuity and Discontinuity: The Debate Throughout Church History." In *Continuity and Discontinuity: Perspectives on the Relationship Between the Old and New Testaments*, Essays in Honor of S. Lewis Johnson, Jr., ed. John S. Feinberg, 17–36. Wheaton: Crossway Books, 1988.

Pritchard, Clive. "Overseas approaches to decision making." In *Cost-Effectiveness Thresholds: Economic and Ethical Issues*, ed. Adrian Towse, Clive Pritchard and Nancy Devlin, 56–68. London: King's Fund, 2003.

Rae, Scott B. "Money Matters in Health Care." In *Cutting-Edge Bioethics: A Christian Exploration of Technologies and Trends*, ed. John Kilner, C. Christopher Hook and Diann B. Uustal, 103–15. Grand Rapids: Eerdmans, 2002.

Rawls, John. "A Theory of Justice." In *Moral Philosophy: Selected Readings*, ed. George Sher, 453–72. San Diego, CA: Harcourt Brace Jovanovich, Publishers, 1987.

Romer, Paul M. "The Politics of Entitlement." In *Individual and Social Responsibility: Child Care, Education, Medical Care, and Long-Term Care in America*, ed. Victor R. Fuchs, 195–228. Chicago: The University of Chicago, 1996.

Rutecki, Gregory W. "Guidelines for Gatekeepers." In *The Changing Face of Health Care*, ed. John F. Kilner, Robert D. Orr and Judith Allen Shelly, 136–44. Grand Rapids: Eerdmans, 1998.

Singer, Peter. "What's Wrong with Killing." In *Writings on an Ethical Life*, ed. Peter Singer, 125–45. New York: HarperCollins, 2000.

Stoneking, Carole Bailey. "Modernitiy: The Social Construction of Aging." In *Growing Old In Christ*, ed. Stanley Hauerwas, Carole Bailey Stoneking, Keith G. Meador and David Cloutier, 63–89. Grand Rapids: Eerdmans, 2003.

"Utilitarianism." In *The Oxford Dictionary of Philosophy*. Oxford: Oxford University Press, 1994.

Vincent, Marvin R. "2 John 2:1, The Elder." *Word Studies in the New Testament*, vol. II, The Writings of John, 392. McLean: MacDonald Publishing Co. 2003.

Waltke, Bruce K. "Kingdom Promises as Spiritual," In *Continuity and Discontinuity: Perspectives on the Relationship Between the Old and New Testaments*. Essays in Honor of S. Lewis Johnson, Jr., ed. John S. Feinberg, 263–88. Wheaton: Crossway, 1988.

Wolterstorff, Nicholas P. "Justice and Peace," In *New Dictionary of Christian Ethics & Pastoral Theology*, ed. David J. Atkinson and David H. Field, 15–20. Downers Grove: InterVarsity, 1995.

Wheeler, Sonda Ely. "Broadening Our View of Justice in Health Care." In *The Changing Face of Health Care: A Christian Appraisal of Managed Care, Resource Allocation, and Patient-Caregiver Relationships*, ed. John F. Kilner, Robert D. Orr and Judith Allen Shelly, 63–73. Grand Rapids: Eerdmans, 1998.

White, Barbara J. "A Nurse's Experience." In *The Changing Face of Health Care: A Christian Appraisal of Managed Care, Resource Allocation, and Patient-Caregiver Relationships*, ed. John F. Kilner, Robert D. Orr, and Judith Allen Shelly, 17–24. Grand Rapids: Eerdmans, 1998.

Wilkins Michael J. and J. P. Moreland. "Introduction: The Furor Surrounding Jesus." In *Jesus Under Fire: Modern Scholarship Reinvents the Historical Jesus*, Michael J. Wilkins and J. P. Moreland, 17–50. Grand Rapids: Zondervan, 1995.

Williams, Alan. "The Importance of Quality of Life in Policy Decisions." In *Quality of life: Assessment and Application*, ed. Stuart R. Walker and Rachel M. Rosser, 282–312. Boston: MTP Press Limited, 1988.

Wing, A. J. "QALY." In *New Dictionary of Christian Ethics & Pastoral Theology*, ed. David Atkinson, and David Field, 714–15. Downers Grove, IL: InterVarsity, 1995.

Periodicals

Anderson, Terry. "George Grant and Religious Social Ethics in Canada." *Religious Studies Review* 6 (1980): 118–25.

Andolsen, Barbara. "Justice, Gender, and the Frail Elderly: Reexamining the Ethic of Care." *Journal of Feminist Studies in Religion* 9 (1993): 127–45.

Arrow, Kenneth. "Uncertainty and the Welfare Economics of Medical Care." *American Economic Review* 53 (1963): 941–69.

Becker, Arthur H. "Values and Aging." *Theological Education* 16 (1980): 341–45.

Block, Daniel I. *Genesis: The Beginning of What?* Paper Presented at The Southern Baptist Theological Seminary Supervised Ministry Experience Seminar, 20 August 2001.

Burkett, Elizabeth S. "Malpractice Problems Shouldn't Hurt Patients." *Business First of Columbus,* Opinion, Letter to the Editor, 29 July 2002.

Bibliography

Callahan, Daniel. "Caring for an Aging World: Allocating Scarce Resources." *Hastings Center Report* 24 (1994): 3–41.
Cheshire, William P. "Twigs of Terebinth: The Ethical Origins of the Hospital in the Judeo-Christian Tradition." *Ethics and Medicine* 19 (2003):143–54.
Clinton, Hillary Rodham. "'Commonsense' reform for health care." *The Courier-Journal*, 25 April 2004, sec. D.
Cohen, Joshua. "Preferences, Need and QALYs." *Journal of Medical Ethics* 22 (1996): 267–72.
Connolly, Ceci. "Health Care's Soaring Cost Takes a Toll. Squeeze Hits Workers, Firms and Government." *Washington Post*, 9 July 2002, 10 (A).
Cook, E. David. "Shalom and Justice in Health Care." *The Southern Baptist Journal of Theology* (200) 4: 60–75.
Cupit, Geoffrey. "Justice, Age, and Veneration." *Ethics* 108 (1998): 702–18.
Davia, Joy. "Doctors Struggle with Different Malpractice Problems: Some See Leaving as Only Alternative." *Sunday Gazette-Mail*, Health Notes, 7 April 2002.
Dowie, Jack. "Analyzing health outcomes." *Journal of Medial Ethics* 27 (2001): 245–50.
Eisenberg, Daniel and Maggie Seiger. "The Doctor Won't See You Now." *Time* 161 (9 June 2003): 46–50.
Eisenberg, Leon. "Health Care: For Patients or for Profits?" *American Journal of Psychiatry* 143 (1985): 1015.
Fuchs, Victor R. "The Clinton Plan: A Researcher Examines Reform." *Health Affairs* 13 (1994): 102–14.
Hardwig, John. "Is There a Duty to Die?" *Hastings Center Report* 27 (1997): 34–42.
Harris, John. "QALYfying the value of life." *Journal of Medical Ethics* 13 (1987): 117–23.
Hyder, Adnan, Guida Rotllant, and Richard H. Morrow. "Measuring the Burden of Disease." *American Journal of Public Health* 88 (1998): 196–202.
Jacob, Melvin R. "Ethical Boundaries and Health Maintenance Organization (HMO) Expectations: Who Draws the Line?" *The Journal of Pastoral Care* 55 (2001): 281.
Kass, Leon R. "L'Chaim and Its Limits: Why Not Immortality?" *First Things* 113 (2001): 17–24.
Kapp, Marshall B. "Health Car Rationing in the United States: a Contemporary Jewish Perspective." *Journal of Psychology and Judaism* 15 (1991): 149–57.
Keshavjee, Salmaan. "Medicine and money: the ethical transformation of medical practice." *Medical Education* 38 (2004): 271–75.
Kilner, John F. "The Ethical Legitimacy of Excluding the Elderly When Medical Resources are Limited." *Annual of the Society of Christian Ethics* (1988): 179–203.
_____. "Age_Based Rationing of Health Care." *Dignity* (Fall 2001): 1.
Lantos, John. "RVUs Blues: How Should Docs Get Paid." *Hastings Center Report* 33 (2003): 37–45.

McLeod, Beth Witrongen. "Relationship—Centered Care." *Noetic Sciences Review* 48 (1999): 36–43.
"Medicare's 30th." *U.S. News & World Report* 119: 5 (1995): 13.
Menzel, Paul, Marthe R. Gold, and Erick Nord. "Toward a Broader View of Values in Cost-Effectiveness Analysis of Health." *Hastings Center Report* 29 (May–June 1999): 7–15.
Payne, Franklin E., Jr. "Counter Point to Teach Us to Number Our Days." *Journal of Biblical Ethics in Medicine* 6 (1992): 103–4.
Pellegrino, Edmund D. and others. "Must the Church be Mute Lest Its Truths be Distorted? A Response to Engelhardt." *Christian Bioethics* 8: 43–47.
Richardson, Jeff. "Linking Health Outcomes to Funding." Working paper presented to the Australian Outcomes Conference in July 1999. *Centre for Health Program Evaluation*, West Heidelberg, Australia.
Rutecki, Gregory W. "Rationing Medical Care to the Elderly Revisited: Futility as a Just Criterion." *Journal of Biblical Ethics in Medicine* 7 (1993): 67–74.
Rutecki, Gregory W. and John D. Geib. "Teach Us to Number Our Days: Age and the Rationing of Medical Care: Use of a Biblical Valuation of Personhood." *Journal of Biblical Ethics in Medicine* 6 (1992): 95–102.
Serafini, Marilyn W. "Medicare's Challenge." *National Journal* 32 (2000): 1602–7.
Siegler, Mark. "Should Age Be a Criterion in Health Care?" *The Hastings Center Report* 14 (1984): 24–27.
Sims, Sandy. "Medical associations say that exodus of California doctors is epidemic." Part 2. *The Sunnyvale Sun*, News, 07 February 2001.
Stone, John E. and Jackson H. Day. "Double Punch." *Christian Social Action* 17 (2004): 13–16.
"The Nursing Shortage & You." *USA Weekend*, 29–31 August 2003: 6–7.
Weinstein, Milton C. "Should Physicians be Gatekeepers of Medical Resources?" *Journal of Medical Ethics* 27 (2001): 268–74.
Weiss, Michael J. "Inconspicuous Consumption: Health Care: The Growing Cost of Feeling Good." *American Demographics* 24 (Apr 2002): 34–38.
Wimberly, Anne E. Streaty. "Caring as Honoring." *Christian Reflection: A Series in Faith and Ethics*, Baylor University (2003): 9–17.

Internet Articles
"Allocation of Limited Medical Resources." *American Medical Association* [on-line]. Accessed 21 July 2004. Available from http://www.ama-assn.org/ama/pub/ category/8388.html; Internet.
Amos, Jonathan. "US Healthcare in 'Danger of Collapse." *BBC News World Edition*, 14 February 2003, In Depth: Denver 2003 [newspaper on-line]. Accessed 15 February 2003. Available from http://news.bbc.co.uk/2/hi/in_depth/sci_tech/2003/denver_ 2003/2760101.stm; Internet.
Andre, Claire and Manuel Velasquez. "System Overload: Pondering the Ethics of American's Health Care System." *Issues in Ethics* 3 (1990): 3 [on-line]. Accessed 04 June 2004. Available from http://www.scu.edu/ethics/publications/iie/v3n3/ system.html; Internet.

Bibliography

Appel, Yehuda. "Kedoshim (Leviticus 19–20), Retirement." *Appel's Parsha Page* [on-line]. Accessed 25 March 2004. Available from http://www.aish.com/torahportion/appel/Retirement.asp; Internet.

Associated Press. "Oregon Health Care Plan Rejected." *The Olympian*, Front Page, 06 November 2002 [on-line]. Accessed 04 April 2003. Available from http>//www.theolympian.com/home/news/20021106/ frontpage/3437_Printer.shtml; Internet.

Bailey, Ronald. "The Pursuit of Happiness, Peter Singer Interviewed." *Reasononline* (December 2000) [journal on-line]. Accessed 8 March 2002. Available from http://www.reason.com/ 0012/rb.the.shtml; Internet.

Cain, Brad "Oregon considers Universal Health Plan." *The Telegraph*, 08 October 2002; [on-line]. Accessed 04 April 2003. Available from http//www.macon.com/mld/ macon/ news/ nation/4239062.html; Internet.

Calvin, John. "The First Commandment of which is the Fifth of the Law; The Fifth Commandment." *Christian Classic Ethereal Library* [on-line]. Accessed 30 December 03. Available from http://www.ccel.org/c/calvin/comment#/comm_vol05/htm/ii.htm; Internet.

Charles, J. Daryl. "Articulating a Distinctly Christian Approach to Suffering." *The Center for Bioethics and Human Dignity*, Commentary, 10 February 2004 [on-line]. Accesses 24 February 2004. Available from http://www.cbhd.com/resources/ endoflife/charles_2004- 02-10_print.htm; Internet.

Chetwynd, Sue. "Priorities in Healthcare: An Ethical and Legal Framework," Warwick & Keele Universities [on-line]. Accessed 15 April 2004. Available from http://www.le.ac.uk/sm.LWMS/resources/ethics/Priori-5.doc; Internet.

Coile, Russell C. Jr. "Futurescan 2002: A Forecast of Healthcare Trends (2002–2006)." *Great Boards* May 2002: 3–4 [on-line]. Accessed 05 April 2003. Available from http://www.great.boards.org; Internet.

Conley, Ronald. "Veterans health care funding slaughtered in rush for pork." *The American Legion Magazine* 154 (May 2003) [on-line]. Accessed 08 Aug 03. Available from http://www.legion.org/pub_relations/pr_releasecontent.php?id=a59; Internet.

_____. "A System Worth Saving." *The American Legion Magazine* 154 (May 2003) [on-line]. Accessed 08 Aug 03. Available from http://www.legion.org/publications/pubs_2003/pubs_may03_ system.htm [Internet].

Davis, Sam. "Ageism and its implications for the health care of older people." *Northern Health* [on-line]. Accessed 25 May 2004. Available from http://www.nh.org.au/research_edu/resbecc/research_becc_ageing.htm; Internet.

Edwards, Jonathan. *Christian Charity or The Duty of Charity to the Poor, Explained and Enforced* [on-line]. Accessed 25 Aug 2004. Available from http://www.biblebb.com/files/edwards/charity.htm; Internet.

"Employers Leading the Charge to Control Health Care Costs." *SmartPros* [on-line journal]. Accessed 29 Aug 2003. Available from http://www.smartpros.com/x38246.xml; Internet.

"Expected Utility Theory." *A Dictionary of Psychology*, ed. Andrew M. Colman. Oxford: Oxford University Press, 2001, *Oxford Reference Online*, Oxford University Press [on-line]. Accessed 08 Aug 03. Available from http://www.oxfordreference.com/views/INTRY.html?subview=Main&entry=t87.002943; Internet.

Fairlamb, David. "No Doctor in the House: The Shortage Will Only Get Worse," *Business Week Online*, 4 Feb 2002 [on-line]. Accessed 16 October 2002. Available from http://www.businessweek.com:print/magazine/content/02_05/c3768044.htm? mainwindow; Internet.

Garratt, Andrew and others. "Quality of life measurement: Bibliographic study of patient assessed health outcome measures." *British Medical Journal* 324 (2002) [on-line]. Accessed 11 February 2004. Available from http://bmj.bmjjournals.com/cgi/reprint/ 324/7351/1417; Internet.

Graham, John D. "An Investor's Look at Life-Saving Opportunities," Risk in Perspective, *Harvard Center for Risk Analysis* 7 (Feb 1999) [on-line]. Accessed 23 September 2003. Available from http://www.hcra.harvard.edu/pdf/February1999.pdf; Internet.

Green, Martin. *Economics of Health Care*, 3rd ed., Office of Health Economics, (London: Industry Supports Education, 2003), 10 [on-line]. Accessed 06 September 2003. Available from http://www.oheschools.org; Internet.

Harris, Brian. *Quantifying Health Outcomes*, University of California, Berkeley (2004) [on-line]. Accessed17 March 2003. Available from http://psg-mac43ucsf.edu/ticr/syllabus/courses/10/2004/01/13/Lecture/notes/Utilities %20and%20QALYS.ppt; Internet.

"Health Care Rationing: Needs and Options." *709 Health Law Syllabus* (19 Sept 2002), Boston University School of Public Health [on-line]. Accessed 21 April 2003. Available from http://www.bumc.bu.edu/Departments/PageMain.asp?Department ID=95 &Page=6616; Internet.

"Health Maintenance Organizations," *Minnesota Historical Society* [on-line]. Accessed 21 April 2003. Available from http://www.mnhs.org/library/tips/history_topics/ 87hmos.html; Internet.

"Health Related Quality of Life—Questions & Answers." *The Quality of Life Instruments Database* [on-line]. Accessed 4 June 2003. Available from http://www.qolid.org/public/questions.html; Internet.

Heller, James G. "Will public health survive QALYs," *Clinical Pharmacology 2002* (Spring 2003) 9.1 [on-line]. Accessed 4 June 2003. Available from http://www. pulsus.com./clin-pha/01_01/hell_ed.htm; Internet.

"History of Facilities Management." *Office of Facilities Management* [on-line]. Accessed 02 July 2003. Available from http://www.va.gov/facmgt/aboutfm/history.asp; Internet.

Iglesias, Theresa. "Medicine's Intrinsic Good." Commentary 09 September 2003, *The Center for Bioethics and Human Dignity* [on-line]. Accessed 24 October 2003. Available from http://www.cbhd.org/resources/bioethics/iglesias_2003-09-09_ print.htm; Internet.

Bibliography

Justine Jenkins, "The Ethical QALY," *Quality of Life News Letter* 7–8 (Jun 93–Jan 94):1 [on-line]. Accessed 02 October 02. Available from http://www.mapi-research-inst.com/pdf/art/qol7_1.pdf; Internet.

Kattan, Michael W. and others. *Time trade-off utility modified to accommodate degenerative and life-threatening conditions*, Harvard University [on-line]. Accessed 14 March 2004. Available from http://www.mgh.harvard.edu/PDF_ Repository/ D010001204.pdf; Internet.

Keeler, William H. "A Catholic Appeal: Leadership for the Common Good." *Office for Social Justice: Catholic Social Teaching* [on-line]. Accessed 29 March 2004. Available from http://www.osjsp.org/cst/keeler.htm; Internet.

Kelley, David. "Altruism and Capitalism." *The Objectivist Center, IOS Journal* 5 [on-line]. Accessed 21 May 2004. Available from http://www.objectivistcenter.org/text/dkelley_altruism-capitalism.asp?navigator; Internet.

Kenneth J. Arrow, 1921- [on-line]. Accessed 10 December 2003. Available from http://cepa.newschool.edu/het/profiles/arrow.htm; Internet.

Malek, Mo. "Implementing QALYs." *Hayward Medical Communications* (March 2001) 2, no. 1 [on-line]. Accessed 02 August 2002. Available from http://www.evidence-based-medicine.co.uk; Internet.

Marazzo, Donald P. "Quality of Life, " *Quality of Life Series—Summary Report* (1998), Dialogue Series 1997 [on-line]. Accessed 1 August 2002. Available from http://pitt.edu-uclid?QOL.htm; Internet.

Markle Foundation. "Connecting for Health . . . A Public–Private Collaborative Convened by the Markle Foundation." *Connection for Health* [on-line]. Accessed 02 March 200. Available from http://www.connectingforhealth.org/aboutus/; Internet.

Mayer, David N. "Clinton Health Plan: The Wrong Prescription." *On Principle* 2 (1994):1 [on-line]. Accessed; 22 April 2003. Available from http://www.ashbrook.org/ publicat/onprin/v2n1/mayer.html; Internet.

"Medicare: Why Do We Have Medicare Part A and Part B?" *ElderWeb* [on-line]. Accessed 19 June 2003. Available from http://www. elderweb.com; Internet.

"Modern Hermeneutics: Lesson 1: Legitimate Contrasted with Illegitimate." *Bible Studies at The Moorings* [on-line]. Accessed 30 March 2004. Available from http://www.themoorings.org/doctrine/issues/hermeneutics/intent.html; Internet.

National Institute for Clinical Excellence and National Co-ordinating Centre for Research Methodology, *What is the Value to Society of a QALY? Issues Raised and Recommendations for How to Address Them* (Norwich: University of East Anglia, 2003), 2 [on-line]. Accessed 23 September 2003. Available from http://www.publichealth.bham.ac.uk/nccm/ PDFs%20and%20 documents/GL_AQLY_report_Feb03.pdf; Internet.

Newport, Ceri Phillips. "So What is a QALY?" *Bandolier Library* [on-line]. Accessed 1 August 2002. Available from http://www.jr2ox.ac.uk/bandolier/band24/b24-7.html; Internet.

No Pure Strategy Is Stable [on-line]. Accessed 07 April 2004. Available from http://www.urticator.net/essay/4/427/html; Internet.

O'Dea, Des. "Putting a value on 'a life saved': Should the value vary with age?" Paper given at the *New Zealand Association of Economists' Conference*, Wellington, NZ, 26–28 June 2002 [on-line]. Accessed 12 October 03. Available from http://nzae. org.nz/ files/no.43(PAPER)-odea.pdf; Internet.

"Our 10 Principles," *The Heart of the Eden Alternative* (2001) [on-line]. Accessed 6 March 2002. Available from http://www.edenalt.com/hom/index.html; Internet.

Padfield, David. *The Care of the Elderly*, (2001) [on-line]. Accessed 24 March 2004. Available from http://www.padfield.com/tracts/elderly.pdf; Internet.

Pallarito, Karen. "US Health Worker Shortage Endangers Public," *Yale New Haven Health*, Health News, Today's Health News, Reuters 05 Sept 2002 [on-line]. Accessed 05 April 2003. Available from http://yalenewhavenhealth.org/Health New/Reuters/ NewsStory0905200240.html; Internet.

Palmer, John L. and Thomas R. Saving, "A Summary of the 2003 ANNUAL REPORTS Social Security and Medicare Boards of Trustees." *Status of the Social Security and Medicare Programs* [on-line]. Accessed 25 June 2003. Available from http://www.ssa.gov/OACT /TRSUM/trsummary.html; Internet.

Phillips, Ceri. "So what is a QALY?" *Bandolier Library Search* [on-line]. Accessed 17 July 02. Available from http://www.jr2.ox.ac.uk/bandolier/band24/b24-7.html; Internet.

_____, and Guy Thompson. "What is a QALY," *Hayward Medical Communications* (May 2001) vol. 1, no. 6 [on-line]. Accessed 02 August 2002; available from http://www. evidence-based-medicine.co.uk; Internet.

"Preference or Utilities." Quality of Life Resources, *American Thoracic Society*, (2003) [on-line]. Accessed 10 October 2003. Available from http://www.atsqol.org/utility. asp; Internet.

"Prescription Drugs." Center on an Aging Society, Georgetown University, *Data Profile* 5, (Sept 2002) [on-line]. Accessed 04 Aug 2003. Available from http://ihcrp. georgetown.du/agingsociety/ pubhtml/rxdrugs/rxdrugs.html; Internet.

"Principles of Distributive Justice." Healthcare Issues, *Ascension Health* [on-line]. Accessed 04 June 2004. Available from http://www.ascensionhealth.org/ethics/public/key_principles/distributive_justice.asp; Internet.

"Quality Adjusted Life Years." *A Dictionary of Sociology*, ed., Gordon Marshall. Oxford: Oxford University Press, 1998. *Oxford Reference Online*, Oxford University Press [on-line]. Accessed 08 August 2003. Available from http:// www.oxfordreference. com/ views/ENTRY.html?subview=Main&entry=t8 8.001836; Internet.

Bibliography

"Quality-adjusted life years." *A Dictionary of Nursing.* Oxford: Oxford University Press, 2003. *Oxford Reference Online,* Oxford University Press [on-line]. Accessed 08 August 2003. Available from http://www.oxfordreference.com/views/ENTRY.html?subview=Main&entry=t62.007626; Internet.

"Section 6: Principles of Justice." *Continuing Education for Case Managers, Social Workers, Rehab Nurses, and Life Care Planners* [on-line]. Accessed 15 April 2004. Available from http://www.ceus4casemanagers.com/ET1007_Section6.html; Internet.

Singer, Peter. "Living and Dying." (Abstract) (Interview) In *Psychology Today* 32 (1999) [journal on-line]. Accessed 8 March 2002. Available from http://www.findarticles.com/cfdls/1175m/132/53479124/print.jhtml; Internet.

Schwartz, Alan. *MHPE 494: Medical Decision Making.* Lecture notes (Spring 1999) [on-line]. Accessed 23 September 2003. Available from http://www.araw.mede.uic.edu/~alansz/ courses/mhpe494/week10.html; Internet.

_____. "Cost-Effectiveness Analysis." *MHPE 494: Medical Decision Making,* week 10, University of Chicago [on-line]. Accessed 24 September 2003. Available from http://araw.mede.uic.edu/~alansz/courses/mhpe494/week10.html; Internet.

Smith, Christopher. "Veterans Deserve Guaranteed Access to Health Care." *The American Legion Magazine* 154 (May 2003) [on-line]. Accessed 08 Aug 03. Available from http://www.legion.org/publications/pubs_2003/pubs_may03 _healthcare. htm; Internet.

"Strategy." *PlanetMath.Org* [on-line]. Accessed 23 February 2004. Available from http://planetmath.org/encyclopedia/Strategy2.html, Internet.

"Study Predicts Another year of Sharp Increases in Medical Premiums." *SmartPros* [on-line journal]. Accessed 29 Aug 2003. Available from http://www.smartpros.com/ x40106.xml; Internet.

Sullivan, Martha, and others. "Stepping Out on Faith: Geriatric Mental Health in 2015." *The Future of Aging in New York State* [on-line]. Accessed 24 May 2004. Available from http://aging.state.ny.us/explore/project2015/artmentalhealth.htm; Internet.

"The Scripture," *Baptist Faith and Message 2000* [on-line]. Accessed 22 March 2004. Available from http://www.sbc.net/bfm/bfm2000.asp; Internet.

The von Neuman-Morgenstern Expected Utility Theory [on-line]. Accessed 10 December 2003. Available from http://cepa.newschool.edu/het/essays/uncert/vnmaxioms. htm; Internet.

Ubel, Peter A. "Understanding and Improving Resource Allocation Decisions." *VA Center for Practice Management and Outcomes Research* [on-line]. Accessed 2 July 2003. Available from http:// www.hsrd.ann-arbor.med.va.gov /ubel_cda.htm; Internet.

"Utility Theory," *A Dictionary of Psychology,* ed. Andrew M. Colman (Oxford: Oxford University Press, 2001), *Oxford Reference Online,* Oxford University Press [on-line]. Accessed 08 August 03. Available from; http://www.oxfordreference.com/ views/ENTRY.html?subview=Main&entry=t87.008710; Internet.

Vann, Korky. "Nation Faces Shortage of Doctors to Treat Geriatric Patients." *Hartford Courant*, 20 Feb 2001 [on-line]. Accessed 11 October 2002. Available from http:// www.HartfordCourant.com; Internet.

Ventegodt, Soren, Measuring the Quality of Life From Theory to Practice," *Quality-of-Life Research Center*, Denmark, (1995) [on-line]. Accessed 10 October 2003. Available from http://home2inet.tele.dk/fclk/mql_eng.htm; Internet.

Walters, Stephen J. and John E. Brazier. "What is the relationship between the minimally important difference and the health state utility values? The case of the SF-6D." *Health Qual Life Outcomes* 2003; 1 (1): 4 [on-line]. Accessed 25 September 2003. Available from http://www.pubmedcentral.gov/articlerender.fcgi?tool=pmcentrez& artid=155547; Internet.

Weisstein, Eric W. "Mixed Strategy." *MathWorld*—A Wolfram Web Resource [on-line]. Accessed 23 February 2004. Available from http://mathworld.wolfram.com/ MixedStrategy.html; Internet.

"What Is Hospice & Palliative Care?" *National Hospice and Palliative Care Organization* [on-line]. Accessed 06 April 2004. Available from http:// www.nhpco. org/i4a/ pages/index.cfm?pageid=3281; Internet.

White, Ronald F. "The Principle of Justice." Ron White's Philosophy and Ethics Homepage, *College of Mount St. Joseph* [on-line]. Accessed 04 June 2004. Available from http://www.msj.edu/white/justice.htm; Internet.

"WHO definition of Health." *2003 World Health Organization* [on-line]. Accessed 02 March 2004. Available from http://www.who.int/about/definition/en/; Internet.

"Years of Healthy Life." *Bureau of Business & Economic Research, University of Madison* [on-line]. Accessed 02 October 2003. Available at http://www.bber.umt.edu/healthcare/healthyyears.htm; [Internet].

"Years of Healthy life—Selected States, United States, 1993–1995." *MMWR Weekly* 47: 5 [on-line]. Accessed 02 October 2003. Available from http:// www.cdc.gov/mmwr/ preview/ mmwrhtml/00050833; Internet.

Dissertations

Fairbairn, A. M. *Studies in the Life of Christ* as quoted in Orville Ernest Daniel, "Corban." Ph.D. diss., The Southern Baptist Theological Seminary, 1929.

Gentry, Jerry Lynn. "Narrative Ethics and Economic Justice: Toward an Ethic of Inclusion." Ph.D. diss., The Southern Baptist Theological Seminary, 1989.

Holmes, Ann Michele. "Uses and Abuses of QALY Analysis." Ph.D. diss., University of British Columbia, 1992.

Safranyik, Gina Diane. "Macro-allocation of Health Care Resources: A Computer Simulation Comparing a Utilitarian and a Deontological Approach." Ph.D. diss., University of Victoria, 2000.

Shelp, Earl. "An Inquiry Into Christian Ethical Sanctions for the "Right To Health Care." Ph.D. diss., The Southern Baptist Theological Seminary, 1976.

www.ingramcontent.com/pod-product-compliance
Lightning Source LLC
Chambersburg PA
CBHW050847230426
43667CB00012B/2179